# The Melting Pot Genealogical Society

# Membership Pedigree Charts

## First Edition: 1984

## Second Edition: 2013©

## Volume I

## Acknowledgments

Thank you to Charleen Nobles and Loretta Walker for all the proofing you did.

~ 5 ~

# How to Use This Book

Member pedigrees are in member number order.

Locate Surname in the index and turn to refer to page listed.

Some members have chosen not to have certain personal information listed.  For those who wish to get in touch with these members, email our library at **MPGS@ATT.net** and your request will be forwarded to that member.

# TABLE OF CONTENTS

# MEMBERS PEDIGREES

Pedigree Chart No. ........

Date 1982

Name of Compiler Mrs. Jane Barnes

Address

City

Person No. 1 on this chart is the same person as _____ on chart No.

No.

　b　Date of Birth
　p.b　Place of Birth
　m.　Date of Marriage
　d.　Date of Death
　p.d　Place of Death

1 Jane Nelson

　b. 20 Dec. 1927
　p.b. Pond Creek, OK
　m. 14 June 1947
　d.
　p.d.

2 Leslie H. Nelson
　(Father of No. 1)
　b. 6 Oct. 1900
　p.b. Columbia, OK.
　d. 15 May 1925

3 Maggie May Blaikie
　(Mother of No. 1)
　b. 19 June 1899
　p.b. Dennison, KS
　d. 13 Oct. 1929
　p.d. Perry, OK

Wm. Jackson Barnes
　(Husband of Wife of No. 1)
　b. 2 Sept. 1927
　p.b. Mena, AR
　d.

4 George M. Nelson
　(Father of No. 2)
　b. 18 Aug 1874
　p.b. MO.
　m. 2 Feb. 1896
　d. 11 July 1959
　p.d. Tonkawa, OK

5 Nellie Beatty Moore
　(Mother of No. 2)
　b. 4 Nov. 1877
　p.b. South Haven, KS
　d. 10 Nov. 1953
　p.d. Oklahoma City, OK

6 Frank Francis Blaikie
　(Father of No. 3)
　b. 5 Oct. 1862
　p.b. Coldingham, Scotland
　m. 2 Oct. 1895
　d. 15 Nov. 1941
　p.d. Springtown, AR

7 Flora A. Mulanax
　(Mother of No. 3)
　b. 28 Aug. 1878
　p.b. Denison, KS
　d. 12 Jan. 1953
　p.d. Springtown, AR

8 Jonas Monroe Nelson
　(Father of No. 4)
　b. 2 Aug. 1833
　p.b. Green Co., Ohio
　m. June 1861
　d. 25 Feb. 1915
　p.d. Salt Fork, OK

9 Ellen A. Hillyer
　(Mother of No. 4)
　b.
　p.b.
　d. 22 Apr. 1875
　p.d.

10 James Oliver Moore
　(Father of No. 5)
　b. 30 Apr. 1857
　p.b. Burlington, KS
　m. 18 Mar. 1877
　d. 20 July 1936
　p.d. Canton, OK.

11 Susan Eugenia Moseley
　(Mother of No. 5)
　b. 18 Apr. 1856
　p.b. South Haven, KS
　d. 17 Jan. 1937
　p.d. Cresant, OK.

12 Robert Blaikie
　(Father of No. 6)
　1828
　p.b. Chrinside, Scotland
　m. 24 Apr. 1849
　d. 4 Jan. 1908
　p.d. Ayton Mains, Scotland

13 Jane Steele
　(Mother of No. 6)
　1827
　p.b. Coldingham, Scotland
　d. 19 Oct. 1833
　p.d. Fouldin Deans, Scotland

14 John Greenbury Mulanax
　(Father of No. 7)
　b. 27 Aug. 1856
　p.b. Columbia, MO
　m. 5 Sept. 1877
　d. 20 Aug. 1930
　p.d. Denison, KS

15 Flora Ellen Kirkpatrick
　(Mother of No. 7)
　b. 27 Dec. 1858
　p.b. Ohio
　d. 20 June 1889
　p.d. Denison, KS

16 Henry Nelson
　(Father of No. 8)
　Continued on chart ____

17 Elizabeth Metsker
　(Mother of No. 8)
　Continued on chart ____

18 Voris Hillyer
　(Father of No. 9)
　Continued on chart ____

19 Sarah Ann Crane
　(Mother of No. 9)
　Continued on chart ____

20 W. G. Moore
　(Father of No. 10)
　Continued on chart ____

21 Ann
　(Mother of No. 10)
　Continued on chart ____

22 Jessie M. Moseley
　(Father of No. 11)
　Continued on chart ____

23 Susan Archibald
　(Mother of No. 11)
　Continued on chart ____

24
　(Father of No. 12)
　Continued on chart ____

25
　(Mother of No. 12)
　Continued on chart ____

26
　(Father of No. 13)
　Continued on chart ____

27
　(Mother of No. 13)
　Continued on chart ____

28 Miles Elliott Mulanax
　(Father of No. 14)
　Continued on chart ____

29 Rachel E. Miller
　(Mother of No. 14)
　Continued on chart ____

30 James Wylie Kirkpatrick
　(Father of No. 15)
　Continued on chart ____

31 Eleanor Ann Lyons
　(Mother of No. 15)
　Continued ____

# Pedigree Chart No........

Date 16 Nov. 1981
Name of Compiler  Charles Bolton
Address
City
Person No. 1 on this chart is the same person as _____ on chart No.
No. ___

b.  Date of Birth
p.b. Place of Birth
m.  Date of Marriage
d.  Date of Death
p.d. Place of Death

**1 Charles Everett Bolton**
b. 19 May 1934
p.b. Combes,Cameron, TX
m. (2) 1 Jan. 1976
d.
p.d.

**2 Charles Emmett Bolton** (Father of No. 1)
b. 7 Feb. 1913
p.b. San Saba Co., TX
m. (1) 5 Mar. 1931
d.
p.d.

**3 Mildred Irene Hand** (Mother of No. 1)
b. 27 Jan. 1914
p.b. Stephens Co., TX
d.
p.d.

**(2) Nova Allein Sharp** (Husband or Wife of No. 1)
b. 6 Sept. 1923
p.b. Harrison Co., MO.
d.

**4 George Alexander Bolton** (Father of No. 2)
b. 5 Aug. 1875
p.b. Devine, Medina, TX
m. 27 Dec. 1905 Lampasas,TX
d. 3 July 1955 bur. Brownwood
p.d. Ft. Worth, Tarrant, TX

**5 Martha Jane Gage** (Mother of No. 2)
b. 25 April 1888
p.b. Grayson Co., TX
d. 2 Feb.1952 bur.Brownwood
p.d. Ft. Worth,Tarrant,TX

**6 John William Hand** (Father of No. 1)
b. 16 Dec. 1890
p.b. Stephens Co., TX
m. 30 Dec. 1909
d. 26 June 1950 bur.Combes
p.d. Harlingen,Cameron,TX

**7 Hattie Theo Maupin** (Mother of No. 3)
b. 16 July 1893
p.b. Comanche Co., TX
d. 18 Aug 1980 bur.Combes
p.d.Harlingen,Cameron, TX

**8 J. W. Bolton** (Father of No. 4)
b.
p.b. ? GA.?
m. 31 Mar 1870 Bexar Co.,TX
d. 1875
p.d. TX.

**9 Sarah Jane Riggs** (Mother of No. 4)
b. 13 Apr. 1853
p.b. Montgomery Co., AR
d. 1883 Devine,Medina,TX
p.d. "

**10 Thomas Washington Gage** (Father of No. 5)
b. 18 May 1854
p.b. Fayette Co., TX
m. 20 June 1878
d. 19 Apr. 1919 bur.Bend
p.d. San Saba Co., TX

**11 Matilda Jane Brazil** (Mother of No. 5)
b. 12 Feb. 1860
p.b. Union, Saline, AR
d. 30 Apr.1925 bur.Bend
p.d. San Saba Co., TX

**12 James Jonathon Hand** (Father of No. 6)
b. 26 Dec. 1849
p.b. Carroll Co., GA
m. (4) 12 Sept. 1888
d. 26 Mar.1924 bur.Harlingen
p.d. Harlingen,Cameron,TX

**13 Martha Emma Dooley** (Mother of No. 6)
b. 3 Feb. 1868
p.b. Matagorda Co., TX
d. 18 Oct. 1939 bur. Harl.
p.d. Harlingen,Cameron,TX

**14 Flavius Josephus Maupin** (Father of No. 7)
b. 28 Oct. 1847
p.b. MO.
m. 12 Feb.1869 Tarrant,TX
d. 10 July 1924 bur.Acker
p.d.Stephens Co., TX

**15 Sarah Louise French** (Mother of No. 7)
b. 8 Dec. 1851
p.b. MO.
d. 27 Oct.1925 bur.Acker
p.d. Stephens Co., TX

**16** (Father of No. 8)
_____ Continued on chart _____

**17** (Mother of No. 8)
_____ Continued on chart _____

**18 Alexander Gray Riggs** (Father of No. 9)
b.1816 N C     Compiled on chart
d.ca 1859 Ouachita Co.,AR

**19 Jane** (Mother of No. 9)
b.ca181? Ouachita Co.,AR
d.ca1859 Ouachita Co.,AR

**20 Henry Salem Gage** (Father of No. 10)
b. 1829 TN    Continued on chart
d.5 Feb. 1852 Fayette Co., TX

**21 Rebecca Jane Nettles** (Mother of No. 10)
b. 1833      Continued on chart
d. 7Sept1856 TX

**22 William Merion Brazil** (Father of No. 11)  Saline Co.AR
b.1839
m.27Mar.1859   Continued on chart
d.ca 1863 in service C.S.A.

**23 Mary Ann Brazil** (Mother of No. 11)
1843
d.ca 1860 Saline Co., AR

**24 James Hodges Hand** (Father of No. 12)  Carroll Co.GA
1817
m.1839 GA    Continued on chart
d. 1863 Randolph Co., AL

**25 Harriet Narciza White** (Mother of No. 12)  Carroll Co.GA
1823
d. 1886 Hamilton Co., TX

**26 Jesse Dooley** (Father of No. 13)
1832 ALA.
d. 1897 TX     Continued on chart

**27 Sarah Jane Chandler** (Mother of No. 13)  Macon Co.GA
1842
d. 1918 Stephens Co., TX

**28 Wilkinson Maupin** (Father of No. 14)
ca 1813 MO.
m. (2)1846 Frankline Co.,MO.

**29 Louisa Valentine** (Mother of No. 14)
1827 MO.
d. Stephens Co., TX 1912

**30 Josiah T. French** (Father of No. 15)
1821 N.Y.
m. (2)1849 MO.   Continued on chart

**31 Martha E. Valentine** (Mother of No. 15)
1833       Continued

# Pedigree Chart No. 1

Date Aug. 1983
Name of Compiler: F. E. Brown
Address
City
Person No. 1 on this chart is the same person as ____ on chart No. ____

No.
b.  Date of Birth
p.b. Place of Birth
m.  Date of Marriage
d.  Date of Death
p.d Place of Death

**1 — Francis Emory Brown**
b. 27 Aug 1908
p.b. Brown's Crossing, GA (Baldwin Co.)
m. 1 Sept 1934 Gulfport, MS
d.
p.d.

**2 — Robert Barron Brown** (Father of No. 1)
b. 2 May 1870
p.b. Brown's Crossing, GA
m. 15 Feb 1900
d. 29 Apr 1925
p.d. Milledgeville, GA

**3 — Elizabeth Combs Winn** (Husband or Wife of No. 1)
b. 4 June 1915
p.b. Grenada, MS
d.

**4 — Robert Richard Brown** (Father of No. 2)
b. 29 Oct 1843
p.b. Brown's Crossing, GA
m. 20 Oct 1868
d. 16 Feb 1915
p.d. Brown's Crossing, GA
bur. Milledgeville, GA

**5 — Mary Eliz. Finney** (Mother of No. 2)
b. 13 Dec 1843
p.b. Haddock, Jones Co. GA
d. 6 Feb 1910
p.d. Brown's Crossing, GA
bur. Milledgeville, GA

**6 — Micajah Thomas Rogers** (Father of No. 3)
b. 29 Jan 1847
p.b. Warren Co., GA
m. 17 Feb 1875
d. 4 June 1911
p.d. Warrenton, GA
bur. Warrenton, GA

**7 — Sallie Celeste Darden** (Mother of No. 3)
b. 26 June 1853
p.b. Wilkes Co., GA
d. 24 May 1927
p.d. Atlanta, GA
bur. Warrenton, GA

**8 — David Pinckney Brown** (Father of No. 4)
b. 22 Aug 1813
p.b. Jones Co., GA
m. 1 Dec 1836
d. 19 June 1875
p.d. Fortville, GA (Jones Co)

**9 — Lucetta Hutchings** (Mother of No. 4)
b. 6 July 1814
p.b. Jones Co., GA
d. 19 June 1868
p.d. Fortville, Jones Co. GA

**10 — James Henry Finney** (Father of No. 5)
b. 5 May 1813
p.b. Jones Co., GA
m. 23 Dec 1832
d. 1 Nov 1877
p.d. Jones Co., GA

**11 — Julia Ann Morris** (Mother of No. 5)
b. 9 Feb 1817
p.b.
d. 31 May 1880
p.d.

**12 — Drury Wooten Rogers** (Father of No. 6)
b. 2 Dec 1815
p.b. Warren Co., GA
m. 28 Feb 1843
d. 1 June 1895
p.d. Warren Co., GA

**13 — Martha Virginia Turk** (Mother of No. 6)
b. 1 March 1822
p.b. Baldwin Co., GA
d. 20 July 1870
p.d. Warren Co., GA

**14 — Dr. William Boliver Darden** (Father of No. 7)
b. 22 Mar 1828
p.b. GA
m. 30 Oct 1850
d. 21 Mar 1885
p.d. Warren Co. bur. Norwood, GA

**15 — Mary Eliz. Wright** (Mother of No. 7)
b. 16 Dec 1830
p.b.
d. 22 Apr 1908
p.d. Warrenton, GA

**16 — Robert Brown** (Father of No. 8)
b. 28 Oct 1786  b. VA
d. 6 Nov 1855
Continued on chart 8

**17 — Martha (Patsy) Hall** (Mother of No. 8)
b. 11 Feb 1794
d. 1 Dec 1853
Continued on chart 8

**18 — Robert Hutchings** (Father of No. 9)
b. 27 Aug 1780  b. in VA
d. 27 Nov 1847
Continued on chart 2

**19 — Drucilla Bonner** (Mother of No. 9)
b. 18 May 1784  b. in GA
d. 18 Feb 1839
Continued on chart 3

**20 — Benjamin Finney** (Father of No. 10)
b. 1785
d. 18 Dec 1840
Continued on chart 8a

**21 — Sarah Taylor** (Mother of No. 10)
b. 22 Apr 1792
d. 11 Feb 1853
Continued on chart 8a

**22 — Jeremiah Morris** (Father of No. 11)
m. 25 Jan 1816 Jones Co., GA
Continued on chart 8b

**23 — Nancy Haskins** (Mother of No. 11)
Continued on chart 8b

**24 — Micajah (Michael) Rogers** (Father of No. 12)
m. 22 Oct 1800
d. Oct 1839 Warren Co. GA
Continued on chart 9

**25 — Ellen McFarland** (Mother of No. 12)
Continued on chart 9

**26 — Thomas Turk** (Father of No. 13)
b. 27 Nov 1792
d. 27 Apr 1880
Continued on chart

**27 — Rebecca Johnson** (Mother of No. 13)
b. 13 Dec 1796
d. 4 Mar 1864
Continued on chart

**28 — Zachariah Darden** (Father of No. 14)
b. 1775/6 VA
m. 1803
d. 24 Dec 1851
Continued on chart 11

**29 — Nancy O. Ellington** (Mother of No. 14)
b. 1785 VA
d. 1 Jul 1861 GA
Continued on chart 11

**30 — John Wright** (Father of No. 15)
Barbour Co., AL
Continued on chart 13

**31 — Sarah Webb Dozier** (Mother of No. 15)
Continued on chart 13

# Pedigree Chart No. 1

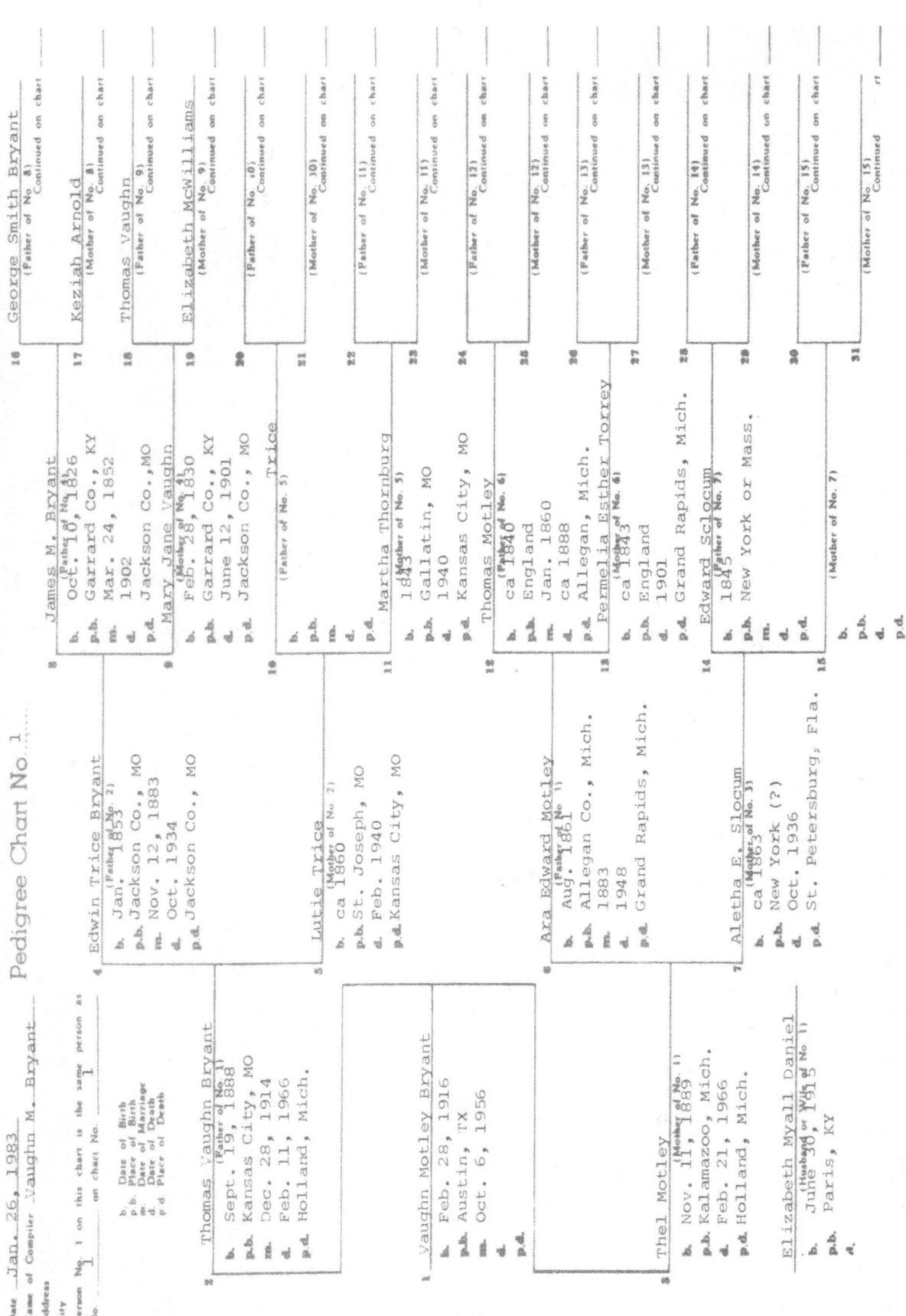

Date: Jan. 26, 1983
Name of Compiler: Vaughn M. Bryant
Address:
City:
Person No. 1 on this chart is the same person as No. _____ on chart No. _____

b. Date of Birth
p.b. Place of Birth
m. Date of Marriage
d. Date of Death
p.d. Place of Death

**1** Vaughn Motley Bryant
b. Feb. 28, 1916
p.b. Austin, TX
m. Oct. 6, 1956
d.
p.d.

**2** Thomas Vaughn Bryant (Father of No. 1)
b. Sept. 19, 1888
p.b. Kansas City, MO
m. Dec. 28, 1914
d. Feb. 11, 1966
p.d. Holland, Mich.

**3** Thel Motley (Mother of No. 1)
b. Nov. 11, 1889
p.b. Kalamazoo, Mich.
d. Feb. 21, 1966
p.d. Holland, Mich.

**4** Edwin Trice Bryant (Father of No. 2)
b. Jan. 1853
p.b. Jackson Co., MO
m. Nov. 12, 1883
d. Oct. 1934
p.d. Jackson Co., MO

**5** Lutie Trice (Mother of No. 2)
b. ca 1860
p.b. St. Joseph, MO
d. Feb. 1940
p.d. Kansas City, MO

**6** Ara Edward Motley (Father of No. 3)
b. Aug. 1861
p.b. Allegan Co., Mich.
m. 1883
d. 1948
p.d. Grand Rapids, Mich.

**7** Aletha E. Slocum (Mother of No. 3)
b. ca 1863
p.b. New York (?)
d. Oct. 1936
p.d. St. Petersburg, Fla.

**8** James M. Bryant (Father of No. 4)
b. Oct. 10, 1826
p.b. Garrard Co., KY
m. Mar. 24, 1852
d. 1902
p.d. Jackson Co., MO

**9** Mary Jane Vaughn (Mother of No. 4)
b. Feb. 28, 1830
p.b. Garrard Co., KY
d. June 12, 1901
p.d. Jackson Co., MO

**10** Trice (Father of No. 5)
b.
p.b.
m.
d.
p.d.

**11** Martha Thornburg (Mother of No. 5)
b. 1843
p.b. Gallatin, MO
d. 1940
p.d. Kansas City, MO

**12** Thomas Motley (Father of No. 6)
b. ca 1840
p.b. England
m. Jan. 1860
d. ca 1888
p.d. Allegan, Mich.

**13** Permelia Esther Torrey (Mother of No. 6)
b. ca 1843
p.b. England
d. 1901
p.d. Grand Rapids, Mich.

**14** Edward Slocum (Father of No. 7)
b. 1845
p.b. New York or Mass.
m.
d.
p.d.

**15** Elizabeth Myall Daniel (Husband or Wife of No. 7)
b. June 30, 1915
p.b. Paris, KY
d.

**16** George Smith Bryant (Father of No. 8) Continued on chart

**17** Keziah Arnold (Mother of No. 8) Continued on chart

**18** Thomas Vaughn (Father of No. 9) Continued on chart

**19** Elizabeth McWilliams (Mother of No. 9) Continued on chart

**20** (Father of No. 10) Continued on chart

**21** (Mother of No. 10) Continued on chart

**22** (Father of No. 11) Continued on chart

**23** (Mother of No. 11) Continued on chart

**24** (Father of No. 12) Continued on chart

**25** (Mother of No. 12) Continued on chart

**26** (Father of No. 13) Continued on chart

**27** (Mother of No. 13) Continued on chart

**28** (Father of No. 14) Continued on chart

**29** (Mother of No. 14) Continued on chart

**30** (Father of No. 15) Continued on chart

**31** (Mother of No. 15) Continued

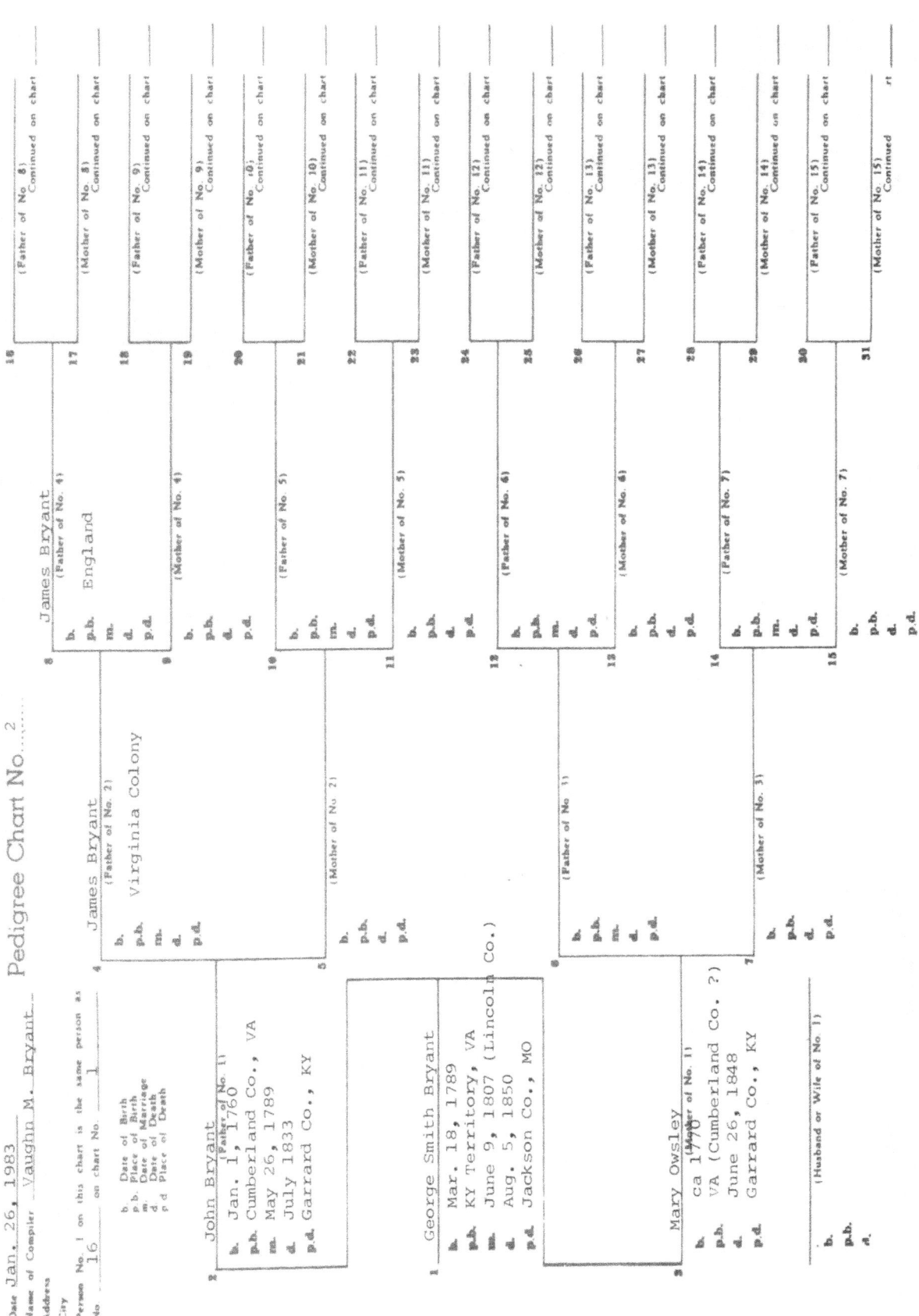

Pedigree Chart No. 2

Date Jan. 26, 1983
Name of Compiler Vaughn M. Bryant
Address
City
Person No. 1 on this chart is the same person as
No. 16 on chart No. 1

b.  Date of Birth
p. b.  Place of Birth
m.  Date of Marriage
d.  Date of Death
p. d.  Place of Death

1  George Smith Bryant
b.  Mar. 18, 1789
p.b.  KY Territory, VA
m.  June 9, 1807 (Lincoln Co.)
d.  Aug. 5, 1850
p.d.  Jackson Co., MO

2  John Bryant (Father of No. 1)
b.  Jan. 1, 1760
p.b.  Cumberland Co., VA
m.  May 26, 1789
d.  July 1833
p.d.  Garrard Co., KY

3  Mary Owsley (Mother of No. 1)
b.  ca 1770
p.b.  VA (Cumberland Co. ?)
d.  June 26, 1848
p.d.  Garrard Co., KY

4  James Bryant (Father of No. 2)
Virginia Colony
b.
p.b.
m.
d.
p.d.

5  (Mother of No. 2)
b.
p.b.
d.
p.d.

6  (Father of No. 3)
b.
p.b.
m.
d.
p.d.

7  (Mother of No. 3)
b.
p.b.
d.
p.d.

8  James Bryant (Father of No. 4)
England
b.
p.b.
m.
d.
p.d.

9  (Mother of No. 4)
b.
p.b.
d.
p.d.

10  (Father of No. 5)
b.
p.b.
m.
d.
p.d.

11  (Mother of No. 5)
b.
p.b.
d.
p.d.

12  (Father of No. 6)
b.
p.b.
m.
d.
p.d.

13  (Mother of No. 6)
b.
p.b.
d.
p.d.

14  (Father of No. 7)
b.
p.b.
m.
d.
p.d.

15  (Mother of No. 7)
b.
p.b.
d.
p.d.

(Husband or Wife of No. 1)

16  (Father of No. 8) Continued on chart
17  (Mother of No. 8) Continued on chart
18  (Father of No. 9) Continued on chart
19  (Mother of No. 9) Continued on chart
20  (Father of No. 10) Continued on chart
21  (Mother of No. 10) Continued on chart
22  (Father of No. 11) Continued on chart
23  (Mother of No. 11) Continued on chart
24  (Father of No. 12) Continued on chart
25  (Mother of No. 12) Continued on chart
26  (Father of No. 13) Continued on chart
27  (Mother of No. 13) Continued on chart
28  (Father of No. 14) Continued on chart
29  (Mother of No. 14) Continued on chart
30  (Father of No. 15) Continued on chart
31  (Mother of No. 15) Continued

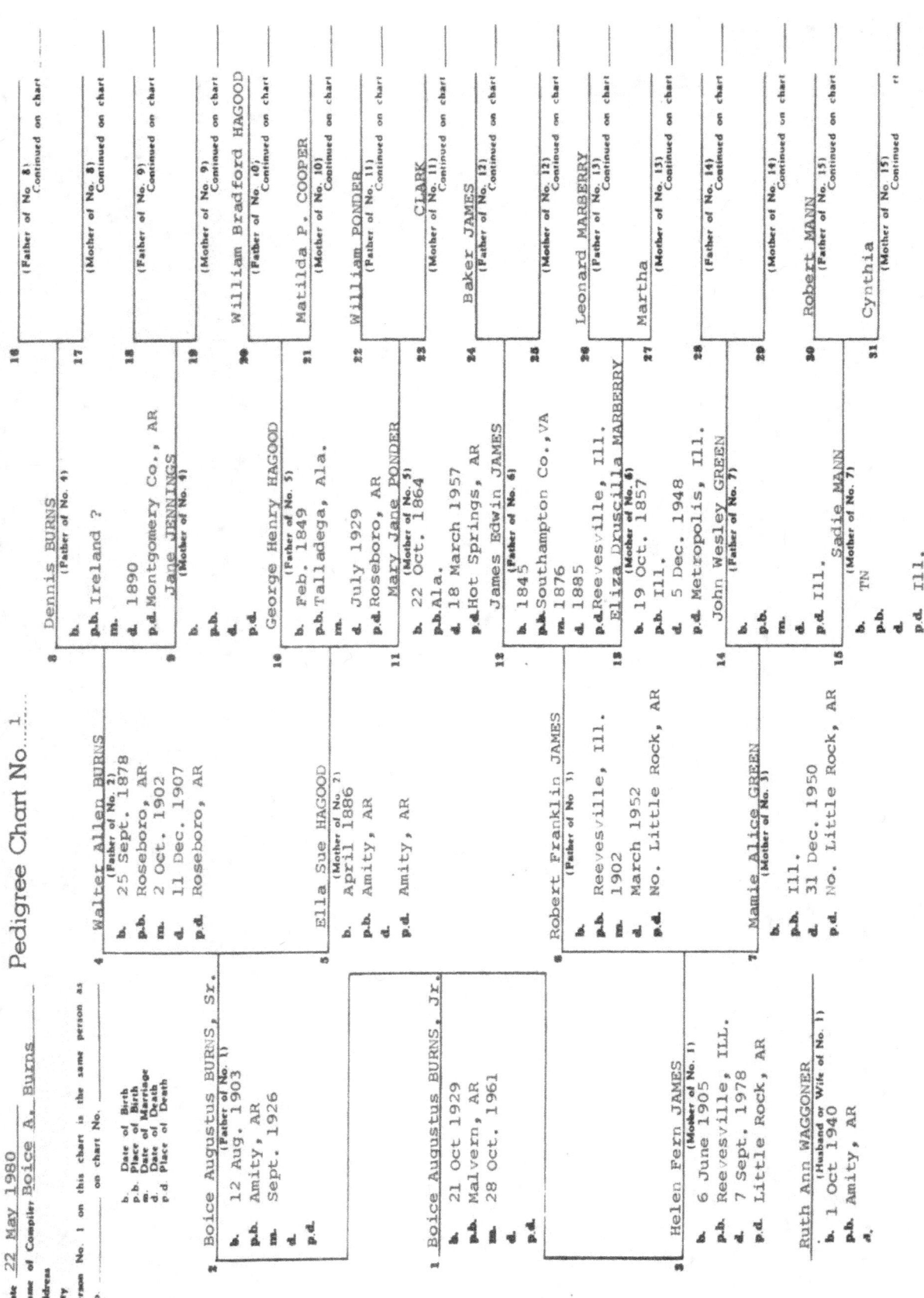

Pedigree Chart No. 1

Date  22 May 1980
Name of Compiler  Boice A. Burns
Address
City
Person No. 1 on this chart is the same person as
No. _____ on chart No. _____

b.   Date of Birth
p.b. Place of Birth
m.   Date of Marriage
d.   Date of Death
p.d  Place of Death

8  Dennis BURNS
   (Father of No. 4)
   b.
   p.b. Ireland ?
   m.
   d.   1890
   p.d. Montgomery Co., AR

9  Jane JENNINGS
   (Mother of No. 4)
   b.
   p.b.
   d.
   p.d.

10 George Henry HAGOOD
   (Father of No. 5)
   b.   Feb. 1849
   p.b. Talladega, Ala.
   m.
   d.   July 1929
   p.d. Roseboro, AR

11 Mary Jane PONDER
   (Mother of No. 5)
   b.   22 Oct. 1864
   p.b. Ala.
   d.   18 March 1957
   p.d. Hot Springs, AR

12 James Edwin JAMES
   (Father of No. 6)
   b.   1845
   p.b. Southampton Co., VA
   m.   1876
   d.   1885
   p.d. Reevesville, Ill.

13 Eliza Druscilla MARBERRY
   (Mother of No. 6)
   b.   19 Oct. 1857
   p.b. Ill.
   d.   5 Dec. 1948
   p.d. Metropolis, Ill.

14 John Wesley GREEN
   (Father of No. 7)
   b.
   p.b.
   m.
   p.d. Ill.

15 Sadie MANN
   (Mother of No. 7)
   b.        TN
   p.b.
   d.
   p.d. Ill.

16
   (Father of No. 8)
   Continued on chart

17
   (Mother of No. 8)
   Continued on chart

18
   (Father of No. 9)
   Continued on chart

19
   (Mother of No. 9)
   Continued on chart

20 William Bradford HAGOOD
   (Father of No. 10)
   Continued on chart

21 Matilda P. COOPER
   (Mother of No. 10)
   Continued on chart

22 William PONDER
   (Father of No. 11)
   Continued on chart

23 CLARK
   (Mother of No. 11)
   Continued on chart

24 Baker JAMES
   (Father of No. 12)
   Continued on chart

25
   (Mother of No. 12)
   Continued on chart

26 Leonard MARBERRY
   (Father of No. 13)
   Continued on chart

27 Martha
   (Mother of No. 13)
   Continued on chart

28
   (Father of No. 14)
   Continued on chart

29
   (Mother of No. 14)
   Continued on chart

30 Robert MANN
   (Father of No. 15)
   Continued on chart

31 Cynthia
   (Mother of No. 15)
   Continued

4  Walter Allen BURNS
   (Father of No. 2)
   b.   25 Sept. 1878
   p.b. Roseboro, AR
   m.   2 Oct. 1902
   d.   11 Dec. 1907
   p.d. Roseboro, AR

5  Ella Sue HAGOOD
   (Mother of No. 2)
   b.   April 1886
   p.b. Amity, AR
   d.
   p.d. Amity, AR

6  Robert Franklin JAMES
   (Father of No. 3)
   b.
   p.b. Reevesville, Ill.
   m.   1902
   d.   March 1952
   p.d. No. Little Rock, AR

7  Mamie Alice GREEN
   (Mother of No. 3)
   b.   Ill.
   p.b.
   d.   31 Dec. 1950
   p.d. No. Little Rock, AR

2  Boice Augustus BURNS, Sr.
   (Father of No. 1)
   b.   12 Aug. 1903
   p.b. Amity, AR
   m.   Sept. 1926
   d.
   p.d.

3  Helen Fern JAMES
   (Mother of No. 1)
   b.   6 June 1905
   p.b. Reevesville, ILL.
   d.   7 Sept. 1978
   p.d. Little Rock, AR

1  Boice Augustus BURNS, Jr.
   b.   21 Oct 1929
   p.b. Malvern, AR
   m.   28 Oct. 1961
   d.
   p.d.

Ruth Ann WAGGONER
   (Husband or Wife of No. 1)
   b.   1 Oct 1940
   p.b. Amity, AR
   d.

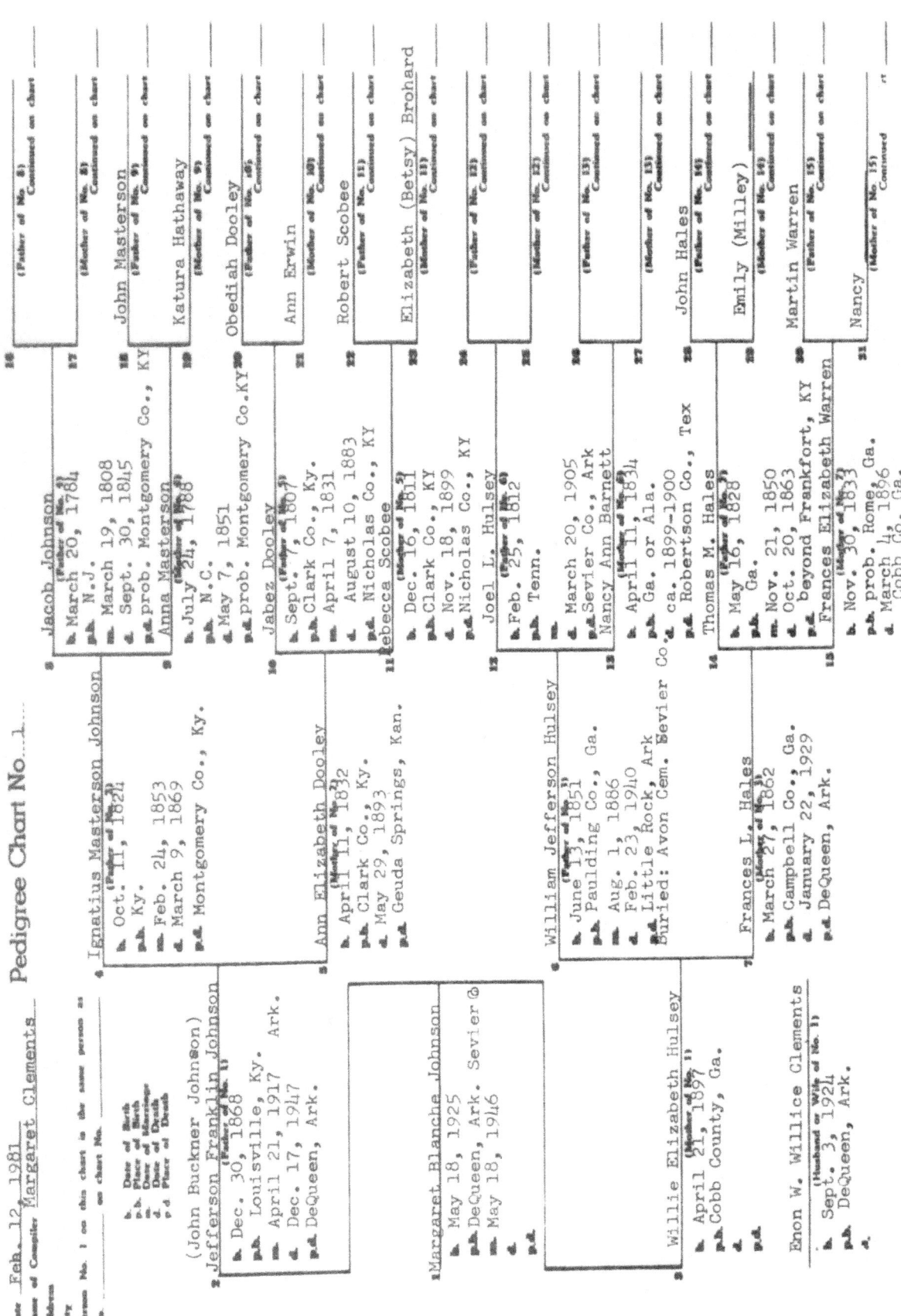

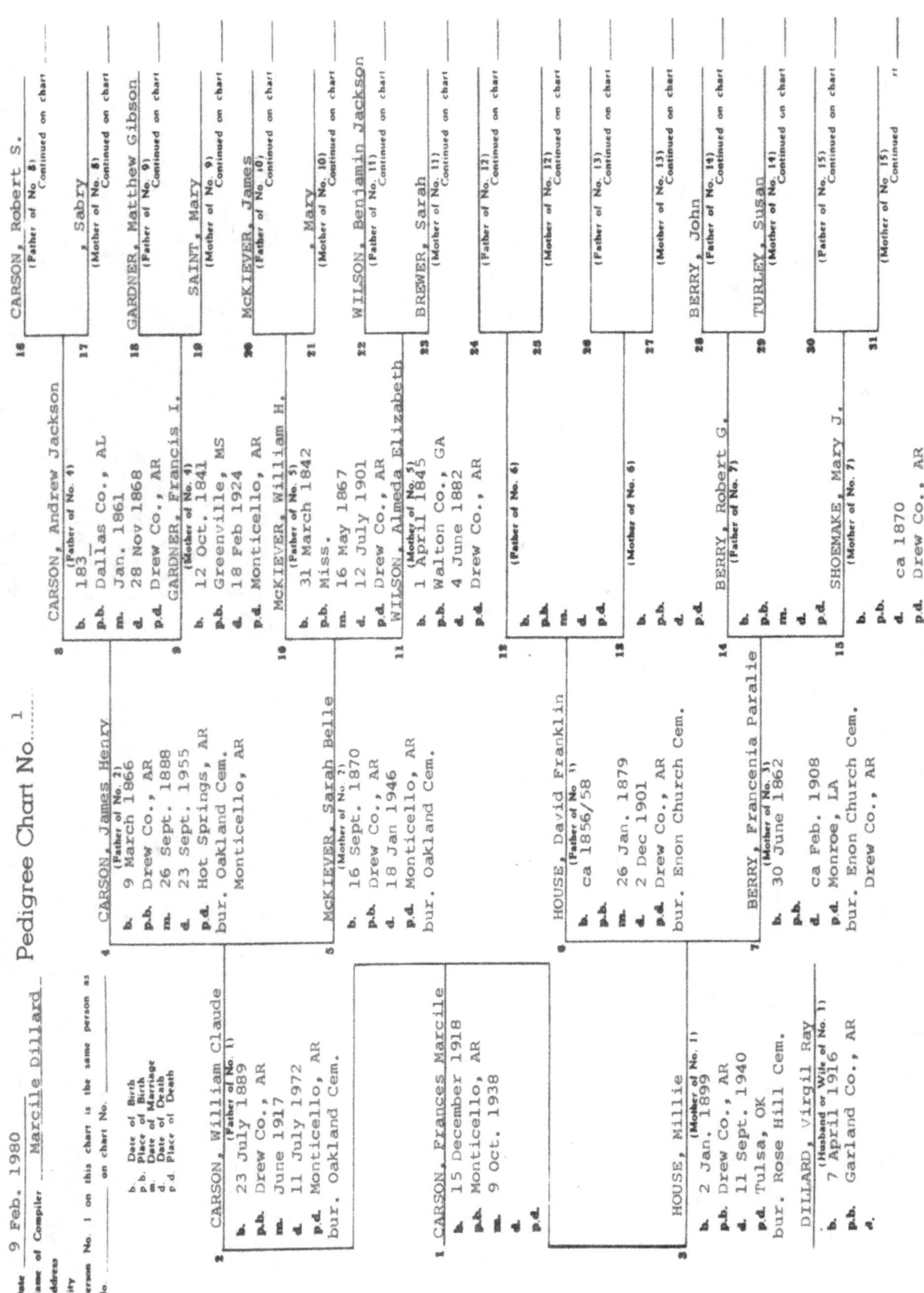

# Pedigree Chart No. 1

Date: 9 Feb. 1980
Name of Compiler: Marcile Dillard
Address:
City:
Person No. 1 on this chart is the same person as ___ on chart No. ___

b. Date of Birth
p.b. Place of Birth
m. Date of Marriage
d. Date of Death
p.d. Place of Death

**1** CARSON, Frances Marcile (Mother of No. 1)
b. 15 December 1918
p.b. Monticello, AR
m. 9 Oct. 1938
d.
p.d.

DILLARD, Virgil Ray (Husband or Wife of No. 1)
b. 7 April 1916
p.b. Garland Co., AR
d.

**2** CARSON, William Claude (Father of No. 1)
b. 23 July 1889
p.b. Drew Co., AR
m. June 1917
d. 11 July 1972
p.d. Monticello, AR
bur. Oakland Cem.

**3** HOUSE, Millie (Mother of No. 1)
b. 2 Jan. 1899
p.b. Drew Co., AR
d. 11 Sept. 1940
p.d. Tulsa, OK
bur. Rose Hill Cem.

**4** CARSON, James Henry (Father of No. 2)
b. 9 March 1866
p.b. Drew Co., AR
m. 26 Sept. 1888
d. 23 Sept. 1955
p.d. Hot Springs, AR
bur. Oakland Cem., Monticello, AR

**5** McKIEVER, Sarah Belle (Mother of No. 2)
b. 16 Sept. 1870
p.b. Drew Co., AR
d. 18 Jan 1946
p.d. Monticello, AR
bur. Oakland Cem.

**6** HOUSE, David Franklin (Father of No. 3)
b. 26 Jan. 1879
p.b.
m.
d. 2 Dec 1901
p.d. Drew Co., AR
bur. Enon Church Cem.

**7** BERRY, Francenia Paralie (Mother of No. 3)
b. 30 June 1862
p.b.
d. ca Feb. 1908
p.d. Monroe, LA
bur. Enon Church Cem. Drew Co., AR

**8** CARSON, Andrew Jackson (Father of No. 4)
b. 183_
p.b. Dallas Co., AL
m. Jan. 1861
d. 28 Nov. 1868
p.d. Drew Co., AR

**9** GARDNER, Francis I. (Mother of No. 4)
b. 12 Oct. 1841
p.b. Greenville, MS
d. 18 Feb 1924
p.d. Monticello, AR

**10** McKIEVER, William H. (Father of No. 5)
b. 31 March 1842
p.b. Miss.
m. 16 May 1867
d. 12 July 1901
p.d. Drew Co., AR

**11** WILSON, Almeda Elizabeth (Mother of No. 5)
b. 1 April 1845
p.b. Walton Co., GA
d. 4 June 1882
p.d. Drew Co., AR

**12** (Father of No. 6)
b. p.b. m. d. p.d.

**13** (Mother of No. 6)

**14** BERRY, Robert G. (Father of No. 7)
b. p.b. m. d. p.d.

**15** SHOEMAKE, Mary J. (Mother of No. 7)
b.
p.b.
d. ca 1870
p.d. Drew Co., AR

**16** CARSON, Robert S. (Father of No. 8) — Continued on chart

**17** ___, Sabry (Mother of No. 8) — Continued on chart

**18** GARDNER, Matthew Gibson (Father of No. 9) — Continued on chart

**19** SAINT, Mary (Mother of No. 9) — Continued on chart

**20** McKIEVER, James (Father of No. 10) — Continued on chart

**21** ___, Mary (Mother of No. 10) — Continued on chart

**22** WILSON, Benjamin Jackson (Father of No. 11) — Continued on chart

**23** BREWER, Sarah (Mother of No. 11) — Continued on chart

**24** (Father of No. 12) — Continued on chart

**25** (Mother of No. 12) — Continued on chart

**26** (Father of No. 13) — Continued on chart

**27** (Mother of No. 13) — Continued on chart

**28** BERRY, John (Father of No. 14) — Continued on chart

**29** TURLEY, Susan (Mother of No. 14) — Continued on chart

**30** (Father of No. 15) — Continued on chart

**31** (Mother of No. 15) — Continued

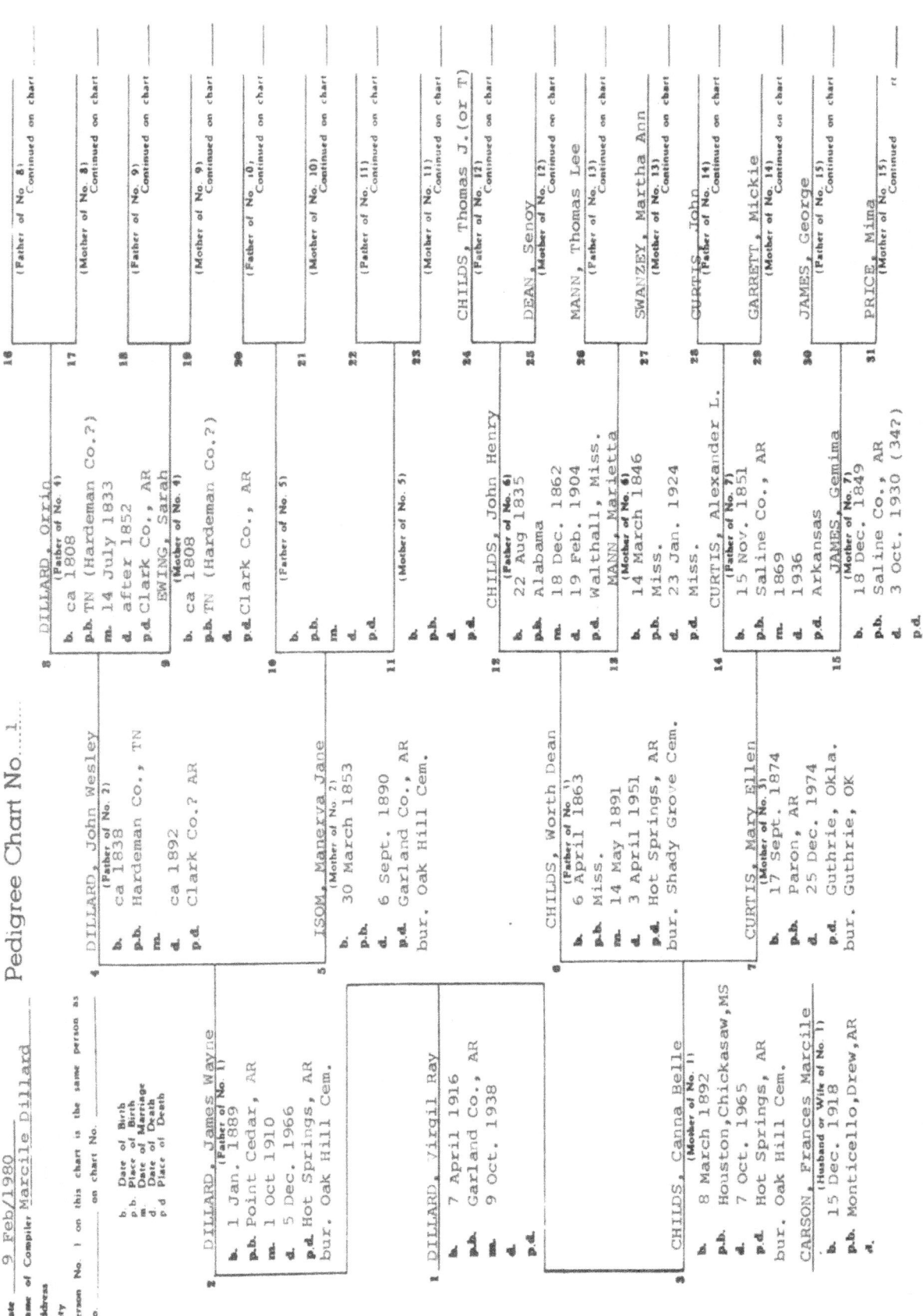

Pedigree Chart No. 1

Date  9 Feb/1980
Name of Compiler: Marcile Dillard
Address
City
Person No. 1 on this chart is the same person as
No. _____ on chart No. _____

b   Date of Birth
p.b  Place of Birth
m   Date of Marriage
d   Date of Death
p.d  Place of Death

1  DILLARD, Virgil Ray
  b.  7 April 1916
  p.b. Garland Co., AR
  m.  7 Oct. 1965
  d.  9 Oct. 1938
  p.d.

2  DILLARD, James Wayne
  (Father of No. 1)
  b.  1 Jan. 1889
  p.b. Point Cedar, AR
  m.  1 Oct 1910
  d.  5 Dec. 1966
  p.d. Hot Springs, AR
  bur. Oak Hill Cem.

3  CHILDS, Canna Belle
  (Mother of No. 1)
  b.  8 March 1892
  p.b. Houston, Chickasaw, MS
  d.  7 Oct. 1965
  p.d. Hot Springs, AR
  bur. Oak Hill Cem.

  CARSON, Frances Marcile
  (Husband or Wife of No. 1)
  b.  15 Dec. 1918
  p.b. Monticello, Drew, AR
  d.

4  DILLARD, John Wesley
  (Father of No. 2)
  b.  ca 1838
  p.b. Hardeman Co., TN
  m.  ca 1892
  d.
  p.d. Clark Co.? AR

5  ISOM, Manerva Jane
  (Mother of No. 2)
  b.  30 March 1853
  p.b.
  d.  6 Sept. 1890
  p.d. Garland Co., AR
  bur. Oak Hill Cem.

6  CHILDS, Worth Dean
  (Father of No. 3)
  b.  6 April 1863
  p.b. Miss.
  m.  14 May 1891
  d.  3 April 1951
  p.d. Hot Springs, AR
  bur. Shady Grove Cem.

7  CURTIS, Mary Ellen
  (Mother of No. 3)
  b.  17 Sept. 1874
  p.b. Paron, AR
  d.  25 Dec. 1974
  p.d. Guthrie, Okla.
  bur. Guthrie, OK

8  DILLARD, Orrin
  (Father of No. 4)
  b.  ca 1808
  p.b. TN (Hardeman Co.?)
  m.  14 July 1833
  d.  after 1852
  p.d. Clark Co., AR

  EWING, Sarah
  (Mother of No. 4)
  b.  ca 1808
  p.b. TN (Hardeman Co.?)
  d.
  p.& Clark Co., AR

10
  b.
  p.b.
  m.
  d.
  p.d.

11
  b.
  p.b.
  (Mother of No. 5)

12  CHILDS, John Henry
  (Father of No. 6)
  b.  22 Aug 1835
  p.b. Alabama
  m.  18 Dec. 1862
  d.  19 Feb. 1904
  p.d. Walthall, Miss.

13  MANN, Marietta
  (Mother of No. 6)
  b.  14 March 1846
  p.b. Miss.
  d.  23 Jan. 1924
  p.d. Miss.

14  CURTIS, Alexander L.
  (Father of No. 7)
  b.  15 Nov. 1851
  p.b. Saline Co., AR
  m.  1869
  d.  1936
  p.d. Arkansas

15  JAMES, Gemima
  (Mother of No. 7)
  b.  18 Dec. 1849
  p.b. Saline Co., AR
  d.  3 Oct. 1930 (347)
  p.d.

16  _____ (Father of No. 8)    Continued on chart
17  _____ (Mother of No. 8)    Continued on chart
18  _____ (Father of No. 9)    Continued on chart
19  _____ (Mother of No. 9)    Continued on chart
20  _____ (Father of No. 10)   Continued on chart
21  _____ (Mother of No. 10)   Continued on chart
22  _____ (Father of No. 11)   Continued on chart
23  _____ (Mother of No. 11)   Continued on chart
24  CHILDS, Thomas J. (or T)  (Father of No. 12)   Continued on chart
25  DEAN, Senoy  (Mother of No. 12)   Continued on chart
26  MANN, Thomas Lee  (Father of No. 13)   Continued on chart
27  SWANZEY, Martha Ann  (Mother of No. 13)   Continued on chart
28  CURTIS, John  (Father of No. 14)   Continued on chart
29  GARRETT, Mickie  (Mother of No. 14)   Continued on chart
30  JAMES, George  (Father of No. 15)   Continued on chart
31  PRICE, Mima  (Mother of No. 15)   Continued

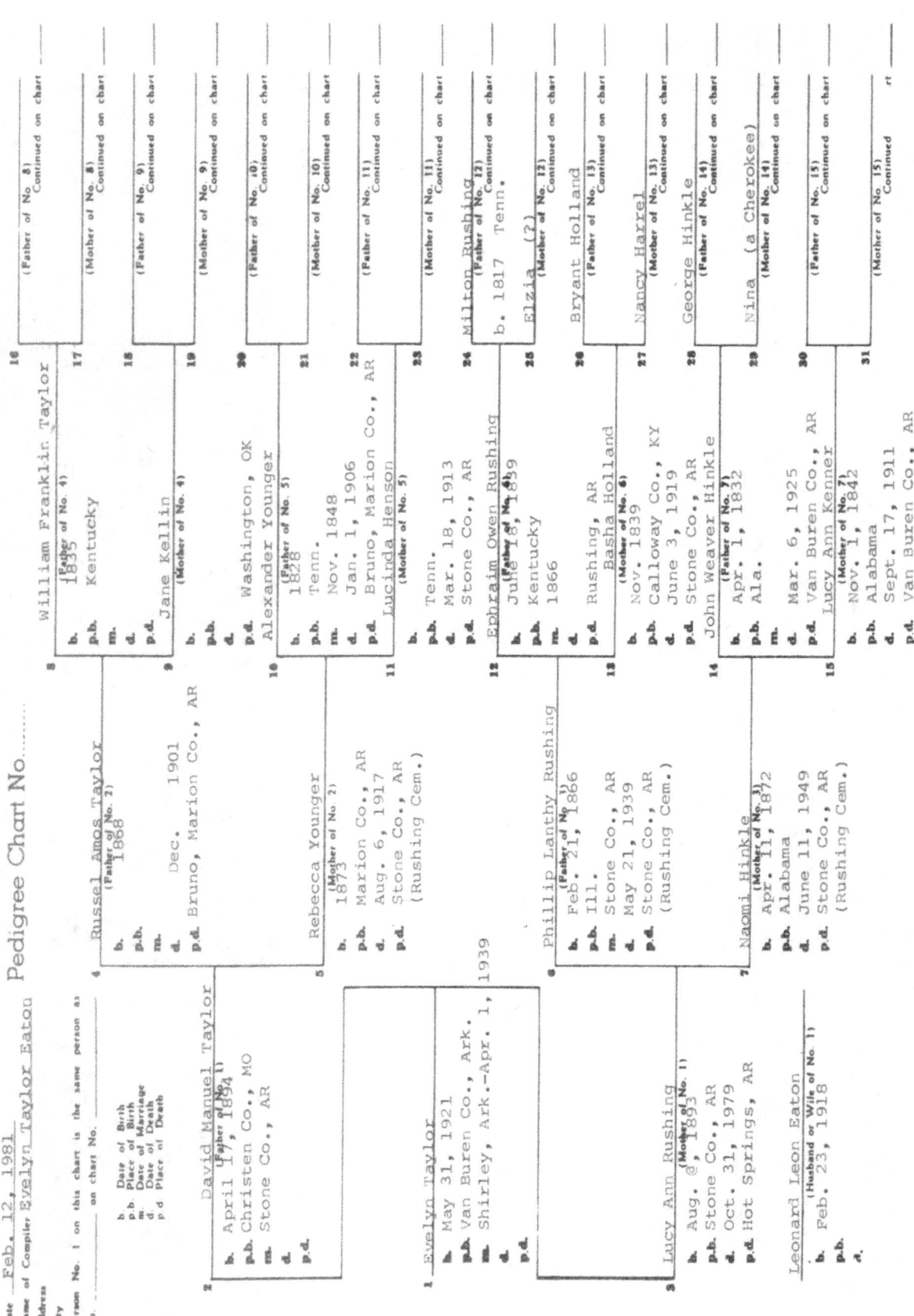

Date __Feb. 12, 1981__    Pedigree Chart No. ..........

Name of Compiler __Evelyn Taylor Eaton__

Address _____

City _____

Person No. 1 on this chart is the same person as
No. _____ on chart No. _____

   b  Date of Birth
   p.b  Place of Birth
   m.  Date of Marriage
   p.d  Place of Death

**2** David Manuel Taylor *(Father of No. 1)*
b. April 17, 1894
p.b. Christen Co., MO
m. Stone Co., AR
d.
p.d.

**1** Evelyn Taylor
b. May 31, 1921
p.b. Van Buren Co., Ark.
m. Shirley, Ark.–Apr. 1, 1939
d.
p.d.

**3** Lucy Ann Rushing *(Mother of No. 1)*
b. Aug. @, 1893
p.b. Stone Co., AR
d. Oct. 31, 1979
p.d. Hot Springs, AR

Leonard Leon Eaton *(Husband or Wife of No. 1)*
b. Feb. 23, 1918
p.b.
d.

**4** Russel Amos Taylor *(Father of No. 2)*
b. 1868
p.b.
m.
d. Dec. 1901
p.d. Bruno, Marion Co., AR

**5** Rebecca Younger *(Mother of No. 2)*
b. 1873
p.b. Marion Co., AR
d. Aug. 6, 1917
p.d. Stone Co., AR (Rushing Cem.)

**6** Phillip Lanthy Rushing *(Father of No. 3)*
b. Feb. 21, 1866
p.b. Ill.
m. Stone Co., AR
d. May 21, 1939
p.d. Stone Co., AR (Rushing Cem.)

**7** Naomi Hinkle *(Mother of No. 3)*
b. Apr. 11, 1872
p.b. Alabama
d. June 11, 1949
p.d. Stone Co., AR (Rushing Cem.)

**8** William Franklin Taylor *(Father of No. 4)*
b. 1835
p.b. Kentucky
m.
d.
p.d.
(Father of No. 8) Continued on chart _____ **16**
(Mother of No. 8) Continued on chart _____ **17**

**9** Jane Kellin *(Mother of No. 4)*
b.
p.b.
d.
p.d. Washington, OK
(Father of No. 9) Continued on chart _____ **18**
(Mother of No. 9) Continued on chart _____ **19**

**10** Alexander Younger *(Father of No. 5)*
b. 1828
p.b. Tenn.
m. Nov. 1848
d. Jan. 1, 1906
p.d. Bruno, Marion Co., AR
(Father of No. 10) Continued on chart _____ **20**
(Mother of No. 10) Continued on chart _____ **21**

**11** Lucinda Henson *(Mother of No. 5)*
b. Tenn.
p.b.
d. Mar. 18, 1913
p.d. Stone Co., AR
(Father of No. 11) Continued on chart _____ **22**
(Mother of No. 11) Continued on chart _____ **23**

**12** Ephraim Owen Rushing *(Father of No. 6)*
b. June 18, 1839
p.b. Kentucky
m. 1866
d.
p.d. Rushing, AR
(Father of No. 12) Continued on chart _____ **24** Milton Rushing b. 1817 Tenn.
(Mother of No. 12) Continued on chart _____ **25** Elzia (?)

**13** Basha Holland *(Mother of No. 6)*
b. Nov. 1839
p.b. Calloway Co., KY
d. June 3, 1919
p.d. Stone Co., AR
(Father of No. 13) Continued on chart _____ **26** Bryant Holland
(Mother of No. 13) Continued on chart _____ **27** Nancy Harrel

**14** John Weaver Hinkle *(Father of No. 7)*
b. Apr. 1, 1832
p.b. Ala.
m.
d. Mar. 6, 1925
p.d. Van Buren Co., AR
(Father of No. 14) Continued on chart _____ **28** George Hinkle
(Mother of No. 14) Continued on chart _____ **29** Nina (a Cherokee)

**15** Lucy Ann Kenner *(Mother of No. 7)*
b. Nov. 1, 1842
p.b. Alabama
d. Sept. 17, 1911
p.d. Van Buren Co., AR
(Father of No. 15) Continued on chart _____ **30**
(Mother of No. 15) Continued _____ **31**

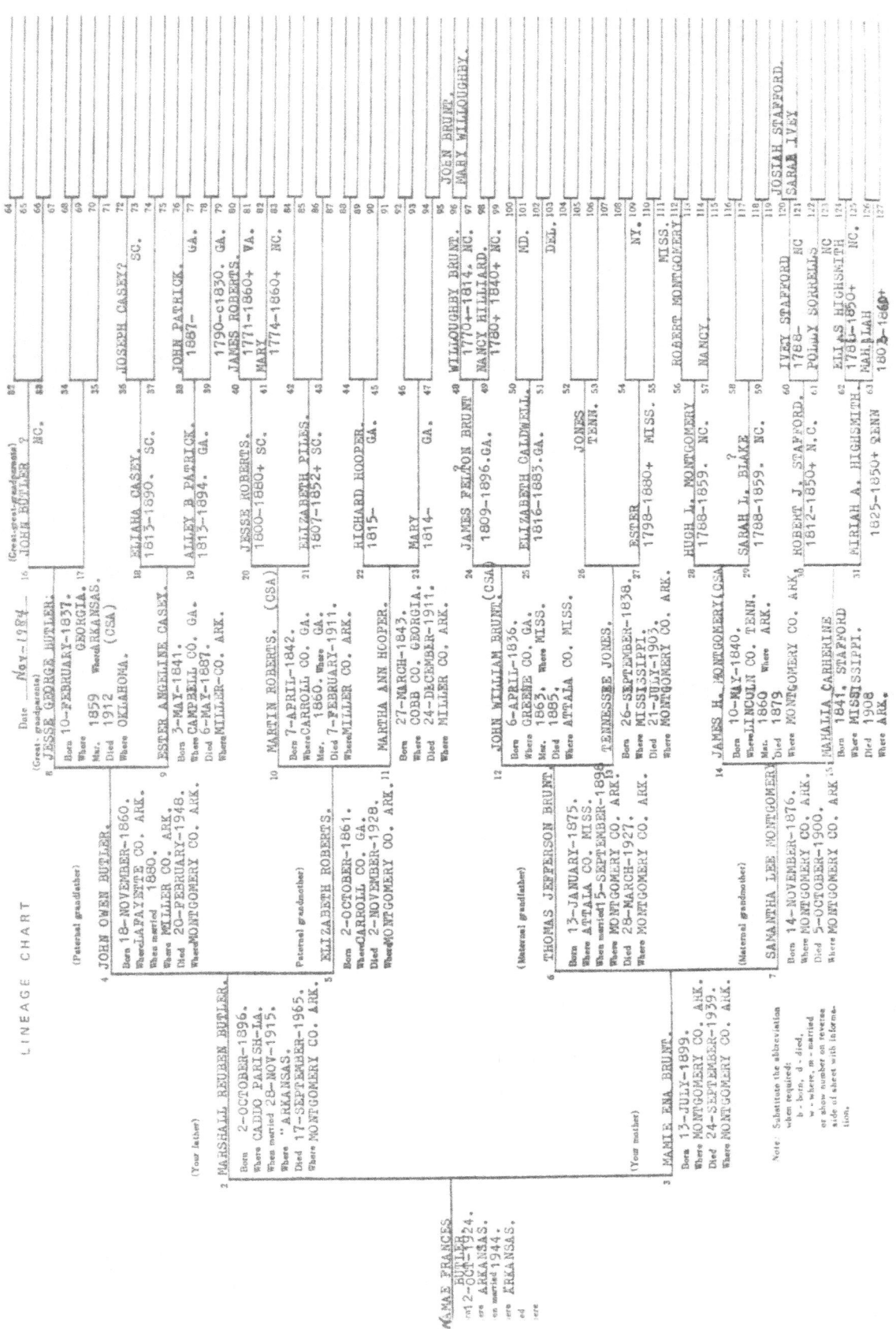

# Pedigree Chart No. 1

Date __May 8, 1982__
Name of Compiler __Richard Greer__
Address _____
City _____
Person No. __1__ on this chart is the same person as
No. _____ on chart No. _____

b.  Date of Birth
p.b.  Place of Birth
m.  Date of Marriage
d.  Date of Death
p.d  Place of Death

**1 Richard D. Greer**
b. April 1, 1952
p.b. Mt. Carmel, Ill.
m. Mar. 15, 1980
d.
p.d.

**2 Masel Amos Greer** (Father of No. 1)
b. Sept. 15, 1903
p.b. Holum, LA.
m. Aug. 4, 1934
d. July 9, 1970
p.d. Norris City, ILL.

**3 Gwendolyn May Snook** (Mother of No. 1)
b. May 23, 1912
p.b. Paonia, CO.
d.
p.d.

**Carol Sue May** (Husband or Wife of No. 1)
b. Jan. 31, 1954
p.b. Columbia, LA.
d.

**4 Sara Amos Greer** (Father of No. 2)
b. Dec. 22, 1877
p.b. Longview, AR
m. Feb. 27, 1901
d. Dec. 15, 1921
p.d. Holum, LA.

**5 Fannie Elvira Volentine** (Mother of No. 2)
b. Mar. 27, 1882
p.b. Holum, LA.
d. 1976
p.d. Mt. Carmel, ILL.

**6 Sidney Earl Snook** (Father of No. 3)
b. May 18, 1885
p.b. Lake City, CO.
m. 1908
d.
p.d. Concord, CA.

**7 Myrtle N. Wade** (Mother of No. 3)
b. Oct. 24, 1889
p.b. Paonia, CO
d. Nov. 1934
p.d. Laverne, CA.

**8 James Fredrick Greer** (Father of No. 4)
b. 1830
p.b. GA
m. Sept. 2, 1851
d.
p.d.

**9 Eliza Rawls** (Mother of No. 4)
b. Mar. 27, 1836
p.b. Hinds Co., MS
d. Sept. 10, 1892
p.d. Longview, AR

**10 Vincent P. Volentine** (Father of No. 5)
b. 1855
p.b. Holum, LA.
m. July 11, 1875
d.
p.d. Lincoln Parish, LA

**11 Jane E. Hamilton** (Mother of No. 5)
b. Nov. 5, 1856
p.b. GA.
d. Sept. 15, 1926
p.d. Holum, LA.

**12 Edmond Snook** (Father of No. 6)
b. March 1849
p.b. Iowa
m.
d. March 1933
p.d. Paonia, CO.

**13 Laura B. Barnaby** (Mother of No. 6)
b.
p.b.
d. 1889
p.d. Grand Junction, CO.

**14 Benjamin F. Wade, Sr.** (Father of No. 7)
b. Iowa
p.b.
m.
d.
p.d. Paonia, CO.

**15 Jessie F. Yoakum** (Mother of No. 7)
b. Iowa
p.b.
d.
p.d. Delta, CO.

**16 Aquilla Greer** (Father of No. 8)
Continued on chart _____

**17 Mary** (Mother of No. 8)
Continued on chart _____

**18 Alexander Rawls** (Father of No. 9)
Continued on chart _____

**19 Anna** (Mother of No. 9)
Continued on chart _____

**20 William Riley Valentine** (Father of No. 10)
Continued on chart _____

**21 Charlottie Poole** (Mother of No. 10)
Continued on chart _____

**22 Joseph Newton Hamilton** (Father of No. 11)
Continued on chart _____

**23 Easter Gilmore** (Mother of No. 11)
Continued on chart _____

**24** (Father of No. 12)
Continued on chart _____

**25** (Mother of No. 12)
Continued on chart _____

**26** (Father of No. 13)
Continued on chart _____

**27** (Mother of No. 13)
Continued on chart _____

**28 Samuel Wade** (Father of No. 14)
Continued on chart _____

**29** (Mother of No. 14)
Continued on chart _____

**30** (Father of No. 15)
Continued on chart _____

**31** (Mother of No. 15)
Continued _____

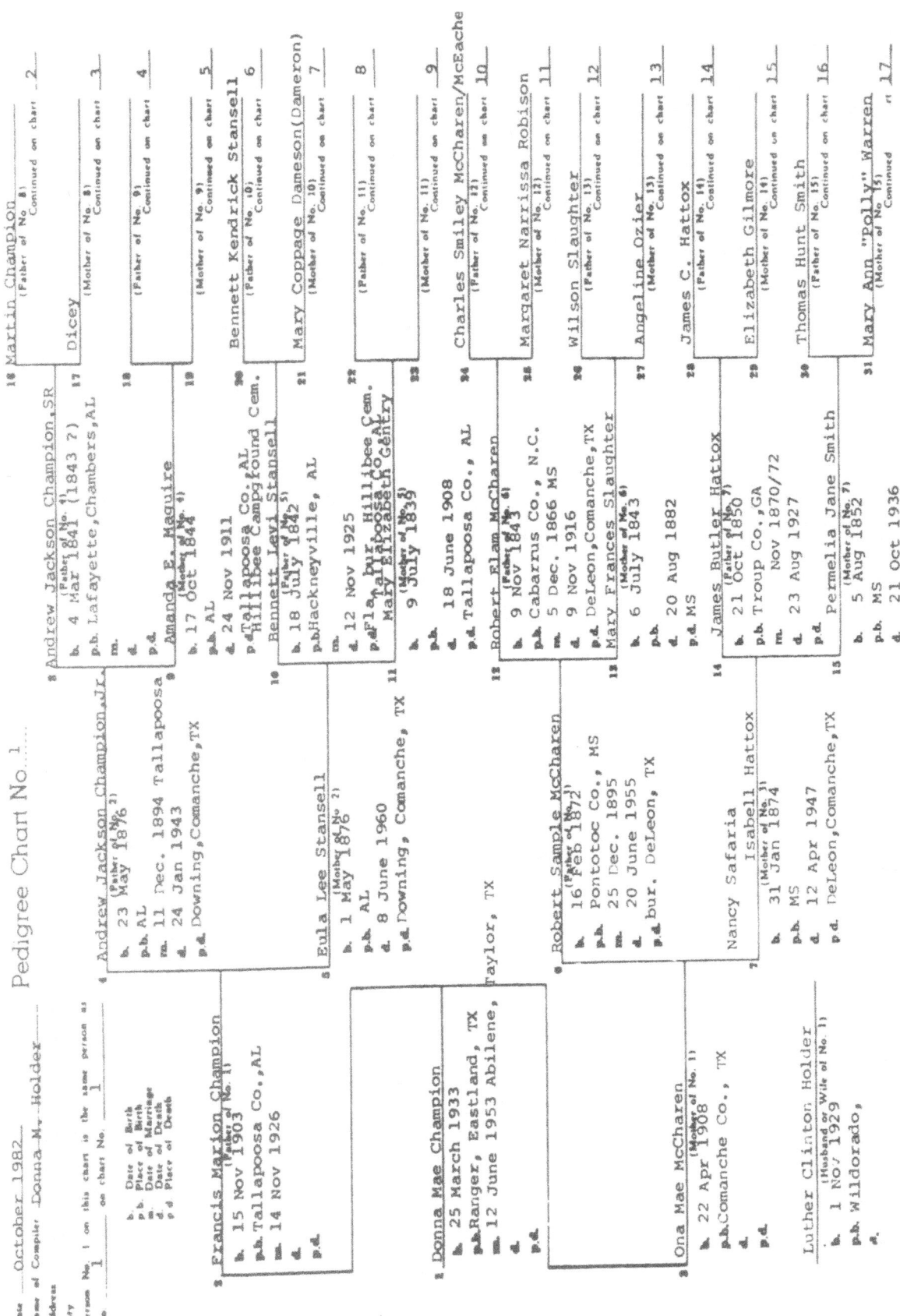

Pedigree Chart No. 1........

Date  October 1982
Name of Compiler  Donna M. Holder
Address
City
Person No. 1 on this chart is the same person as
No. ____ on chart No. __1__

b.  Date of Birth
p.b.  Place of Birth
m.  Date of Marriage
d.  Date of Death
p.d.  Place of Death

1  Donna Mae Champion
b.  25 March 1933
p.b. Ranger, Eastland, TX
m.  12 June 1953 Abilene, Taylor, TX
d.
p.d.

2  Francis Marion Champion (Father of No. 1)
b.  15 Nov 1903
p.b. Tallapoosa Co.,AL
m.  14 Nov 1926
d.
p.d.

3  Ona Mae McCharen (Mother of No. 1)
b.  22 Apr 1908
p.b. Comanche Co., TX
d.
p.d.

Luther Clinton Holder (Husband or Wife of No. 1)
b.  1 Nov 1929
p.b. Wildorado,
d.

4  Andrew Jackson Champion, Jr. (Father of No. 2)
b.  23 May 1876
p.b. AL
m.  11 Dec. 1894 Tallapoosa
d.  24 Jan 1943
p.d. Downing,Comanche,TX

5  Eula Lee Stansell (Mother of No. 2)
b.  1 May 1876
p.b. AL
d.  8 June 1960
p.d. Downing, Comanche, TX

6  Robert Sample McCharen (Father of No. 3)
b.  16 Feb 1872
p.b. Pontotoc Co., MS
m.  25 Dec. 1895
d.  20 June 1955
p.d. bur. DeLeon, TX

7  Nancy Safaria Isabell Hattox (Mother of No. 3)
b.  31 Jan 1874
p.b. MS
d.  12 Apr 1947
p.d. DeLeon,Comanche,TX

8  Andrew Jackson Champion,SR (Father of No. 4)
b.  4 Mar 1841 (1843 ?)
p.b. Lafayette,Chambers,AL
m.
d.
p.d.

9  Amanda E. Maguire (Mother of No. 4)
b.  17 Oct 1844
p.b. AL
d.  24 Nov 1911
p.d. Tallapoosa Co.,AL  Hillibee Campground Cem.

10  Bennett Levi Stansell (Father of No. 5)
b.  18 July 1842
p.b. Hackneyville, AL
m.
d.  12 Nov 1925
p.d. Flat, bur. Hillibee Cem.

Mary Elizabeth Gentry
b.  9 July 1839 (Mother of No. 5)
p.b.
d.  18 June 1908
p.d. Tallapoosa Co., AL

12  Robert Elam McCharen (Father of No. 6)
b.  9 Nov 1843
p.b. Cabarrus Co., N.C.
m.  5 Dec. 1866 MS
d.  9 Nov 1916
p.d. DeLeon,Comanche,TX

13  Mary Frances Slaughter (Mother of No. 6)
b.  6 July 1843
p.b.
d.  20 Aug 1882
p.d. MS

14  James Butler Hattox (Father of No. 7)
b.  21 Oct 1850
p.b. Troup Co.,GA
m.  Nov 1870/72
d.  23 Aug 1927
p.d.

15  Permelia Jane Smith (Mother of No. 7)
b.  5 Aug 1852
p.b. MS
d.  21 Oct 1936

18  Martin Champion (Father of No. 8) _____ 2

17  Dicey (Mother of No. 8) Continued on chart _____ 3

18  (Father of No. 9) Continued on chart _____ 4

19  (Mother of No. 9) Continued on chart _____ 5

Bennett Kendrick Stansell (Father of No. 10) Continued on chart _____ 6

21  Mary Coppage Dameson(Dameron) (Mother of No. 10) Continued on chart _____ 7

22  (Father of No. 11) Continued on chart _____ 8

23  (Mother of No. 11) Continued on chart _____ 9

24  Charles Smiley McCharen/McEache (Father of No. 12) Continued on chart _____ 10

25  Margaret Narrissa Robison (Mother of No. 12) Continued on chart _____ 11

26  Wilson Slaughter (Father of No. 13) Continued on chart _____ 12

27  Angeline Ozier (Mother of No. 13) Continued on chart _____ 13

28  James C. Hattox (Father of No. 14) Continued on chart _____ 14

29  Elizabeth Gilmore (Mother of No. 14) Continued on chart _____ 15

30  Thomas Hunt Smith (Father of No. 15) Continued on chart _____ 16

31  Mary Ann "Polly" Warren (Mother of No. 15) Continued on chart _____ 17

# Pedigree Chart No. 1-A

Date March 24, 1980
Name of Compiler Donna Mae Holder
Address
City
Person No. 1 on this chart is the same person as
No. _____ on chart No. _____

b. Date of Birth
p.b. Place of Birth
m. Date of Marriage
d. Date of Death
p.d Place of Death

1 Luther Clinton Holder
b. 1 Nov 1929
p.b. Wildorado, Texas
m. 12 June 1953
d.
p.d.

2 William Lee Holder (Father of No. 1)
b. 2 Aug 1887
p.b. Parker Co., Texas
m. 11 Dec 1910
d. Archer City, Texas
p.d.

3 Clara Maydell Hill (Mother of No. 1)
b. 30 June 1896
p.b. Parker Co., Texas
d. 29 June 1964
p.d. Archer City, Texas

Donna Mae Champion (Husband or Wife of No. 1)
b. 25 Mar 1933
p.b. Ranger, Texas
d.

4 Laney Clinton Holder (Father of No. 2)
b. 27 Dec 1861
p.b. Perry Co., Tenn.
m. 7 Jan 1883
d. 15 Feb 1934
p.d. Parker Co., Texas

5 Minerva Staggs (Mother of No. 2)
b. 8 Dec 1868
p.b. Parker Co., Texas
d. 26 Feb 1941
p.d. Parker Co., Texas

6 Edwin Luther Hill (Father of No. 3)
b. 22 Aug 1873
p.b. Tenn.
m. 28 May 1961
d.
p.d. Parker Co., Texas

7 Mattie Hemphill (Mother of No. 3)
b. 10 Jan 1877
p.b.
d. 22 July 1955
p.d. Parker Co., Texas

8 Isaac Holder (Father of No. 4)
b. 5 Jan 1833
p.b. Perry Co., Tenn.
m. 8 Feb 1892
p.d. Parker Co., Texas

9 Sarah I. Wiley (Mother of No. 4)
b. 9 June 1829
p.b.
d. 24 Dec 1890
p.d. Parker Co., Texas

10 Noah Staggs (Father of No. 5)
b. 7 Jan 1843
p.b.
m.
d. 3 Mar 1885
p.d. Parker Co., Texas

11 Matilda Moore (Mother of No. 5)
b. Aug 1847
p.b. Ark.
d. 21 Feb 1916
p.d. Parker Co., Texas

12 Leroy I. Hill (Father of No. 6)
b. Sept. 1844
p.b.
m. 1 Feb. 1903
d. Osage, Tenn.
p.d.

13 Mary A. Wilkerson (Mother of No. 6)
b.
p.b.
d.
p.d.

14 James Andrew Hemphill (Father of No. 7)
b.
p.b.
m.
d.
p.d.

15 Rebecca Canifax (Mother of No. 7)
b.
p.b.
d.
p.d.

16 Lane Holder (Father of No. 8)
Continued on chart

17 Rutha (Mother of No. 8)
Continued on chart

18 (Father of No. 9)
Continued on chart

19 (Mother of No. 9)
Continued on chart

20 (Father of No. 10)
Continued on chart

21 (Mother of No. 10)
Continued on chart

22 (Father of No. 11)
Continued on chart

23 (Mother of No. 11)
Continued on chart

24 William B. Hill (Father of No. 12)
Continued on chart

25 Nancy E. (Mother of No. 12)
Continued on chart

26 (Father of No. 13)
Continued on chart

27 (Mother of No. 13)
Continued on chart

28 (Father of No. 14)
Continued on chart

29 (Mother of No. 14)
Continued on chart

30 (Father of No. 15)
Continued on chart

31 (Mother of No. 15)
Continued on chart

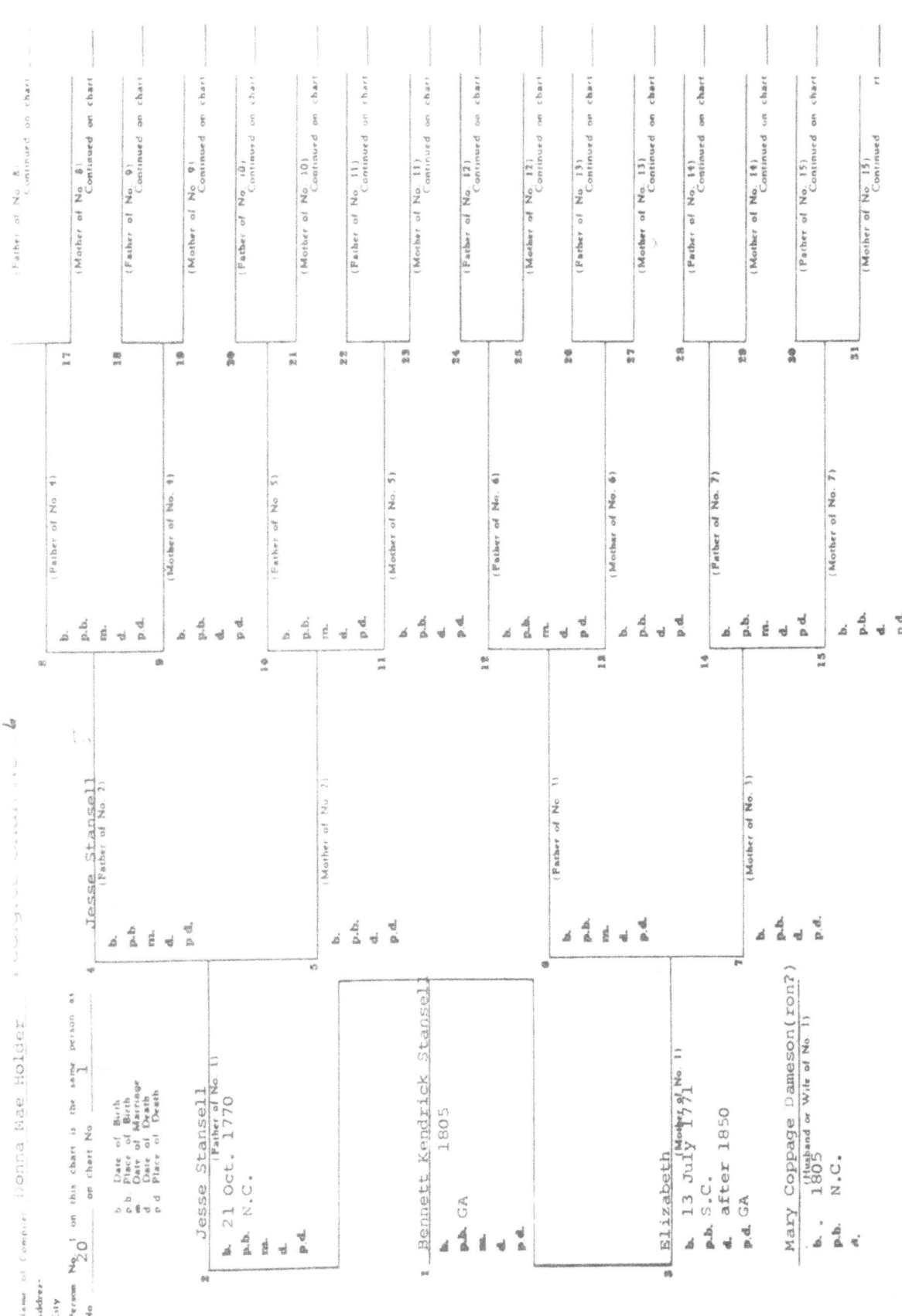

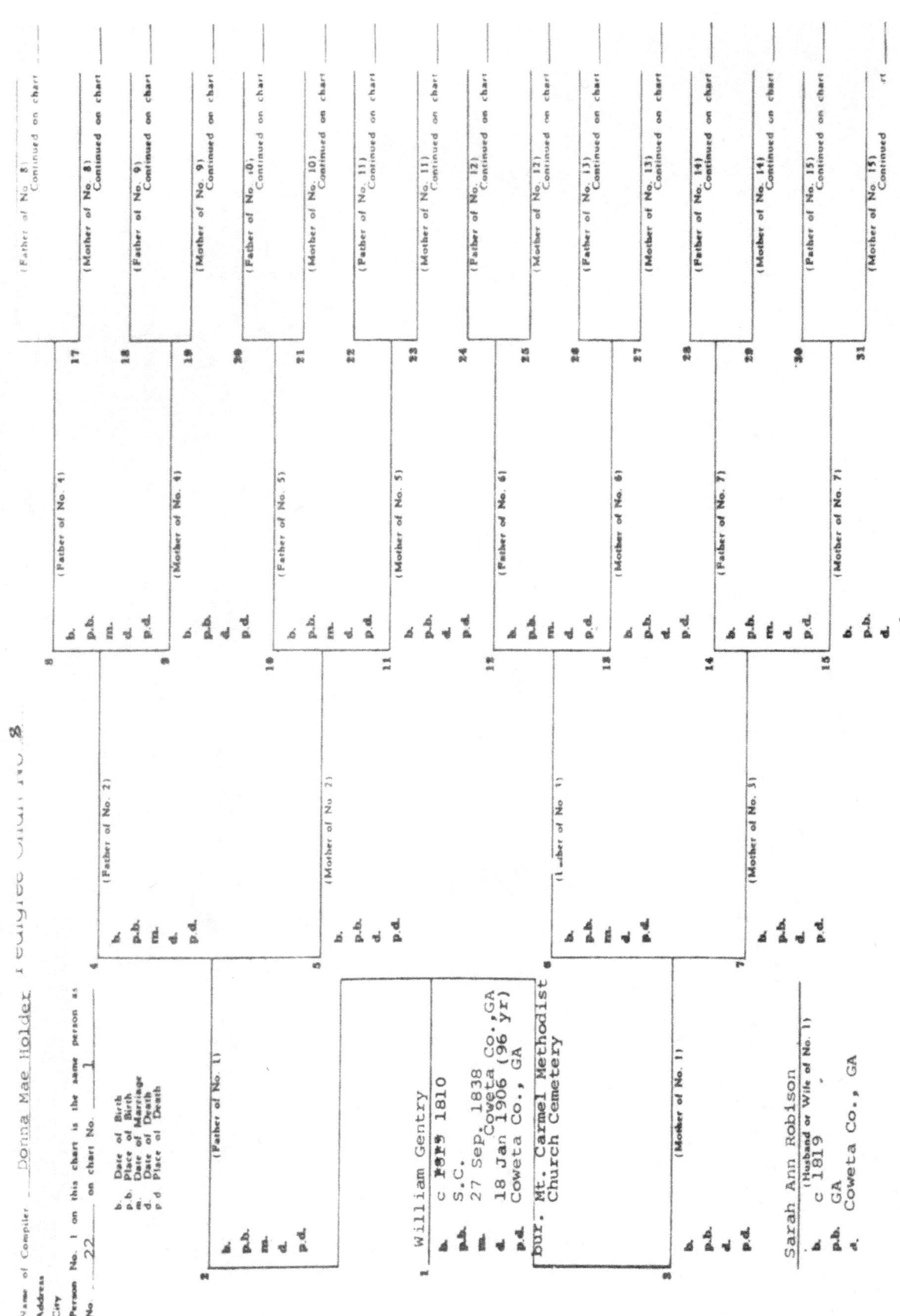

Name of Compiler ___Donna Mae Holder___ Pedigree Chart No. 8

Address

City

Person No. 1 on this chart is the same person as

No. ___22___ on chart No. ___1___

b. Date of Birth
p.b. Place of Birth
m. Date of Marriage
d. Date of Death
p.d Place of Death

1 William Gentry
b. c FEB 1810
p.b. S.C.
m. 27 Sep. 1838 Coweta Co.,GA
d. 18 Jan 1906 (96 yr)
p.d. Coweta Co., GA
bur. Mt. Carmel Methodist Church Cemetery

3 Sarah Ann Robison
(Husband or Wife of No. 1)
b. c 1819
p.b. GA
d. Coweta Co., GA

2 (Father of No. 1)
b.
p.b.
m.
d.
p.d.

3 (Mother of No. 1)
b.
p.b.
d.
p.d.

4 (Father of No. 2)
b.
p.b.
m.
d.
p.d.

5 (Mother of No. 2)
b.
p.b.
d.
p.d.

6 (Father of No. 3)
b.
p.b.
m.
d.
p.d.

7 (Mother of No. 3)
b.
p.b.
d.
p.d.

8 (Father of No. 4)
b.
p.b.
m.
d.
p.d.

9 (Mother of No. 4)
b.
p.b.
d.
p.d.

10 (Father of No. 5)
b.
p.b.
m.
d.
p.d.

11 (Mother of No. 5)
b.
p.b.
d.
p.d.

12 (Father of No. 6)
b.
p.b.
m.
d.
p.d.

13 (Mother of No. 6)
b.
p.b.
d.
p.d.

14 (Father of No. 7)
b.
p.b.
m.
d.
p.d.

15 (Mother of No. 7)
b.
p.b.
d.
p.d.

17 (Father of No. 8) Continued on chart

18 (Mother of No. 8) Continued on chart

19 (Father of No. 9) Continued on chart

20 (Mother of No. 9) Continued on chart

21 (Father of No. 10) Continued on chart

22 (Mother of No. 10) Continued on chart

23 (Father of No. 11) Continued on chart

24 (Mother of No. 11) Continued on chart

25 (Father of No. 12) Continued on chart

26 (Mother of No. 12) Continued on chart

27 (Father of No. 13) Continued on chart

28 (Mother of No. 13) Continued on chart

29 (Father of No. 14) Continued on chart

30 (Mother of No. 14) Continued on chart

31 (Father of No. 15) Continued on chart

(Mother of No. 15) Continued

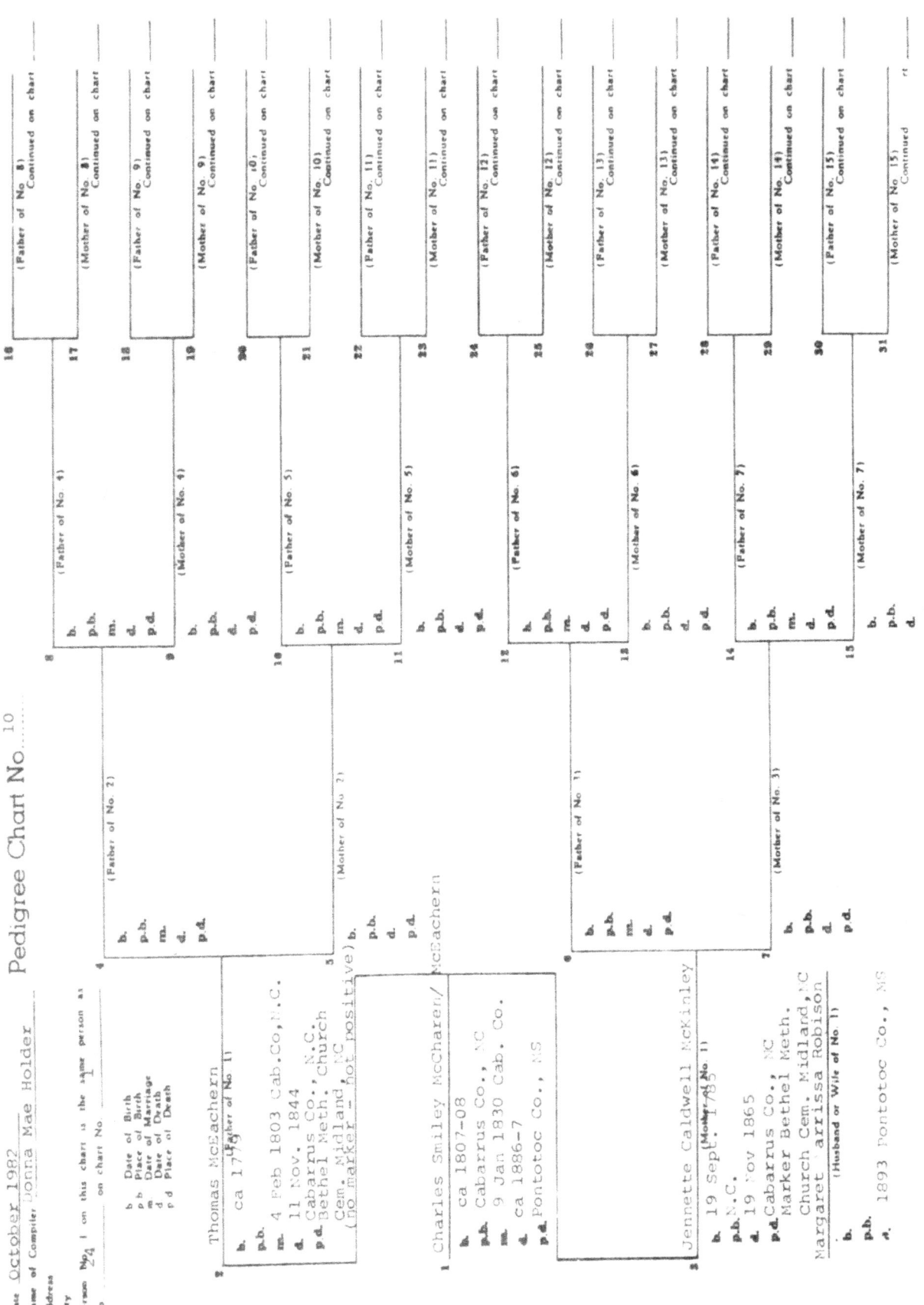

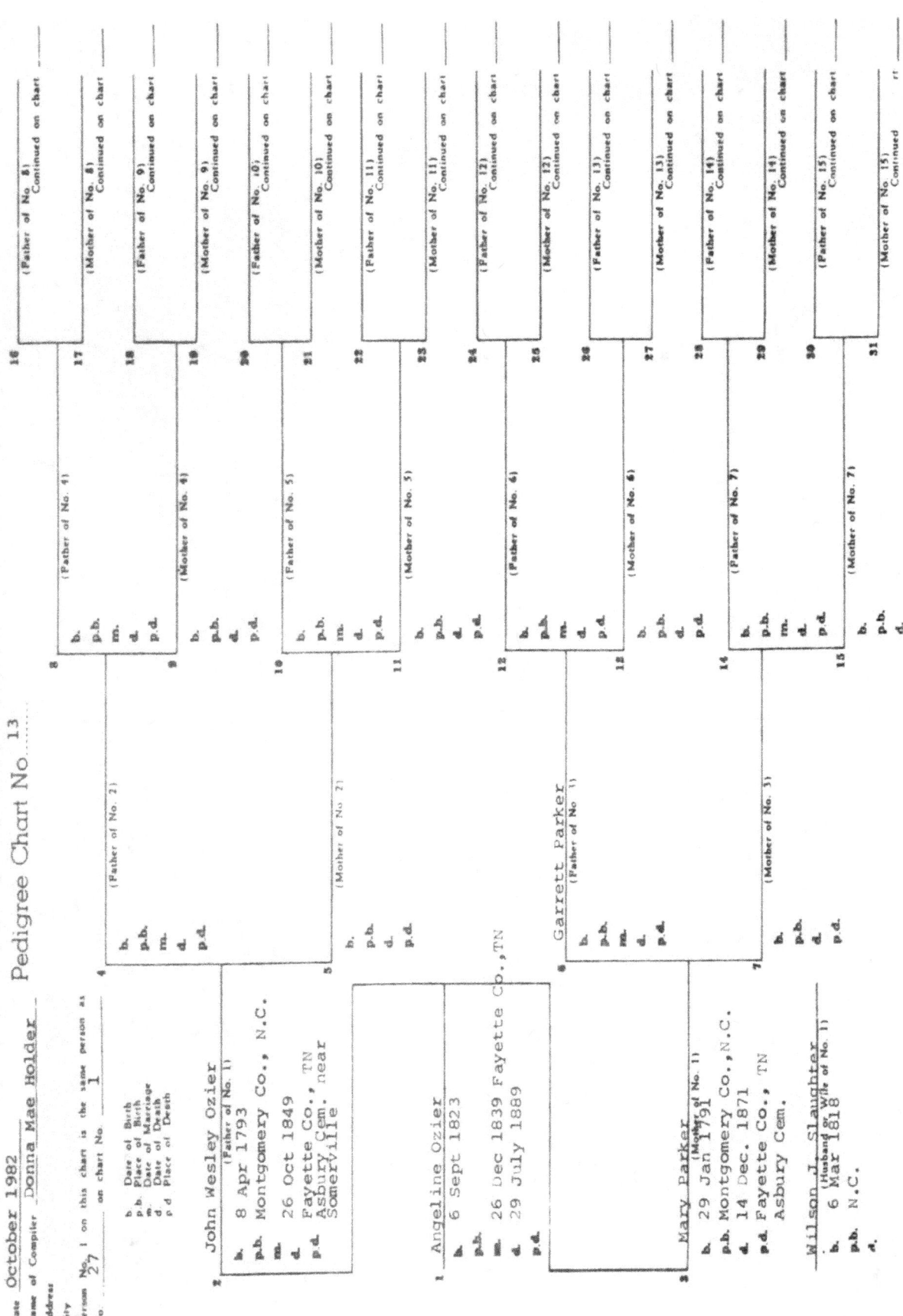

Pedigree Chart No. 13

Date October 1982

Name of Compiler Donna Mae Holder

Address

City

Person No. 1 on this chart is the same person as
No. 27 on chart No. 1

2  John Wesley Ozier (Father of No. 1)
b.  8 Apr 1793
p.b. Montgomery Co., N.C.
m.  26 Oct 1849
d.
p.d. Fayette Co., TN
     Asbury Cem. near
     Somerville

1  Angeline Ozier
b.  6 Sept 1823
p.b.
m.  26 Dec 1839 Fayette Co.,TN
d.  29 July 1889
p.d.

6  Garrett Parker (Father of No. 1)

3  Mary Parker (Mother of No. 1)
b.  29 Jan 1791
p.b. Montgomery Co., N.C.
d.  14 Dec. 1871
p.d. Fayette Co., TN
     Asbury Cem.

Wilson J. Slaughter (Husband or Wife of No. 1)
b.  6 Mar 1818
p.b. N.C.
d.

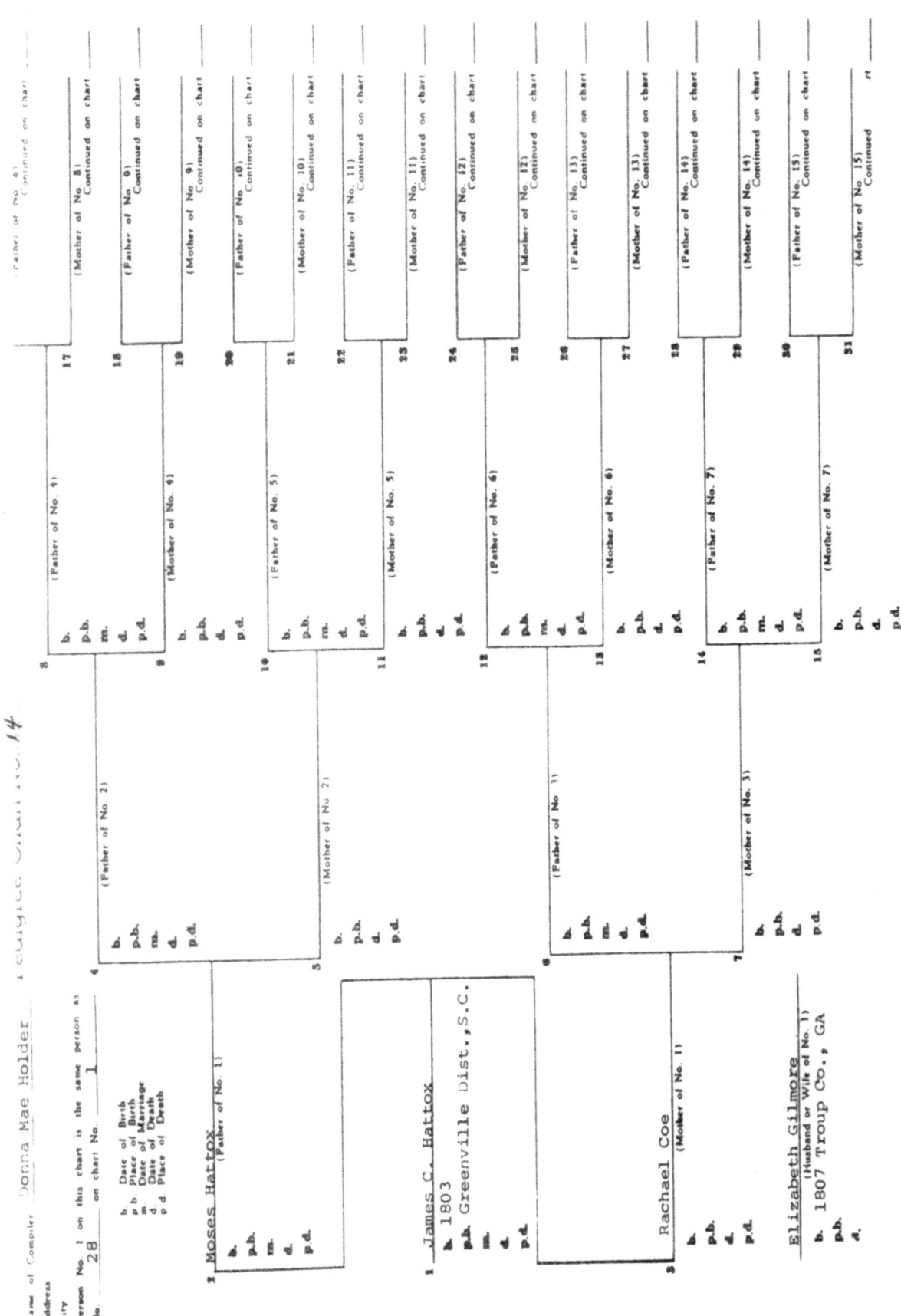

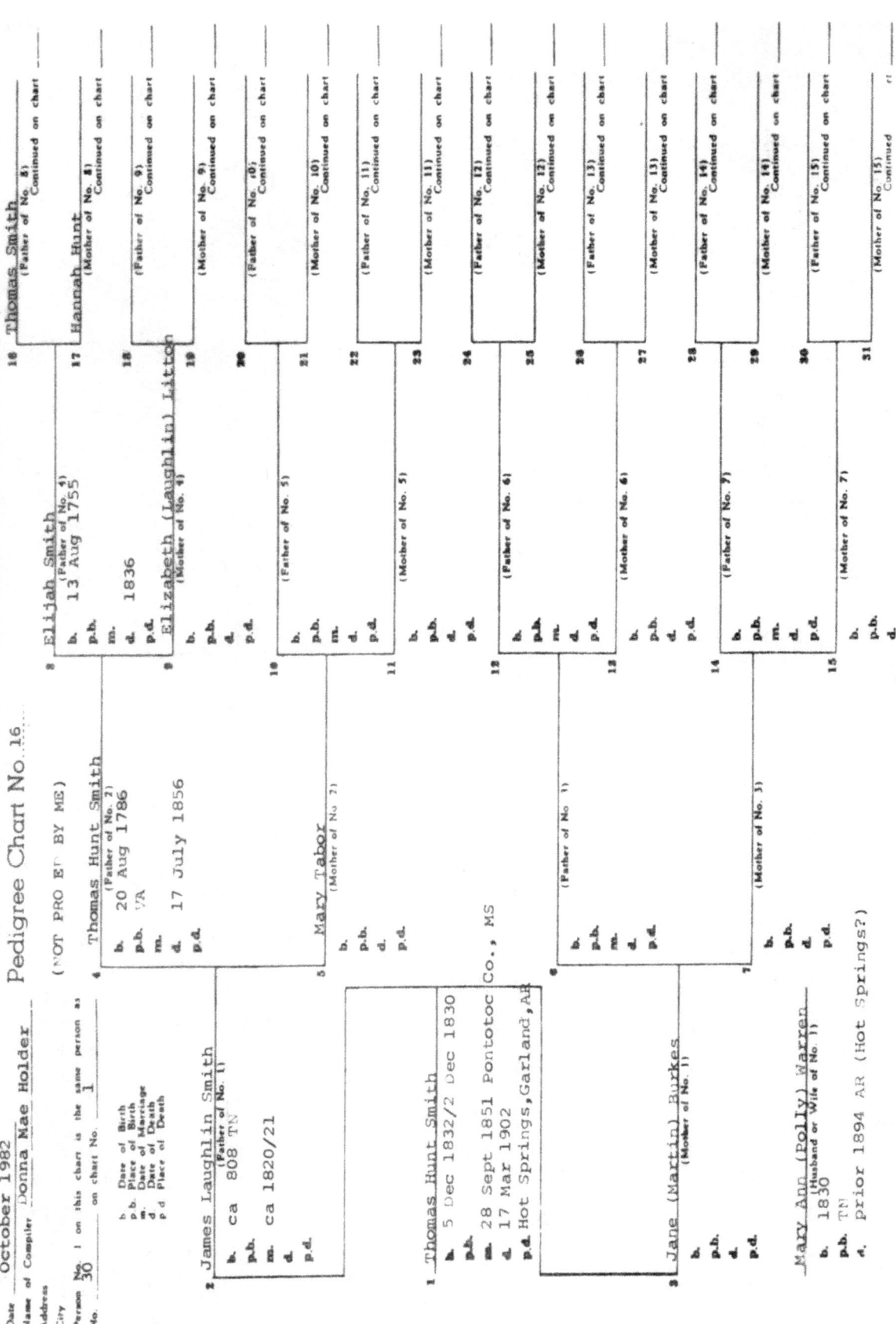

Date __October 1982__        Pedigree Chart No. 16

Name of Compiler __Donna Mae Holder__

Address

City

Person No. __1__ on this chart is the same person as
No. __30__ on chart No. __1__

b.    Date of Birth
p.b.  Place of Birth
m.    Date of Marriage
d.    Date of Death
p.d.  Place of Death

(NOT PROVED BY ME)

8  Elijah Smith
   (Father of No. 4)
   b.   13 Aug 1755
   p.b.
   m.
   d.   1836
   p.d.

9  Elizabeth (Laughlin) Litton
   (Mother of No. 4)
   b.
   p.b.
   d.
   p.d.

4  Thomas Hunt Smith
   (Father of No. 2)
   b.   20 Aug 1786
   p.b.  VA
   m.
   d.   17 July 1856
   p.d.

5  Mary Tabor
   (Mother of No. 2)
   b.
   p.b.
   d.
   p.d.

2  James Laughlin Smith
   (Father of No. 1)
   b.   ca 808 TN
   p.b.
   m.   ca 1820/21
   d.
   p.d.

1  Thomas Hunt Smith
   b.   5 Dec 1832/2 Dec 1830
   p.b.
   m.   28 Sept 1851 Pontotoc Co., MS
   d.   17 Mar 1902
   p.d. Hot Springs,Garland,AR

3  Jane (Martin) Burkes
   (Mother of No. 1)
   b.
   p.b.
   d.
   p.d.

6  (Father of No. 3)
   b.
   p.b.
   m.
   d.
   p.d.

7  (Mother of No. 3)
   b.
   p.b.
   d.
   p.d.

Mary Ann (Polly) Warren
   (Husband or Wife of No. 1)
   b.   1830
   p.b. TN
   d.   prior 1894 AR (Hot Springs?)

18  Thomas Smith
    (Father of No. 8)        Continued on chart ___

17  Hannah Hunt
    (Mother of No. 8)        Continued on chart ___

18  (Father of No. 9)        Continued on chart ___

19  (Mother of No. 9)        Continued on chart ___

20  (Father of No. 10)       Continued on chart ___

21  (Mother of No. 10)       Continued on chart ___

22  (Father of No. 11)       Continued on chart ___

23  (Mother of No. 11)       Continued on chart ___

24  (Father of No. 12)       Continued on chart ___

25  (Mother of No. 12)       Continued on chart ___

26  (Father of No. 13)       Continued on chart ___

27  (Mother of No. 13)       Continued on chart ___

28  (Father of No. 14)       Continued on chart ___

29  (Mother of No. 14)       Continued on chart ___

30  (Father of No. 15)       Continued on chart ___

31  (Mother of No. 15)       Continued

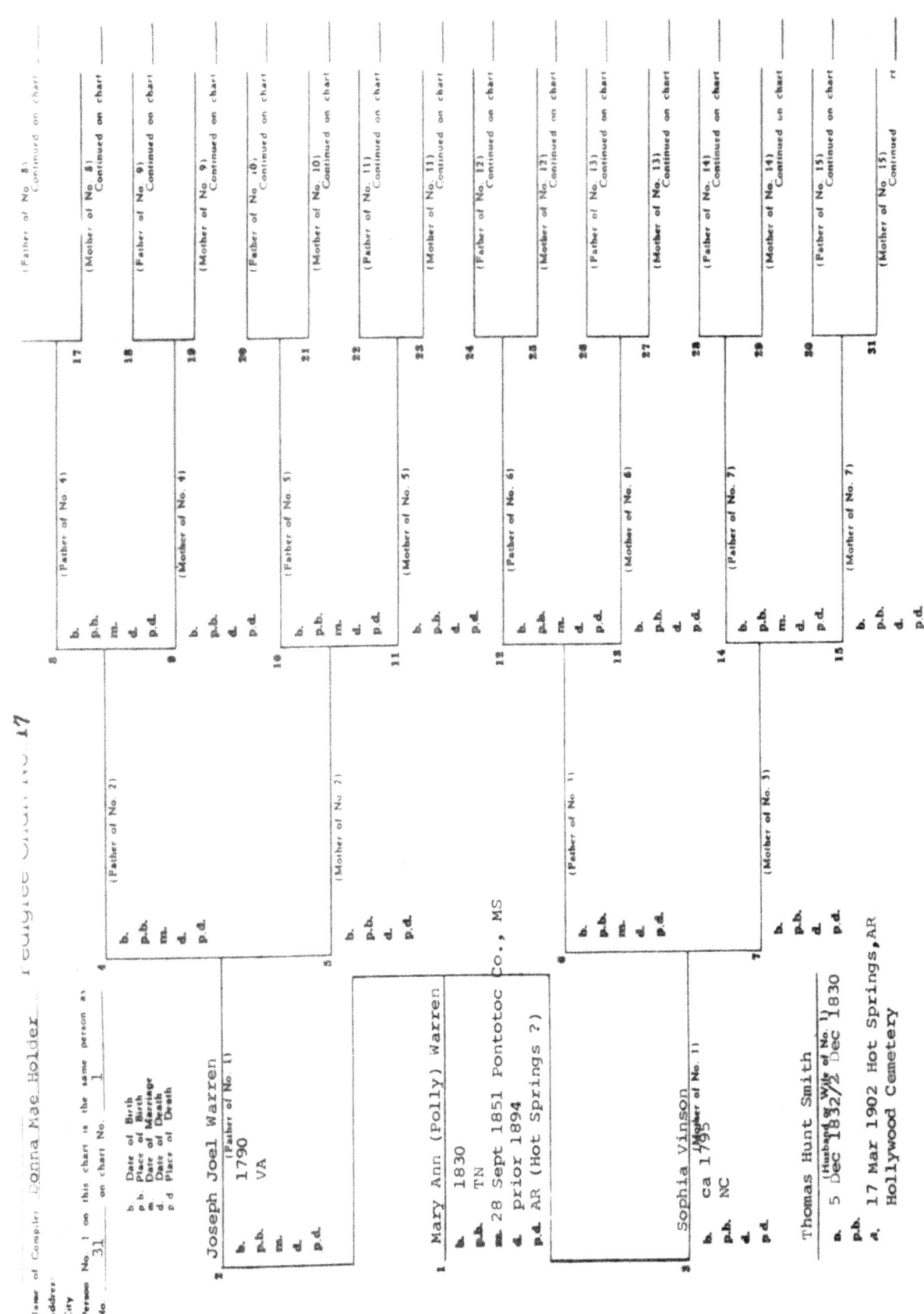

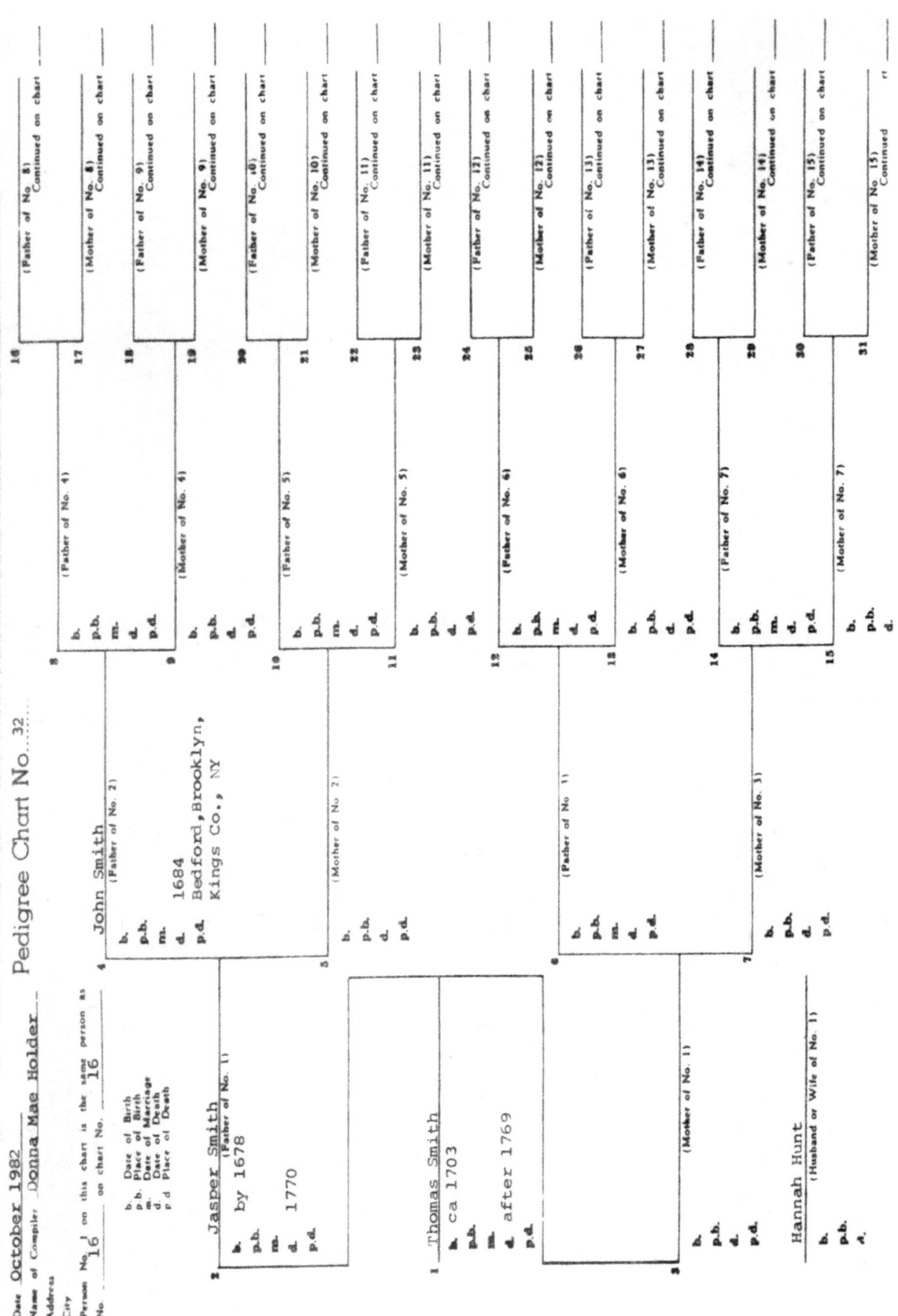

Pedigree Chart No. 32

Date October 1982
Name of Compiler Donna Mae Holder
Address
City
Person No. 1 on this chart is the same person as No. 16 on chart No. 16

b. Date of Birth
p.b. Place of Birth
m. Date of Marriage
d. Date of Death
p.d Place of Death

1 Thomas Smith
b. ca 1703
p.b.
m.
d. after 1769
p.d.

2 Jasper Smith (Father of No. 1)
b. by 1678
p.b.
m.
d. 1770
p.d.

3 (Mother of No. 1)
b.
p.b.
d.
p.d.

Hannah Hunt (Husband or Wife of No. 1)
b.
p.b.
d.

4 John Smith (Father of No. 2)
b.
p.b.
m.
d. 1684
p.d. Bedford, Brooklyn, Kings Co., NY

5 (Mother of No. 2)
b.
p.b.
d.
p.d.

6 (Father of No. 3)
b.
p.b.
m.
d.
p.d.

7 (Mother of No. 3)
b.
p.b.
d.
p.d.

8 (Father of No. 4)
b.
p.b.
m.
d.
p.d.

9 (Mother of No. 4)
b.
p.b.
d.
p.d.

10 (Father of No. 5)
b.
p.b.
m.
d.
p.d.

11 (Mother of No. 5)
b.
p.b.
d.
p.d.

12 (Father of No. 6)
b.
p.b.
m.
d.
p.d.

13 (Mother of No. 6)
b.
p.b.
d.
p.d.

14 (Father of No. 7)
b.
p.b.
m.
d.
p.d.

15 (Mother of No. 7)
b.
p.b.
d.

16 (Father of No. 8) Continued on chart

17 (Mother of No. 8) Continued on chart

18 (Father of No. 9) Continued on chart

19 (Mother of No. 9) Continued on chart

20 (Father of No. 10) Continued on chart

21 (Mother of No. 10) Continued on chart

22 (Father of No. 11) Continued on chart

23 (Mother of No. 11) Continued on chart

24 (Father of No. 12) Continued on chart

25 (Mother of No. 12) Continued on chart

26 (Father of No. 13) Continued on chart

27 (Mother of No. 13) Continued on chart

28 (Father of No. 14) Continued on chart

29 (Mother of No. 14) Continued on chart

30 (Father of No. 15) Continued on chart

31 (Mother of No. 15) Continued

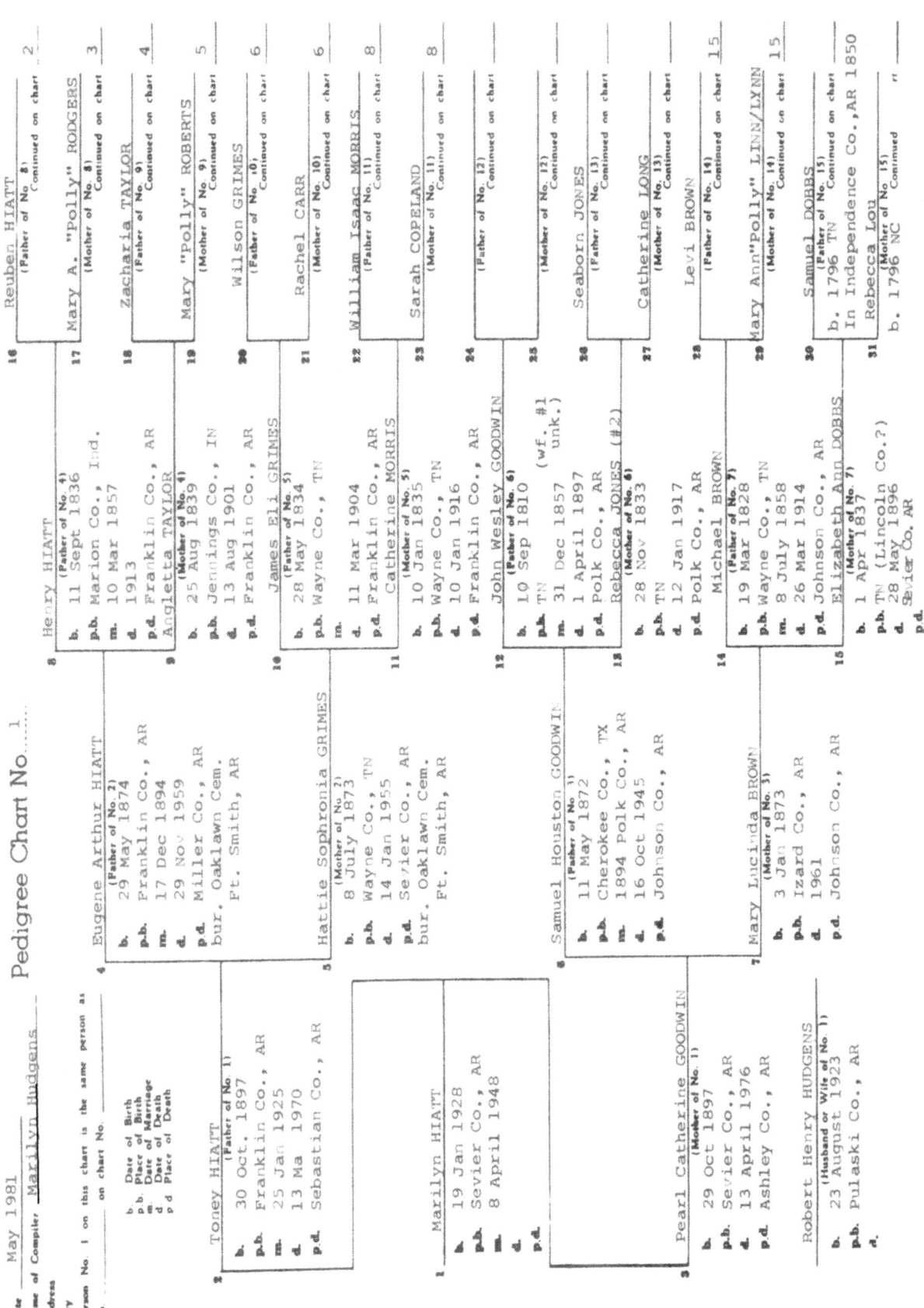

Date __May 1981__
Name of Compiler __Marilyn Hudgens__
Address
City
Person No. 1 on this chart is the same person as ___ on chart No. ___

Pedigree Chart No. 1......

b.   Date of Birth
p.b.   Place of Birth
m.   Date of Marriage
d.   Date of Death
p.d   Place of Death

**1   Marilyn HIATT**
b. 19 Jan 1928
p.b. Sevier Co., AR
m. 8 April 1948
d.
p.d.

**(Husband or Wife of No. 1)   Robert Henry HUDGENS**
m. 23 August 1923
p.b. Pulaski Co., AR
d.

**2   Toney HIATT (Father of No. 1)**
b. 30 Oct. 1897
p.b. Franklin Co., AR
m. 25 Jan 1925
d. 13 Ma 1970
p.d. Sebastian Co., AR

**3   Pearl Catherine GOODWIN (Mother of No. 1)**
b. 29 Oct. 1897
p.b. Sevier Co., AR
d. 13 April 1976
p.d. Ashley Co., AR

**4   Eugene Arthur HIATT (Father of No. 2)**
b. 29 May 1874
p.b. Franklin Co., AR
m. 17 Dec 1894
d. 29 Nov 1959
p.d. Miller Co., AR
bur. Oaklawn Cem. Ft. Smith, AR

**5   Hattie Sophronia GRIMES (Mother of No. 2)**
b. 8 July 1873
p.b. Wayne Co., TN
d. 14 Jan 1955
p.d. Sevier Co., AR
bur. Oaklawn Cem. Ft. Smith, AR

**6   Samuel Houston GOODWIN (Father of No. 3)**
b. 11 May 1872
p.b. Cherokee Co., TX
m. 1894 Polk Co., AR
d. 16 Oct 1945
p.d. Johnson Co., AR

**7   Mary Lucinda BROWN (Mother of No. 3)**
b. 3 Jan 1873
p.b. Izard Co., AR
d. 1961
p.d. Johnson Co., AR

**8   Henry HIATT (Father of No. 4)**
b. 11 Sept 1836
p.b. Marion Co., Ind.
m. 10 Mar 1857
d. 1913
p.d. Franklin Co., AR

**9   Angletta TAYLOR (Mother of No. 4)**
b. 25 Aug 1839
p.b. Jennings Co., IN
d. 13 Aug 1901
p.d. Franklin Co., AR

**10   James Eli GRIMES (Father of No. 5)**
b. 28 May 1834
p.b. Wayne Co., TN
m.
d. 11 Mar 1904
p.d. Franklin Co., AR

**11   Catherine MORRIS (Mother of No. 5)**
b. 10 Jan 1835
p.b. Wayne Co., TN
d. 10 Jan 1916
p.d. Franklin Co., AR

**12   John Wesley GOODWIN (Father of No. 6)**
b. 10 Sep 1810
p.b. TN   (wf. #1 unk.)
m. 31 Dec 1857
d. 1 April 1897
p.d. Polk Co., AR

**13   Rebecca JONES (#2) (Mother of No. 6)**
b. 28 Nov 1833
p.b. Wayne Co., TN
d. 12 Jan 1917
p.d. Polk Co., AR

**14   Michael BROWN (Father of No. 7)**
b. 19 Mar 1828
p.b. Wayne Co., TN
m. 8 July 1858
d. 26 Mar 1914
p.d. Johnson Co., AR

**15   Elizabeth Ann DOBBS (Mother of No. 7)**
b. 1 Apr 1837
p.b. TN (Lincoln Co.?)
d. 28 May 1896
p.d. Sevier Co., AR

**16   Reuben HIATT (Father of No. 8)** — Continued on chart 2
**17   Mary A. "Polly" RODGERS (Mother of No. 8)** — Continued on chart 3
**18   Zacharia TAYLOR (Father of No. 9)** — Continued on chart 4
**19   Mary "Polly" ROBERTS (Mother of No. 9)** — Continued on chart 5
**20   Wilson GRIMES (Father of No. 10)** — Continued on chart 6
**21   Rachel CARR (Mother of No. 10)** — Continued on chart 6
**22   William Isaac MORRIS (Father of No. 11)** — Continued on chart 8
**23   Sarah COPELAND (Mother of No. 11)** — Continued on chart 8
**24   (Father of No. 12)** — Continued on chart
**25   (Mother of No. 12)** — Continued on chart
**26   Seaborn JONES (Father of No. 13)** — Continued on chart
**27   Catherine LONG (Mother of No. 13)** — Continued on chart
**28   Levi BROWN (Father of No. 14)** — Continued on chart
**29   Mary Ann "Polly" LINN/LYNN (Mother of No. 14)** — Continued on chart 15
**30   Samuel DOBBS (Father of No. 15)** — b. 1796 TN In Independence Co., AR 1850 — Continued on chart
**31   Rebecca Lou (Mother of No. 15)** — b. 1796 NC — Continued on chart

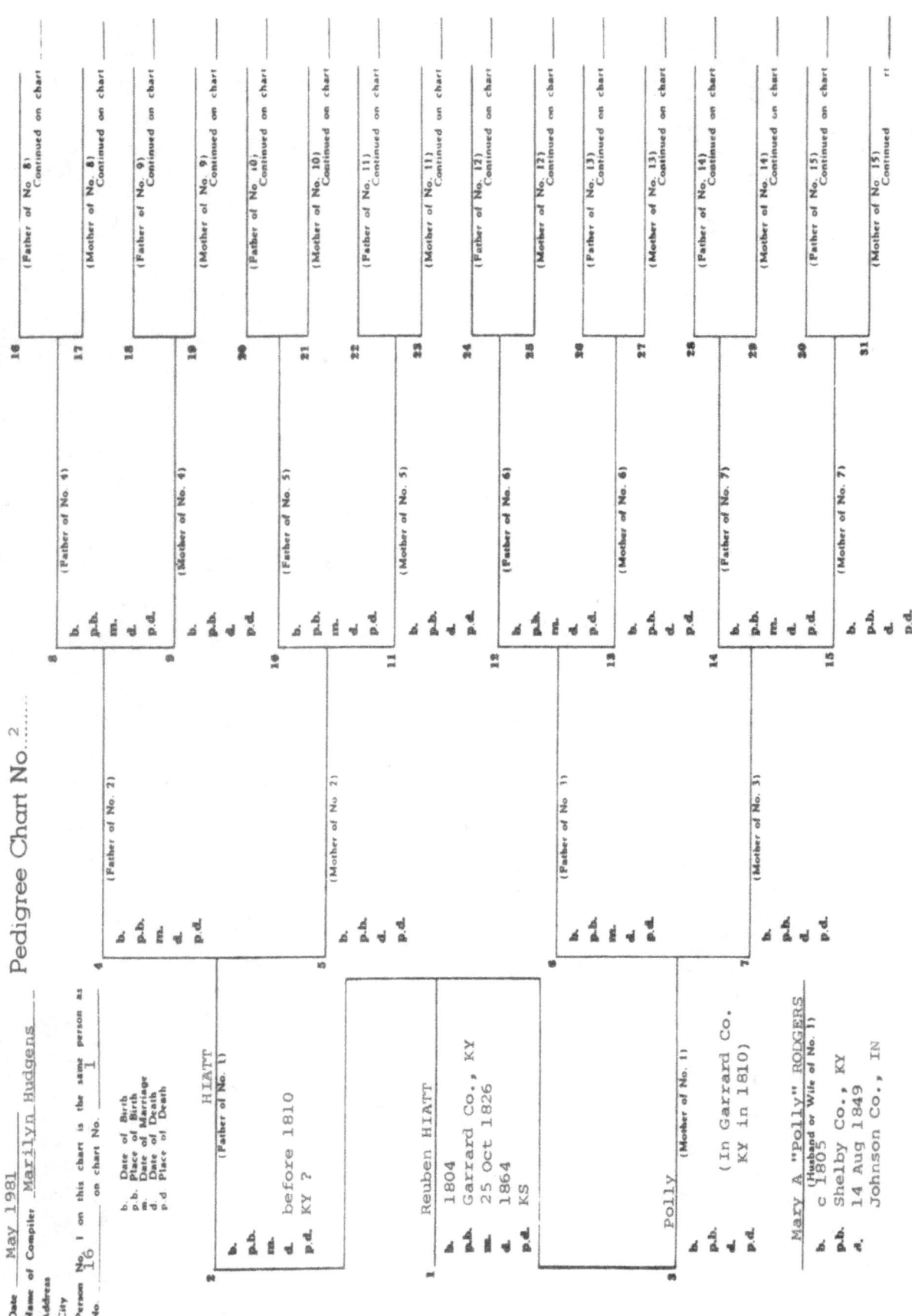

Pedigree Chart No. 2

Date May 1981
Name of Compiler Marilyn Hudgens
Address
City
Person No. 16 on this chart is the same person as No. 1 on chart No.

b. Date of Birth
p.b. Place of Birth
m. Date of Marriage
d. Date of Death
p.d Place of Death

HIATT (Father of No. 1)

2
b.
p.b.
m.
d. before 1810
p.d. KY ?

1
Reuben HIATT
b. 1804
p.b. Garrard Co., KY
m. 25 Oct 1826
d. 1864
p.d. KS

3
Polly (Mother of No. 1)
b.
p.b. (In Garrard Co.
d. KY in 1810)
p.d.

Mary A "Polly" RODGERS (Husband or Wife of No. 1)
b. c 1805
p.b. Shelby Co., KY
d. 14 Aug 1849
Johnson Co., IN

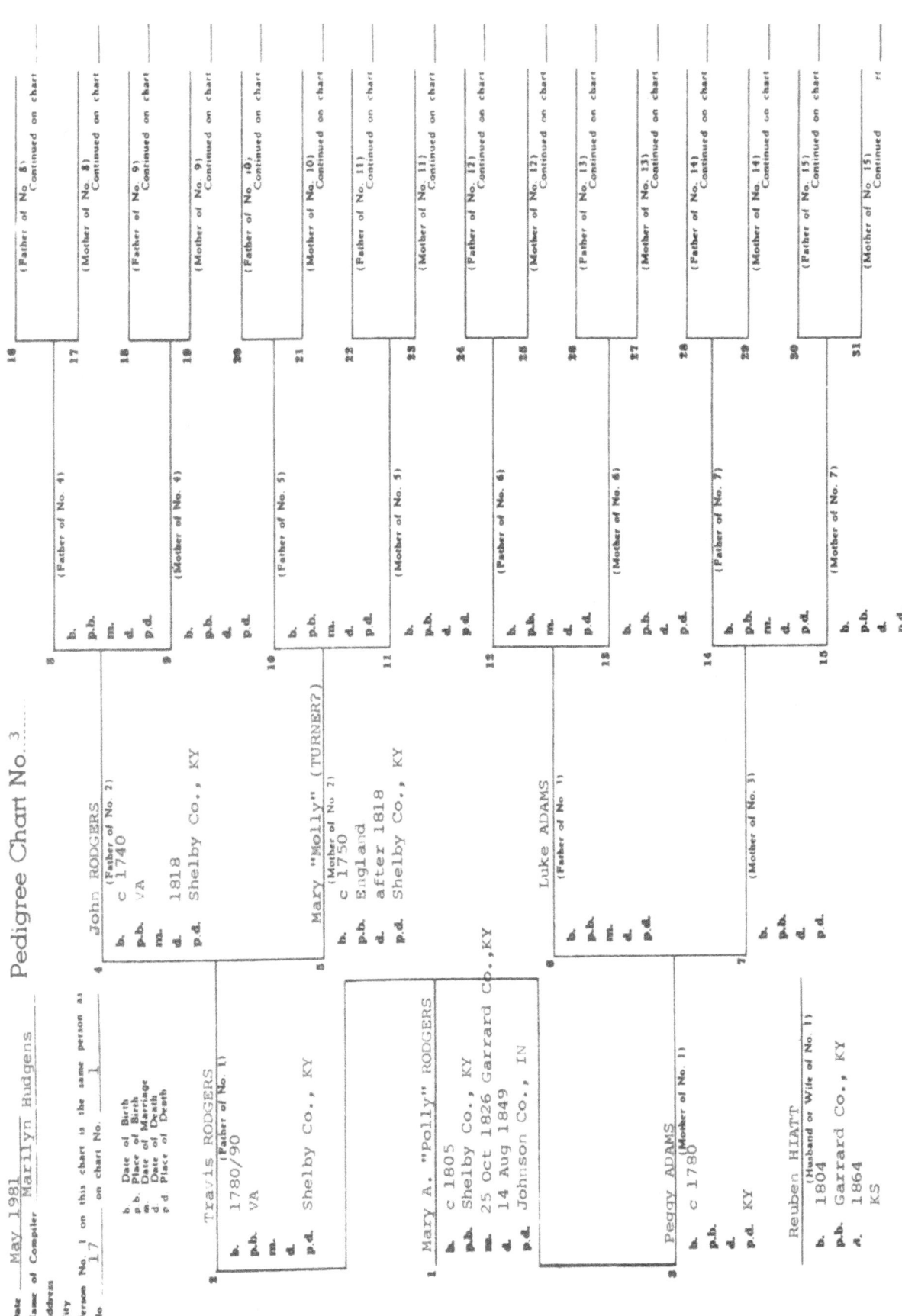

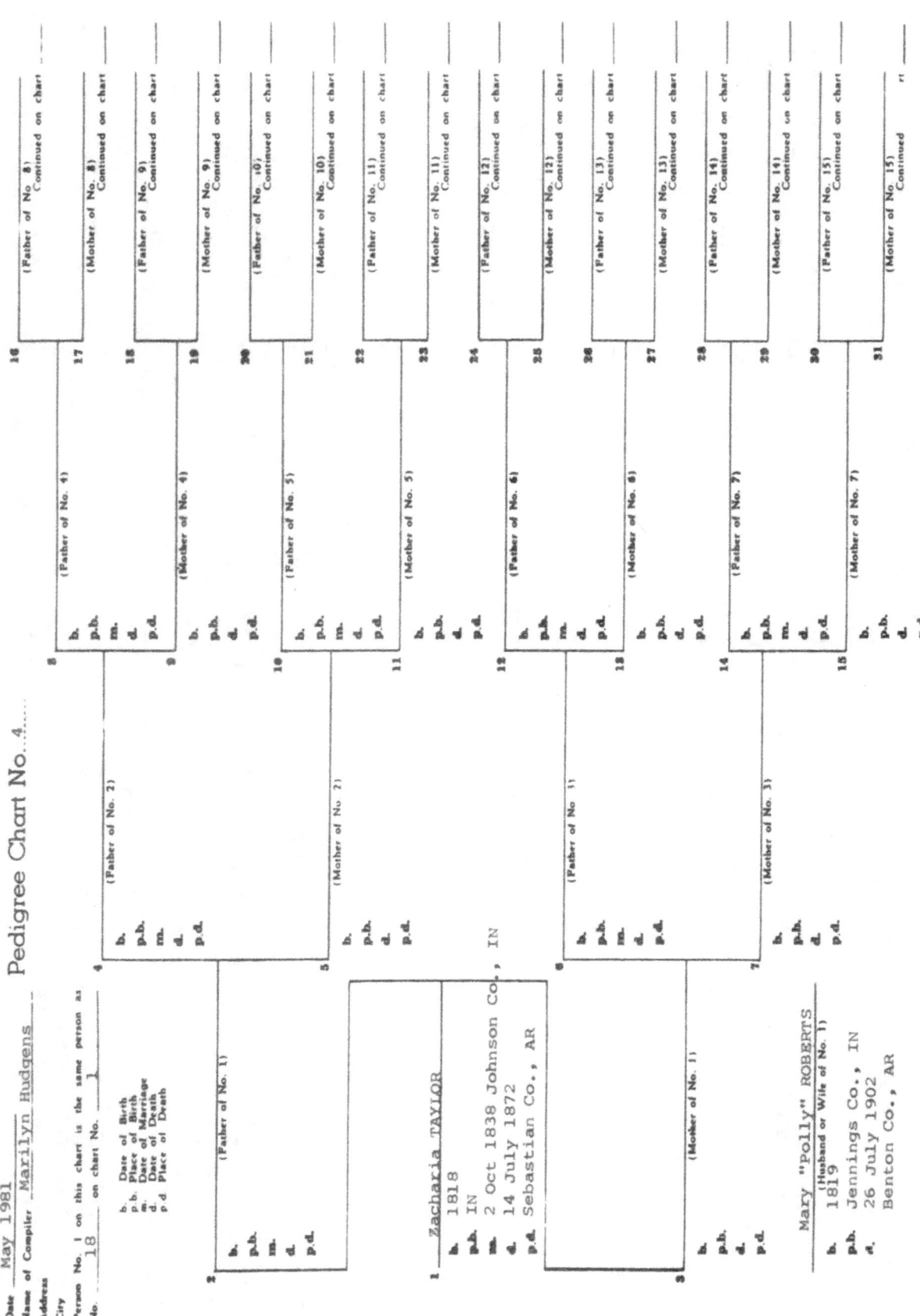

Pedigree Chart No. 4

Date _May 1981_
Name of Compiler _Marilyn Hudgens_
Address
City
Person No. _1_ on this chart is the same person as No. _18_ on chart No. _1_

b.  Date of Birth
p.b. Place of Birth
m.  Date of Marriage
d.  Date of Death
p.d Place of Death

1 Zacharia TAYLOR
b.   1818
p.b. IN
m.  2 Oct 1838 Johnson Co., IN
d.   14 July 1872
p.d. Sebastian Co., AR

Mary "Polly" ROBERTS
(Husband or Wife of No. 1)
b.   1819
p.b. Jennings Co., IN
d.   26 July 1902
Benton Co., AR

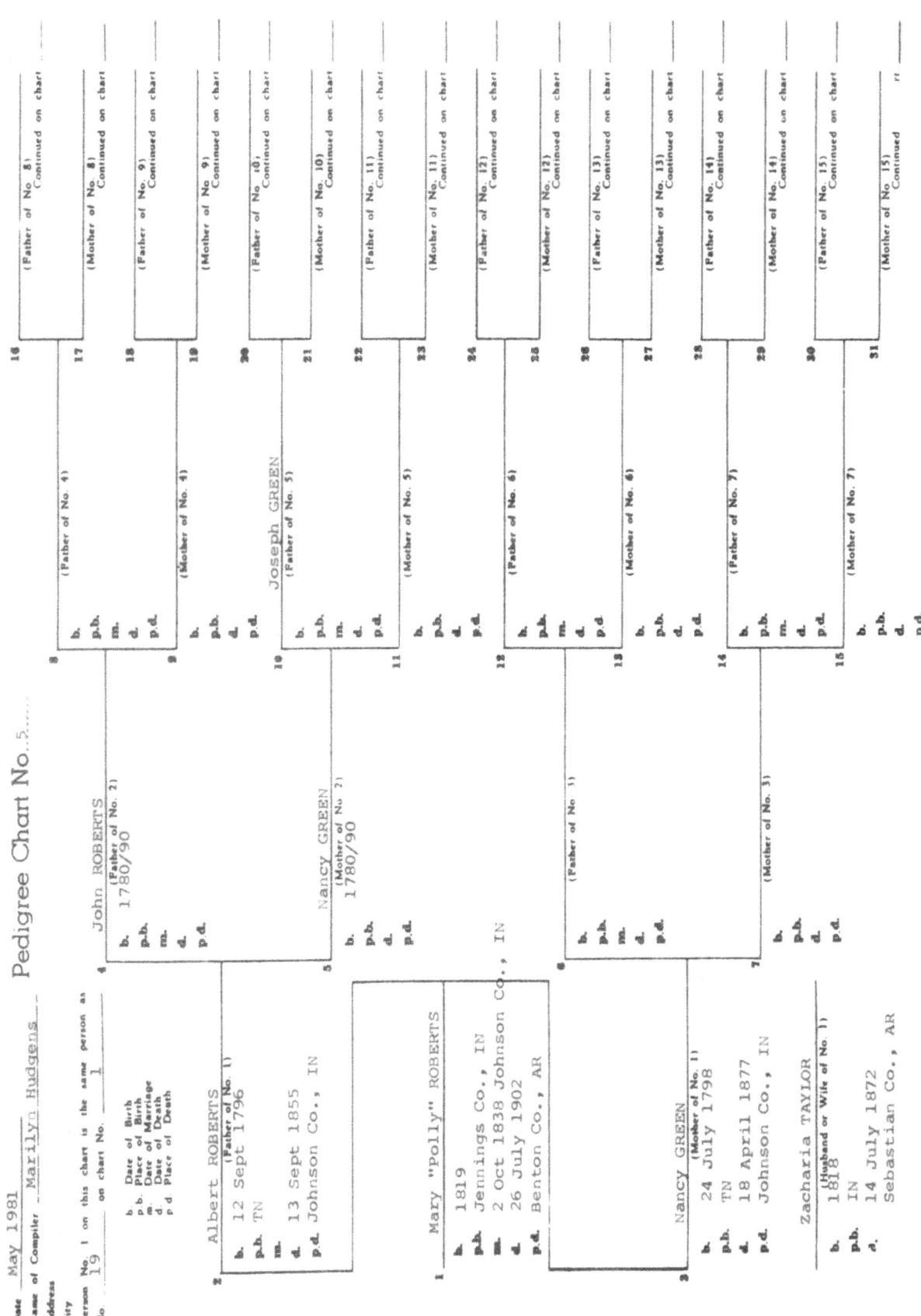

Pedigree Chart No. 5......

Date   May 1981
Name of Compiler - Marilyn Hudgens
Address
City
Person No. 1 on this chart is the same person as
No. 19 on chart No. 1

b.   Date of Birth
p.b. Place of Birth
m.   Date of Marriage
d.   Date of Death
p.d  Place of Death

2  Albert ROBERTS
   (Father of No. 1)
b.   12 Sept 1796
p.b. TN
m.
d.   13 Sept 1855
p.d. Johnson Co., IN

1  Mary "Polly" ROBERTS
b.   1819
p.b. Jennings Co., IN
m.   2 Oct 1838 Johnson Co., IN
d.   26 July 1902
p.d. Benton Co., AR

3  Nancy GREEN
   (Mother of No. 1)
b.   24 July 1798
p.b. TN
d.   18 April 1877
p.d. Johnson Co., IN

   Zacharia TAYLOR
   (Husband or Wife of No. 1)
b.   1818
p.b. IN
d.   14 July 1872
p.d. Sebastian Co., AR

4  John ROBERTS
   (Father of No. 2)
   1780/90
b.
p.b.
m.
d.
p.d.

5  Nancy GREEN
   (Mother of No. 2)
   1780/90
b.
p.b.
d.
p.d.

6  (Father of No. 3)
b.
p.b.
m.
d.
p.d.

7  (Mother of No. 3)
b.
p.b.
d.
p.d.

8  (Father of No. 4)
b.
p.b.
m.
d.
p.d.

9  (Mother of No. 4)
b.
p.b.
d.
p.d.

10  Joseph GREEN
    (Father of No. 5)
b.
p.b.
m.
d.
p.d.

11  (Mother of No. 5)
b.
p.b.
d.
p.d.

12  (Father of No. 6)
b.
p.b.
m.
d.
p.d.

13  (Mother of No. 6)
b.
p.b.
d.
p.d.

14  (Father of No. 7)
b.
p.b.
m.
d.
p.d.

15  (Mother of No. 7)
b.
p.b.
d.
p.d.

16  (Father of No. 8)   Continued on chart

17  (Mother of No. 8)   Continued on chart

18  (Father of No. 9)   Continued on chart

19  (Mother of No 9)   Continued on chart

20  (Father of No. 10)   Continued on chart

21  (Mother of No. 10)   Continued on chart

22  (Father of No. 11)   Continued on chart

23  (Mother of No. 11)   Continued on chart

24  (Father of No. 12)   Continued on chart

25  (Mother of No. 12)   Continued on chart

26  (Father of No. 13)   Continued on chart

27  (Mother of No. 13)   Continued on chart

28  (Father of No. 14)   Continued on chart

29  (Mother of No. 14)   Continued on chart

30  (Father of No. 15)   Continued on chart

31  (Mother of No. 15)   Continued

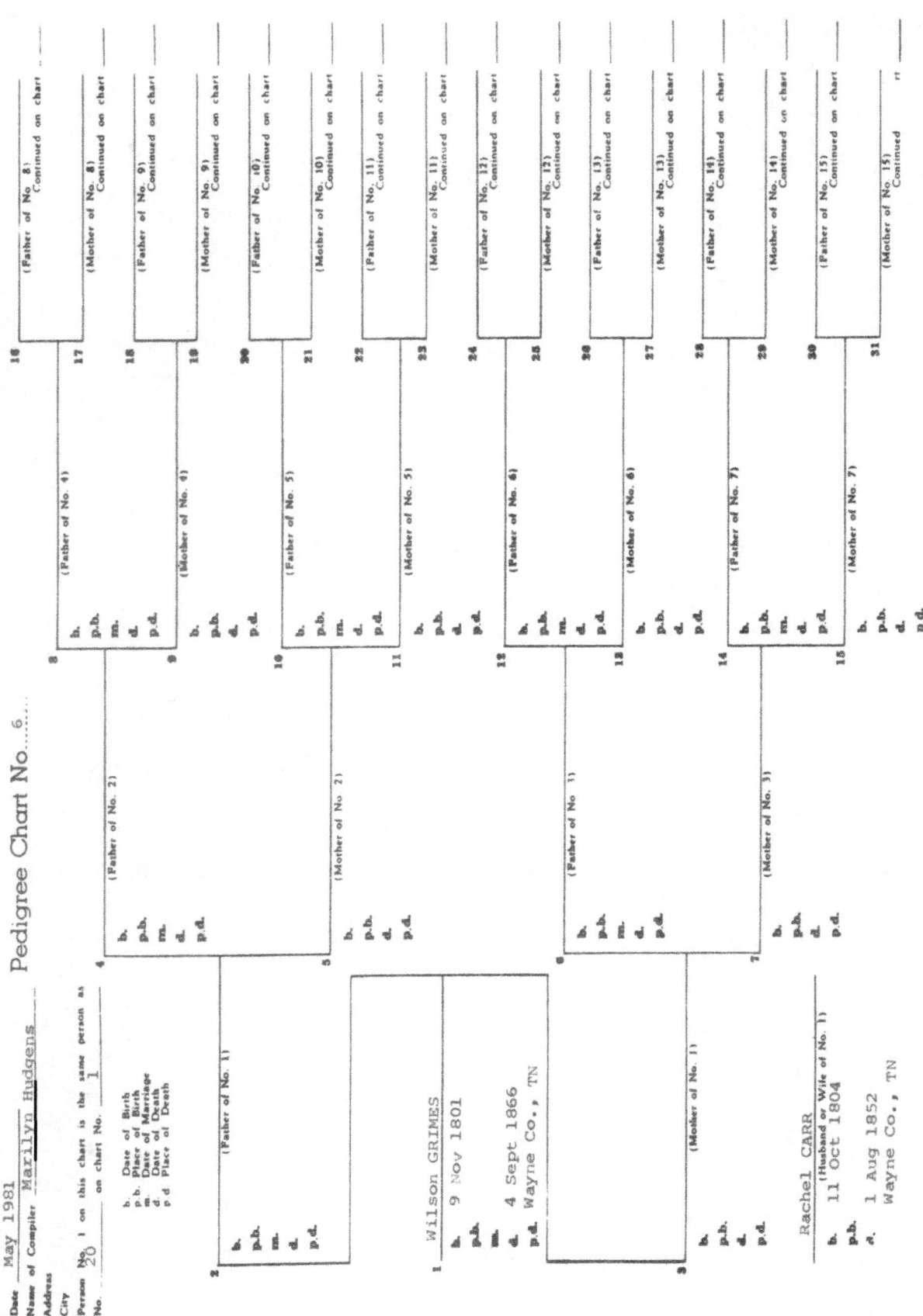

Pedigree Chart No. 6

Date    May 1981
Name of Compiler    Marilyn Hudgens
Address
City
Person No. 1 on this chart is the same person as
No. 20 on chart No. 1

b.   Date of Birth
p.b. Place of Birth
m.   Date of Marriage
d.   Date of Death
p.d. Place of Death

1  Wilson GRIMES
b.   9 Nov 1801
p.b.
m.   4 Sept 1866
p.d. Wayne Co., TN

Rachel CARR
(Husband or Wife of No. 1)
b.   11 Oct 1804
p.b.
d.   1 Aug 1852
       Wayne Co., TN

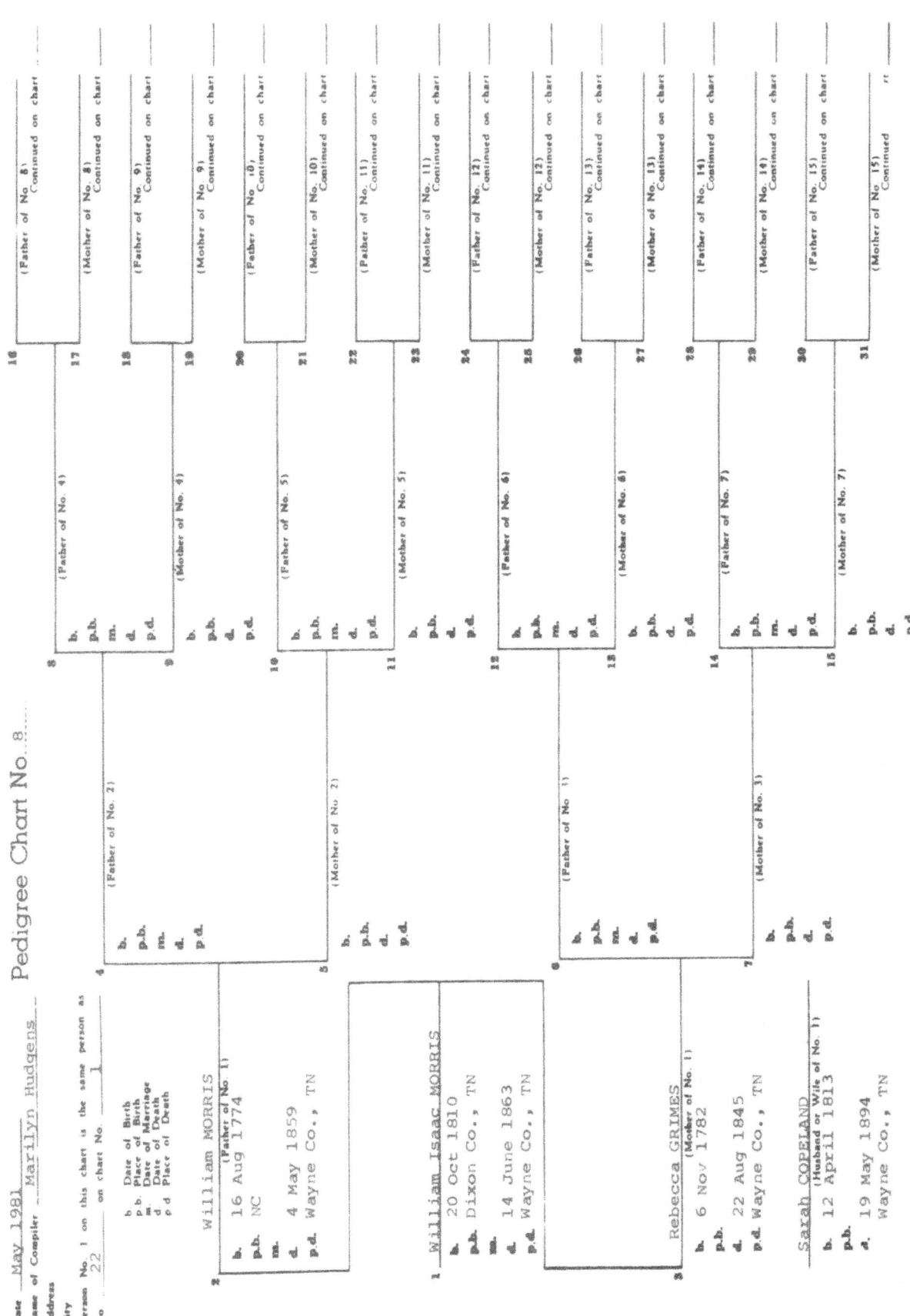

Date  May 1981
Name of Compiler  Marilyn Hudgens
Address
City
Person No. 1 on this chart is the same person as
No. 22 on chart No. 1

b.   Date of Birth
p.b. Place of Birth
m.   Date of Marriage
d.   Date of Death
p.d  Place of Death

Pedigree Chart No. 8

2
William MORRIS
(Father of No. 1)
b.  16 Aug 1774
p.b. NC
m.
d.  4 May 1859
p.d. Wayne Co., TN

1
William Isaac MORRIS
b.  20 Oct 1810
p.b. Dixon Co., TN
m.  14 June 1863
p.d. Wayne Co., TN

3
Rebecca GRIMES
(Mother of No. 1)
b.  6 Nov 1782
p.b.
d.  22 Aug 1845
p.d. Wayne Co., TN

Sarah COPELAND
(Husband or Wife of No. 1)
b.  12 April 1813
p.b.
d.  19 May 1894
Wayne Co., TN

4
(Father of No. 2)
b.
p.b.
m.
d.
p.d.

5
(Mother of No. 2)
b.
p.b.
d.
p.d.

6
(Father of No. 3)
b.
p.b.
m.
d.
p.d.

7
(Mother of No. 3)
b.
p.b.
d.
p.d.

8
(Father of No. 4)
b.
p.b.
m.
d.
p.d.

9
(Mother of No. 4)
b.
p.b.
d.
p.d.

10
(Father of No. 5)
b.
p.b.
m.
d.
p.d.

11
(Mother of No. 5)
b.
p.b.
d.
p.d.

12
(Father of No. 6)
b.
p.b.
m.
d.
p.d.

13
(Mother of No. 6)
b.
p.b.
d.
p.d.

14
(Father of No. 7)
b.
p.b.
m.
d.
p.d.

15
(Mother of No. 7)
b.
p.b.
d.
p.d.

16  (Father of No. 8)
    Continued on chart

17  (Mother of No. 8)
    Continued on chart

18  (Father of No. 9)
    Continued on chart

19  (Mother of No. 9)
    Continued on chart

20  (Father of No. 10)
    Continued on chart

21  (Mother of No. 10)
    Continued on chart

22  (Father of No. 11)
    Continued on chart

23  (Mother of No. 11)
    Continued on chart

24  (Father of No. 12)
    Continued on chart

25  (Mother of No. 12)
    Continued on chart

26  (Father of No. 13)
    Continued on chart

27  (Mother of No. 13)
    Continued on chart

28  (Father of No. 14)
    Continued on chart

29  (Mother of No. 14)
    Continued on chart

30  (Father of No. 15)
    Continued on chart

31  (Mother of No. 15)
    Continued

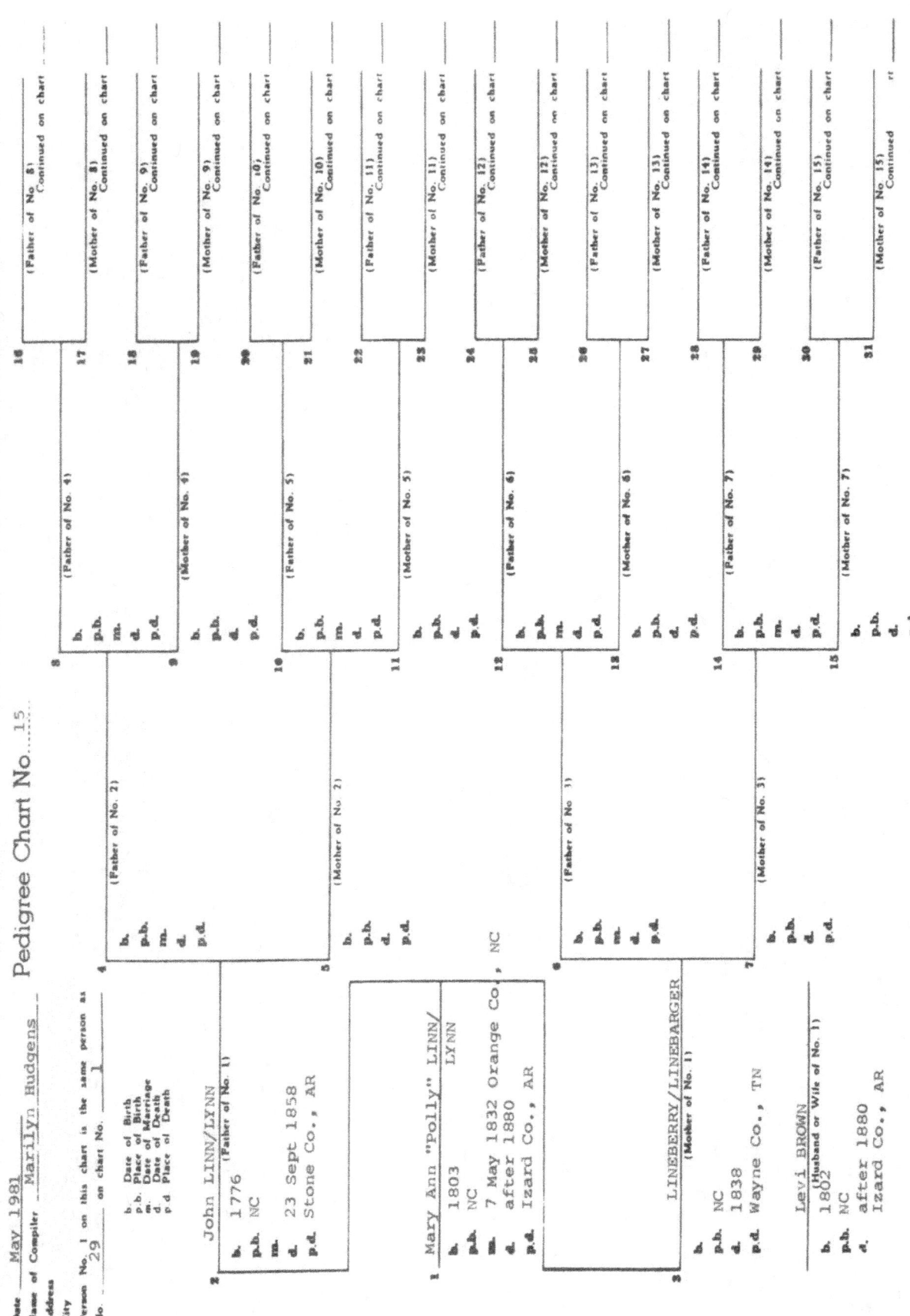

Date 8 August 1983 Pedigree Chart No.........
Name of Compiler Carol Hughes
Address
City
Person No. 1 on this chart is the same person as No............ on chart No.

b. Date of Birth
p.b. Place of Birth
m. Date of Marriage
d. Date of Death
p.d Place of Death

1 Carol D. Heidorn
b. 24 November 1935
p.b. Antioch, Calif.
d.

2 Raymond W. Hughes
b. 28 May 1926
p.b. Shamrock, Ok.
m. (#2)14 Sept. 1968
d.
p.d.

3 Icie Tabitha Rogers
b. 20 June 1902
p.b. Wanette, Ok.
d. 13 January 1961
p.d. Martinez, Calif.

4 James Henry Hughes
b. 26 Sept. 1886
p.b. Paris, Texas
m. 11 Nov. 1917
d. 14 March 1961
p.d. Concord, Calif.

5 Nancy Elizabeth Sparks
b. 25 January 1862
p.b. Kingston, Georgia
d. 24 January 1917
p.d. Morris, Ok.

6 William Monroe Rogers
b. 20 October 1878
p.b. Tuscaloosa, Alabama
m. 24 February 1901
d. 24 October 1959
p.d. Sacramento, Calif.

7 Martha Elvira Adams
b. 12 December 1884
p.b. Jasper, Ar.
d. 18 November 1955
p.d. Sacramento, Calif.

8 Jeremiah Henry Hughes
b. 11 October 1858
p.b. Hackett City, Ar.
m. 8 June 1884
d. 10 January 1917
p.d. Henryetta, Ok.

10 James Sparks
b. 1837
p.b. South Carolina
m. 7 February 1859
d. 1862
p.d. Virginia

11 Eliza J. Purser
b. 1840
p.b. South Carolina
d.

12 William Jarrett Rogers
b. 20 November 1848
p.b. Alabama
m. 7 September 1902
d.

13 Sarah E. McAlester
b. 9 March 1843
p.b. Alabama
d. 28 February 1922
p.d. Oklahoma

14 James Newton Adams
b. 12 February 1853
p.b. Arkansas
m. 29 June 1882
d. 14 March 1916
p.d. Drumright, Ok.

15 Mary Matilda Bailey
b. 14 October 1856
p.b. 18 April 1915
d.

16 (Father of No. 8) Continued on chart
17 (Mother of No. 8) Continued on chart
18 (Father of No. 9) Continued on chart
19 (Mother of No. 9) Continued on chart
20 Drury Sparks (Father of No. 10) Continued on chart
21 Nancy (Mother of No. 10) Continued on chart
22 William Purser (Father of No. 11) Continued on chart
23 Elizabeth (Mother of No. 11) Continued on chart
24 James S. (or) G. Rogers (Father of No. 12) Continued on chart
25 May Hulda (Mother of No. 12) Continued on chart
26 James Ray McAlester (Father of No. 13) Continued on chart
27 Hannah (Mother of No. 13) Continued on chart
28 Joseph Adams (Father of No. 14) Continued on chart
29 Elvira (Mother of No. 14) Continued on chart
30 (Father of No. 15) Continued on chart
31 (Mother of No. 15) Continued

# Pedigree Chart No.

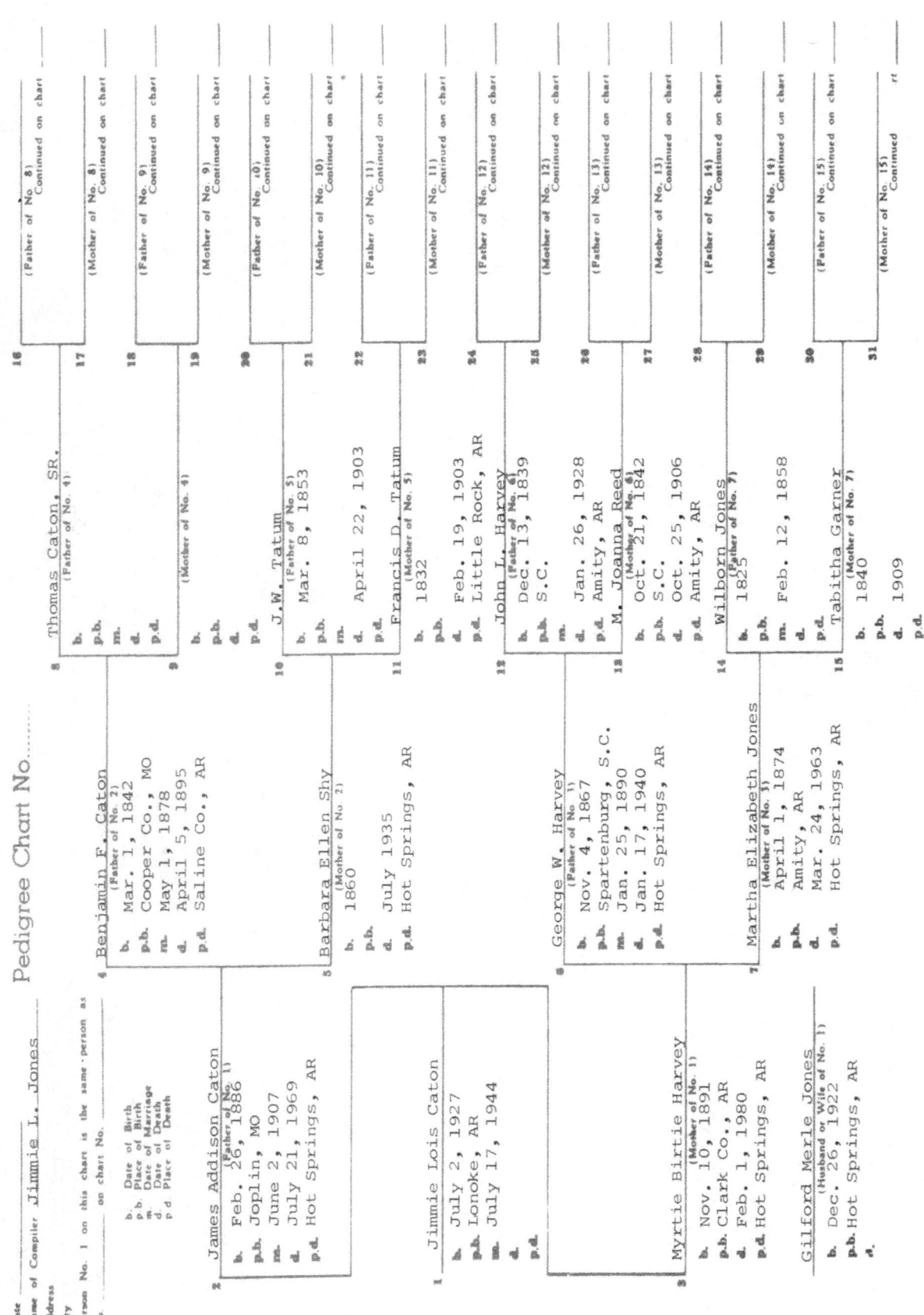

Date
Name of Compiler Jimmie L. Jones
Address
City
Person No. 1 on this chart is the same person as _____ on chart No. _____

No.

b. Date of Birth
p.b. Place of Birth
m. Date of Marriage
d. Date of Death
p.d Place of Death

**1** Jimmie Lois Caton
b. July 2, 1927
p.b. Lonoke, AR
m. July 17, 1944
d.
p.d.

**2** James Addison Caton
(Father of No. 1)
b. Feb. 26, 1886
p.b. Joplin, MO
m. June 2, 1907
d. July 21, 1969
p.d. Hot Springs, AR

**3** Myrtie Birtie Harvey
(Mother of No. 1)
b. Nov. 10, 1891
p.b. Clark Co., AR
d. Feb. 1, 1980
p.d. Hot Springs, AR

Gilford Merle Jones
(Husband or Wife of No. 1)
b. Dec. 26, 1922
p.b. Hot Springs, AR
d.

**4** Benjamin F. Caton
(Father of No. 2)
b. Mar. 1, 1842
p.b. Cooper Co., MO
m. May 1, 1878
d. April 5, 1895
p.d. Saline Co., AR

**5** Barbara Ellen Shy
(Mother of No. 2)
b. 1860
p.b.
d. July 1935
p.d. Hot Springs, AR

**6** George W. Harvey
(Father of No. 1)
b. Nov. 4, 1867
p.b. Spartenburg, S.C.
m. Jan. 25, 1890
d. Jan. 17, 1940
p.d. Hot Springs, AR

**7** Martha Elizabeth Jones
(Mother of No. 3)
b. April 1, 1874
p.b. Amity, AR
d. Mar. 24, 1963
p.d. Hot Springs, AR

**8** Thomas Caton, SR.
(Father of No. 4)
b.
p.b.
m.
d.
p.d.

**9** (Mother of No. 4)
b.
p.b.
d.
p.d.

**10** J.W. Tatum
(Father of No. 5)
b. Mar. 8, 1853
p.b.
m.
d. April 22, 1903
p.d.

**11** Francis D. Tatum
(Mother of No. 5)
b. 1832
p.b.
d. Feb. 19, 1903
p.d. Little Rock, AR

**12** John L. Harvey
(Father of No. 6)
b. Dec. 13, 1839
p.b. S.C.
m.
d. Jan. 26, 1928
p.d. Amity, AR

**13** M. Joanna Reed
(Mother of No. 6)
b. Oct. 21, 1842
p.b. S.C.
d. Oct. 25, 1906
p.d. Amity, AR

**14** Wilborn Jones
(Father of No. 7)
b. 1825
p.b.
m.
d.
p.d.

**15** Tabitha Garner
(Mother of No. 7)
b. Feb. 12, 1858
p.b.
d.
p.d.

**16** (Father of No. 8)
Continued on chart ____

**17** (Mother of No. 8)
Continued on chart ____

**18** (Father of No. 9)
Continued on chart ____

**19** (Mother of No. 9)
Continued on chart ____

**20** (Father of No. 10)
Continued on chart ____

**21** (Mother of No. 10)
Continued on chart ____

**22** (Father of No. 11)
Continued on chart ____

**23** (Mother of No. 11)
Continued on chart ____

**24** (Father of No. 12)
Continued on chart ____

**25** (Mother of No. 12)
Continued on chart ____

**26** (Father of No. 13)
Continued on chart ____

**27** (Mother of No. 13)
Continued on chart ____

**28** (Father of No. 14)
Continued on chart ____

**29** (Mother of No. 14)
Continued on chart ____

**30** (Father of No. 15)
Continued on chart ____

**31** (Mother of No. 15)
Continued on chart ____

# Pedigree Chart No. ........

Date 4 April 1980
Name of Compiler M. Eliz. (Gossett) Mahoney
Address
City
Person No. 1 on this chart is the same person as _____ on chart No.

b.   Date of Birth
p.b. Place of Birth
m.   Date of Marriage
d.   Date of Death
p.d. Place of Death

**1. Mary Elizabeth Gossett**
b. 1 June 1925
p.b. Hot Springs, Ark.
m. 21 July 1950
(2nd) 17 May 1973

**2. Marshall Alfred Gossett** (Father of No. 1)
b. 2 Nov. 1893
p.b. Newark, Ark.
m. 28 Dec 1917
d. 20 Sept 1978
p.d. Hot Springs, Ark.

**3. Maude Pierce** (Mother of No. 1)
b. 10 April 1898
p.b. Cord, Ark.

**Patrick B. Mahoney (2nd)** (Husband of Wife of No. 1)
b. 27 Nov 1902
p.b. W. Chicago, Ill.

**4. Robert Marshall Gossett** (Father of No. 2)
b. 28 Mar 1866
p.b. Newark, Ark.
m. 28 Dec 1892
d. 10 Jan 1948
p.d. Hot Springs, Ark

**5. Mary Lee Matlock** (Mother of No. 2)
b. 7 Feb 1871
p.b. Oil Trough, Ark
d. 2 Dec 1959
p.d. Hot Springs, Ark

**6. Elijah Franklin Pierce** (Father of No. 3)
b. 27 Jan 1868
p.b. TN ?
m. 25 Nov 1891 – Ind. Co
d. 24 June 1908
p.d. Tupelo, Ark.

**7. Clara Delmah Gould** (Mother of No. 3)
b. 19 Nov 1873
p.b. Cord, Ark
d. 9 Nov 1950
p.d. El Dorado, Ark.

**8. Allen Gossett** (Father of No. 4)
b. 11 Sept 1835
p.b. TN
m. 9 Jan 1859 Newark, Ark
d. 13 Jan 1917
p.d. Austin, Ark.

**9. Charlotte Brannon** (Mother of No. 4)
b. 1 Jan 1841
p.b. TN
d. 15 Feb 1913
p.d. Judsonia, Ark

**10. Wm James Clinton Matlock** (Father of No. 5)
b. 1832
p.b. Ala
m. 5 June 1861
d. 1888
p.d. Indep. Co., Ark
Mary Jane Mayhan (wife 1)

**11.** (Mother of No. 5)
b. 1846
p.b. Indep. Co., Ark
d. 1878
p.d. Indep. Co., Ark

**12. John L. Pierce** (Father of No. 6)
b. 10 Jan 1838
p.b. McMinn Co., TN / Athens, TN
m. 29 Apr 1904
p.d. Indep. Co., Ark
Lucy Herod

**13.** (Mother of No. 6)
b. 7 July 1840
p.b. TN
d. 28 June 1904
p.d. Indep. Co., Ark

**14. Wm. Monroe Gould** (Father of No. 7)
b. 7 June 1837
p.b. TN
m. 1 Oct 1868 Cord, Ark.
d. 11 Apr 1889
p.d. Cord, Ark.

**15. Elizabeth Jane Stewart** (Mother of No. 7)
b. 23 Nov 1838
p.b. TN
d. 3 Mar 1912
p.d. Cord, Ark

**16. John Gossett** (Father of No. 8) Continued on chart
bn ca 1800
d Humphreys Co., TN

**17. Frances Owens?** (Mother of No. 8) Continued on chart
bn ca 1802 KY

**18. Williamson Brannon** (Father of No. 9) Continued on chart
b ca 1817 TN
d ca 1885 Indep. Co., Ark

**19. Casandra Cherry** (Mother of No. 9) Continued on chart
b ca 1813 TN
d after 1886 Ark

**20. William Matlock** (Father of No. 10) Continued on chart

**21. Joycie Waldron** (Mother of No. 10) Continued on chart

**22. James Monroe Mayhan** (Father of No. 11) Continued on chart
b ca 1819 TN
m 18 Sept 1842, Ark

**23. Sarah Wylie** (Mother of No. 11) Continued on chart
b ca 1825

**24. Thomas Pierce** (Father of No. 12) Continued on chart
bn TN
d ca 1868

**25. Elizabeth Wyatt** (Mother of No. 12) Continued on chart
bn ca Va 1872

**26.** (Father of No. 13) Continued on chart

**27.** (Mother of No. 13) Continued on chart

**28. Andrew Gould (Gold)** (Father of No. 14) Continued on chart
b ca 1810 TN
D Indep. Co., Ark.

**29. Jane Early** (Mother of No. 14) Continued on chart
b 1810 VA
d 20 Aug 1872 Indep. Co., Ark

**30.** (Father of No. 15) Continued on chart

**31.** (Mother of No. 15) Continued on chart

Pedigree Chart No. 1

Date _____ 1982
Name of Compiler _____ Mrs. Shirley Mazzini
Address
City
Person No. 1 on this chart is the same person as _____ on chart No. _____

No. _____
b.   Date of Birth
p.b. Place of Birth
d.   Date of Death
p.d  Place of Death

**1  Shirley Ann KING**
b.  2 Aug 1947
p.b. Tulare Co., CA
m.
d.
p.d.

Jerry MAZZINI (Husband or Wife of No. 1)
b.
p.b.
d.

**2  Raymond KING** (Father of No. 1)
b.  13 Mar 1923
p.b. Ottawa Co., OK
m.  10 May 1942 Washoe Co., Nev.
d.
p.d.

**3  Agness MEEK** (Mother of No. 1)
b.  15 Mar 1923
p.b. Garland Co., AR
d.
p.d.

**4  Ira Jasper KING** (Father of No. 2)
b.  14 Feb 1885
p.b. Stone Co., MO
m.  11 Nov 1915 Seb.Co.AR
d.  8 May 1961
p.d. Delano, CA

**5  Martha Alice COLE** (Mother of No. 2)
b.  28 July 1889
p.b. Southwest City, MO
d.  21 July 1961
p.d. Tulare Co., CA

**6  Samuel Jones MEEK** (Father of No. 3)
b.  10 Jan 1890
p.b. Logan Co., AR
m.  21 July 1908 Mont.Co.AR
d.  5 Mar 1945
p.d. Stockton, CA

**7  (Nancy) Delaney BATES** (Mother of No. 3)
b.  15 Aug 1889
p.b. Garland Co., AR
d.  3 Mar 1939
p.d. Visalia, CA

**8  Cyron Layfette KING** (Father of No. 4)
b.  1856
p.b. Stone Co., MO
m.  m#2 Melia GARDNER
d.
p.d.

**9  Harriet KERR #1** (Mother of No. 4)
b.  31 May 1850
p.b. MO
d.
p.d.

**10  James Newton COLE** (Father of No. 5)
b.  25 Nov 1853
p.b. Washington Co., AR
m.
d.  26 April 1936
p.d.

**11  Mary A. SCOTT** (Mother of No. 5)
b.  15 Aug 1859
p.b. Washington Co., AR
d.  26 Dec 1935
p.d. Long, OK

**12  James Henry MEEK** (Father of No. 6)
b.  29 Jan 1848
p.b. Choctaw Nation
m.
d.  23 Nov 1930
p.d. Garland Co., AR

**13  Mary F. HILL (BLAKE)** (Mother of No. 6)
b.  1 May 1847
p.b. Miss.
d.  30 June 1920
p.d. Garland Co., AR

**14  James Aaron BATES** (Father of No. 7)
b.  1847
p.b. N.C.
m.  #1 1866 Mont.Co.AR
d.  1897/98
p.d.

**15  Francis M. RILEY #2 wf** (Mother of No. 7)
b.  1845
p.b. Montgomery Co., AR
d.  1898/99
p.d. Garland Co., AR

**16  Geo. Washington KING** (Father of No. 8)
Continued on No. 8 ... 2

**17  Caroline STUBBLEFIELD #1 wf.** (Mother of No. 8)
Continued on No. 8

**18  John Dabney KERR** (Father of No. 9)
d., Civil War Continued on No. 9

**19  Nancy KIRK** (Mother of No. 9)
1821 N.C.  Continued on No. 9
1898 Cape Fair, MO

**20  Henry COLES** (Father of No. 10)
1827 TN  Continued on chart

**21  Mary** (Mother of No. 10)
1827 TN  Continued on chart

**22  James SCOTT** (Father of No. 11)
1833 TN  Continued on chart
1851 Washington Co., AR

**23  Emily HODGES** (Mother of No. 11)
1833 TN  Continued on chart

**24  (Father of No. 12)**
Continued on chart

**25  Martha** (Mother of No. 12)
ca 1829 AL  Continued on chart

**26  (Father of No. 13)**
Continued on chart

**27  (Mother of No. 13)**
Continued on chart

**28  (Father of No. 14)**
Continued on chart

**29  (Mother of No. 14)**
Continued on chart

**30  Thomas Jefferson RILEY** (Father of No. 15)
4 Feb. 1820 Ala.  Continued on chart
Sept. 1879 Garland Co., AR

**31  Nancy Caroline BRADY #2** (Mother of No. 15)
17 June 1832 TN  married
31 Aug 1896 Garland Co., AR

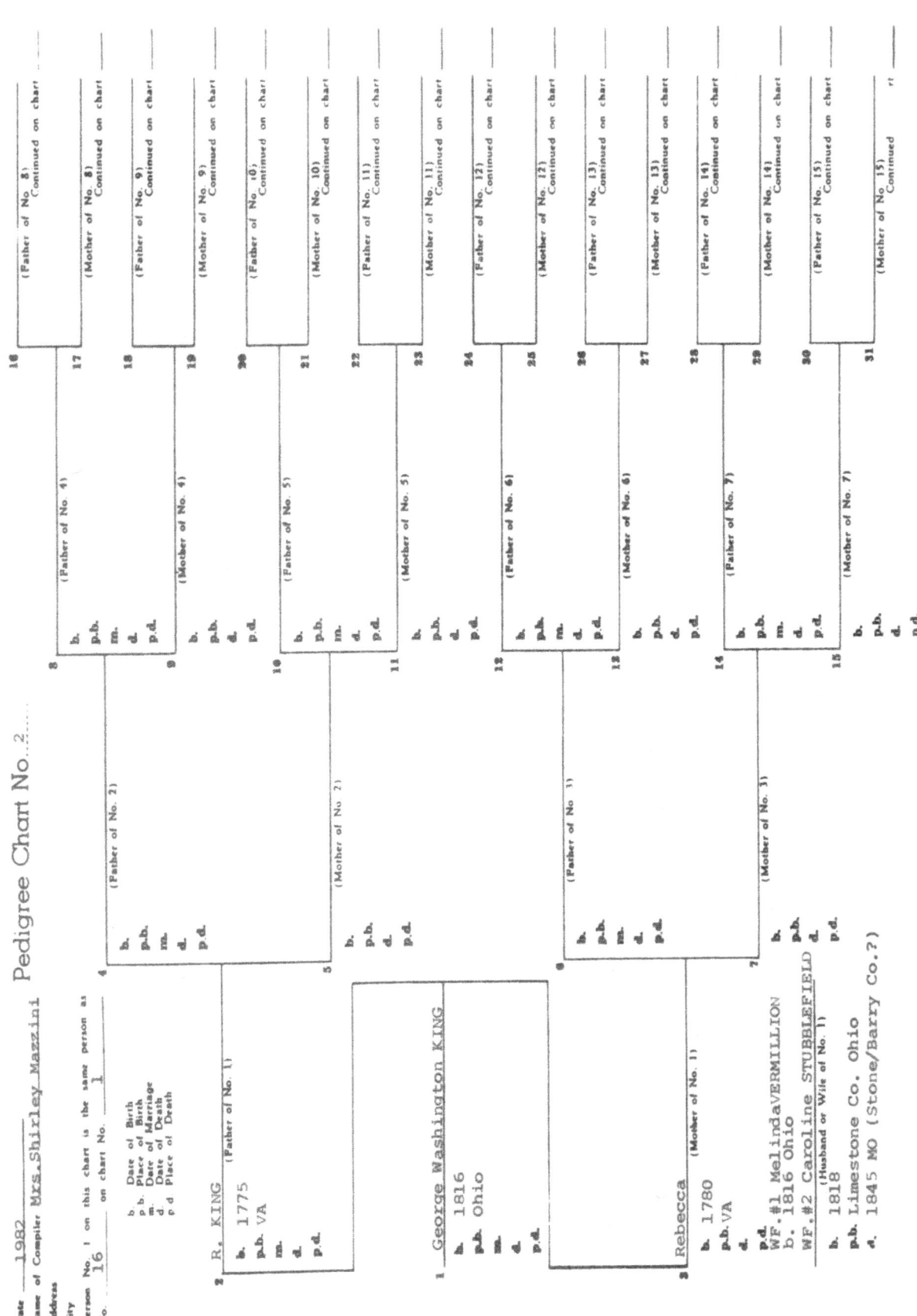

Pedigree Chart No. 2

Date ___1982___
Name of Compiler ___Mrs. Shirley Mazzini___
Address
City
Person No. 1 on this chart is the same person as
No. ___16___ on chart No. ___1___

b.   Date of Birth
p.b. Place of Birth
m.   Date of Marriage
d.   Date of Death
p d  Place of Death

1  George Washington KING
b.   1816
p.b. Ohio
m.
d.
p.d.

2  R, KING  (Father of No. 1)
b.   1775
p.b. VA
m.
d.
p.d.

3  Rebecca  (Mother of No. 1)
b.   1780
p.b. VA
d.
p.d.
WF.#1 Melinda VERMILLION
b. 1816 Ohio
WF.#2 Caroline STUBBLEFIELD   (Husband or Wife of No. 1)
b.   1818
p.b. Limestone Co. Ohio
d.   1845 MO (Stone/Barry Co.?)

# Pedigree Chart No.........

Date March 1982
Name of Compiler Anita Meador
Address
City
Person No. 1 on this chart is the same person as _____ on chart No.

b. Date of Birth
p.b. Place of Birth
m. Date of Marriage
d. Date of Death
p.d Place of Death

**1 Jimmy W. Meador**
b. 29 June 1928
p.b. Johnson Co., TX
m.
d. 29 Oct. 1947
p.d.

**2 Hezekiah Leonard Meador** (Father of No. 1)
b. 4 June 1884
p.b. Johnson Co., TX
m. 13 Dec. 1908
d. 29 Jan. 1965
p.d. Tarrant Co., TX

**3 Maude Mae Ledbetter** (Mother of No. 1)
b. 1 Apr. 1887
p.b. Kaufman Co., TX
d. 15 Nov. 1980
p.d. Johnson Co., TX

**Anita Hazel Jensen** (Husband or Wife of No. 1)
b. 30 Jan. 1931
p.b. Jefferson Co., Mont.
d.

**4 Charles Pinkney Meador** (Father of No. 2)
b. 4 Mar. 1847
p.b. Hot Spring Co., AR
m. 12 June 1873
d. 30 Dec. 1927
p.d. Johnson Co., TX

**5 Nancy Jane Holsenback** (Mother of No. 2)
b. 14 Dec. 1856
p.b. Van Buren Co., AR
d. 23 Nov. 1937
p.d. Johnson Co., TX

**6 Welborn Columbus Ledbetter** (Father of No. 3)
b. 2 June 1848
p.b. Murray Co., GA
m. 19 Nov 1868
d. 23 Dec. 1896
p.d. Kaufman Co., TX

**7 Susan L. Tadlock** (Mother of No. 3)
b. 24 Mar 1850
p.b. Hopkins Co., TX
d. 6 Feb. 1937
p.d. Johnson Co., TX

**8 George Washington Meador** (Father of No. 4)
b. 29 Aug 1813
p.b. ? (S.C.?)
m. (2)26 Apr. 1846, Clark Co., AR
d. 8 Oct. 1885
p.d. Johnson Co., TX
(2) Clarissa Meadows

**9** (Mother of No. 4)
b. 26 Oct. 1826
p.b. ? (AL ?)
d. 3 Oct. 1857
p.d. Johnson Co., TX

**10 Abraham Holsenback** (Father of No. 5)
b. 29 Sept. 1813
p.b.
m.
d. 3 May 1866
p.d. Van Buren Co., AR

**11 Mary "Polly" Pruitt** (Mother of No. 5)
b. 9 Sept. 1814
p.b. Tenn.
d. 12 Nov. 1861
p.d. Johnson Co., TX

**12 Wiley L. Ledbetter** (Father of No. 6)
b. 1824
p.b. N.C.
m. 29 Mar. 1845 GA
d.
p.d.

**13 Mary Ann Strawn** (Mother of No. 6)
b. 1828
p.b. GA
d.
p.d. TX

**14 James Tadlock** (Father of No. 7)
b. 1804
p.b. Barron Co., KY
m.
d.
p.d.

**15 Martha "Betsy" Crisp** (Mother of No. 7)
b. 1807
p.b. KY
d.
p.d.

16 (Father of No. 8) Continued on chart
17 (Mother of No. 8) Continued on chart
18 Clement Meadows (Father of No. 9) Continued on chart
19 Olive ? (Mother of No. 9) Continued on chart
20 (Father of No. 10) Continued on chart
21 (Mother of No. 10) Continued on chart
22 David Pruitt (Father of No. 11) Continued on chart
23 Charlotte Sneed (Mother of No. 11) Continued on chart
24 (Father of No. 12) Continued on chart
25 (Mother of No. 12) Continued on chart
26 (Father of No. 13) Continued on chart
27 (Mother of No. 13) Continued on chart
28 (Father of No. 14) Continued on chart
29 (Mother of No. 14) Continued on chart
30 (Father of No. 15) Continued on chart
31 (Mother of No. 15) Continued

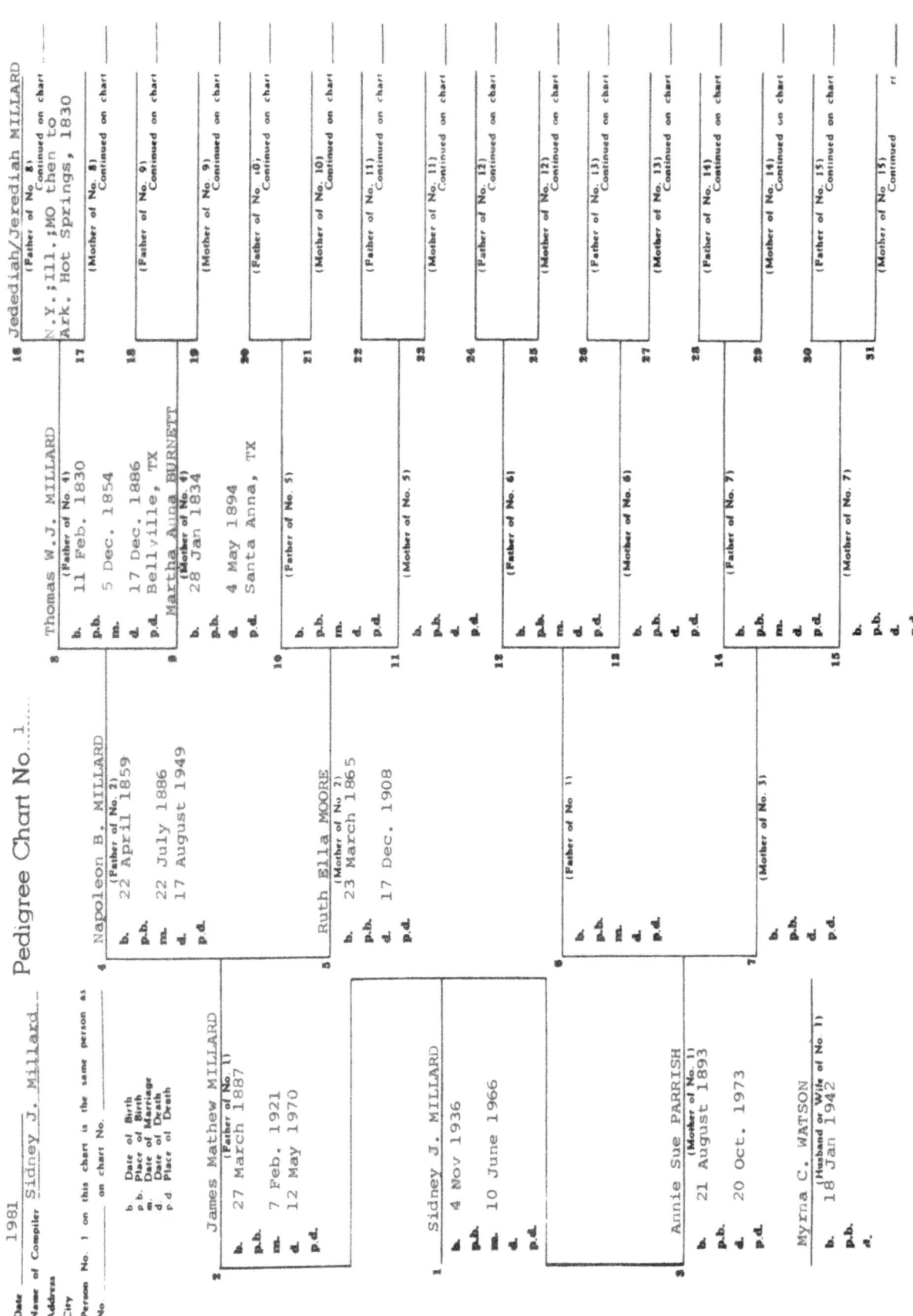

Pedigree Chart No. 1

Date ____ 1981
Name of Compiler ___ Sidney J. Millard
Address ____
City ____
Person No. 1 on this chart is the same person as
No. ____ on chart No. ____

b.   Date of Birth
p.b. Place of Birth
m.   Date of Marriage
d.   Date of Death
p.d  Place of Death

1  Sidney J. MILLARD
b.   4 Nov 1936
p.b.
m.   10 June 1966
d.
p.d.

2  James Mathew MILLARD (Father of No. 1)
b.   27 March 1887
p.b.
m.   7 Feb. 1921
d.   12 May 1970
p.d.

3  Annie Sue PARRISH (Mother of No. 1)
b.   21 August 1893
p.b.
d.   20 Oct. 1973
p.d.

Myrna C. WATSON (Husband or Wife of No. 1)
b.   18 Jan 1942
p.b.
d.

4  Napoleon B. MILLARD (Father of No. 2)
b.   22 April 1859
p.b.
m.   22 July 1886
d.   17 August 1949
p.d.

5  Ruth Ella MOORE (Mother of No. 2)
b.   23 March 1865
p.b.
d.   17 Dec. 1908
p.d.

6  (Father of No. 3)
b.
p.b.
m.
d.
p.d.

7  (Mother of No. 3)
b.
p.b.
d.
p.d.

8  Thomas W.J. MILLARD (Father of No. 4)
b.   11 Feb. 1830
p.b.
m.   5 Dec. 1854
d.   17 Dec. 1886  Bellville, TX
p.d.

9  Martha Anna BURNETT (Mother of No. 4)
b.   28 Jan 1834
p.b.
d.   4 May 1894
p.d. Santa Anna, TX

10  (Father of No. 5)
b.
p.b.
m.
d.
p.d.

11  (Mother of No. 5)
b.
p.b.
d.
p.d.

12  (Father of No. 6)
b.
p.b.
m.
d.
p.d.

13  (Mother of No. 6)
b.
p.b.
d.
p.d.

14  (Father of No. 7)
b.
p.b.
m.
d.
p.d.

15  (Mother of No. 7)
b.
p.b.
d.
p.d.

16  Jedediah/Jerediah MILLARD (Father of No. 8)
N.Y.;Ill.;MO then to Ark. Hot Springs, 1830
Continued on chart ____

17  ____  (Mother of No. 8)  Continued on chart ____

18  (Father of No. 9)  Continued on chart ____

19  (Mother of No. 9)  Continued on chart ____

20  (Father of No. 10)  Continued on chart ____

21  (Mother of No. 10)  Continued on chart ____

22  (Father of No. 11)  Continued on chart ____

23  (Mother of No. 11)  Continued on chart ____

24  (Father of No. 12)  Continued on chart ____

25  (Mother of No. 12)  Continued on chart ____

26  (Father of No. 13)  Continued on chart ____

27  (Mother of No. 13)  Continued on chart ____

28  (Father of No. 14)  Continued on chart ____

29  (Mother of No. 14)  Continued on chart ____

30  (Father of No. 15)  Continued on chart ____

31  (Mother of No. 15)  Continued ____

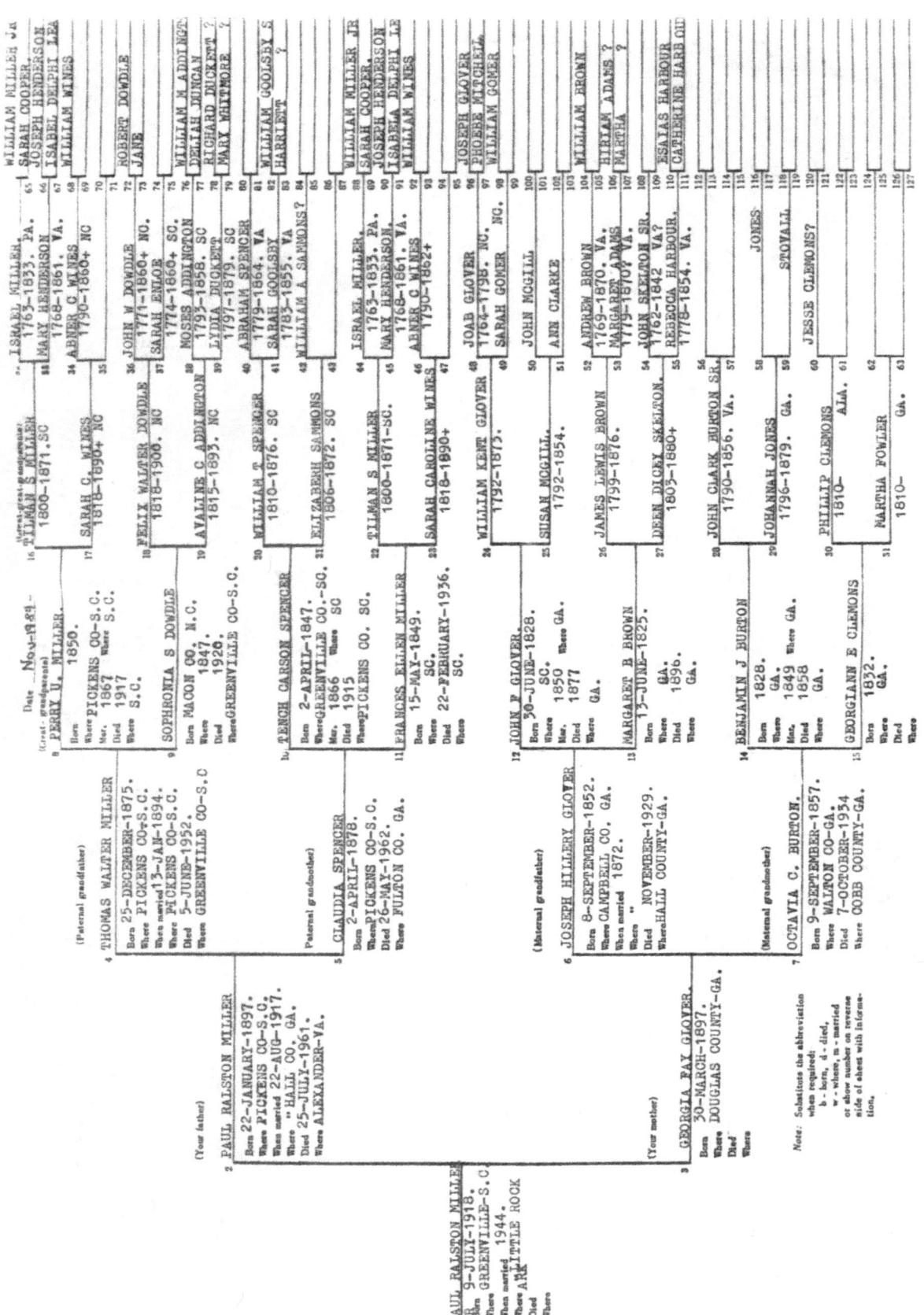

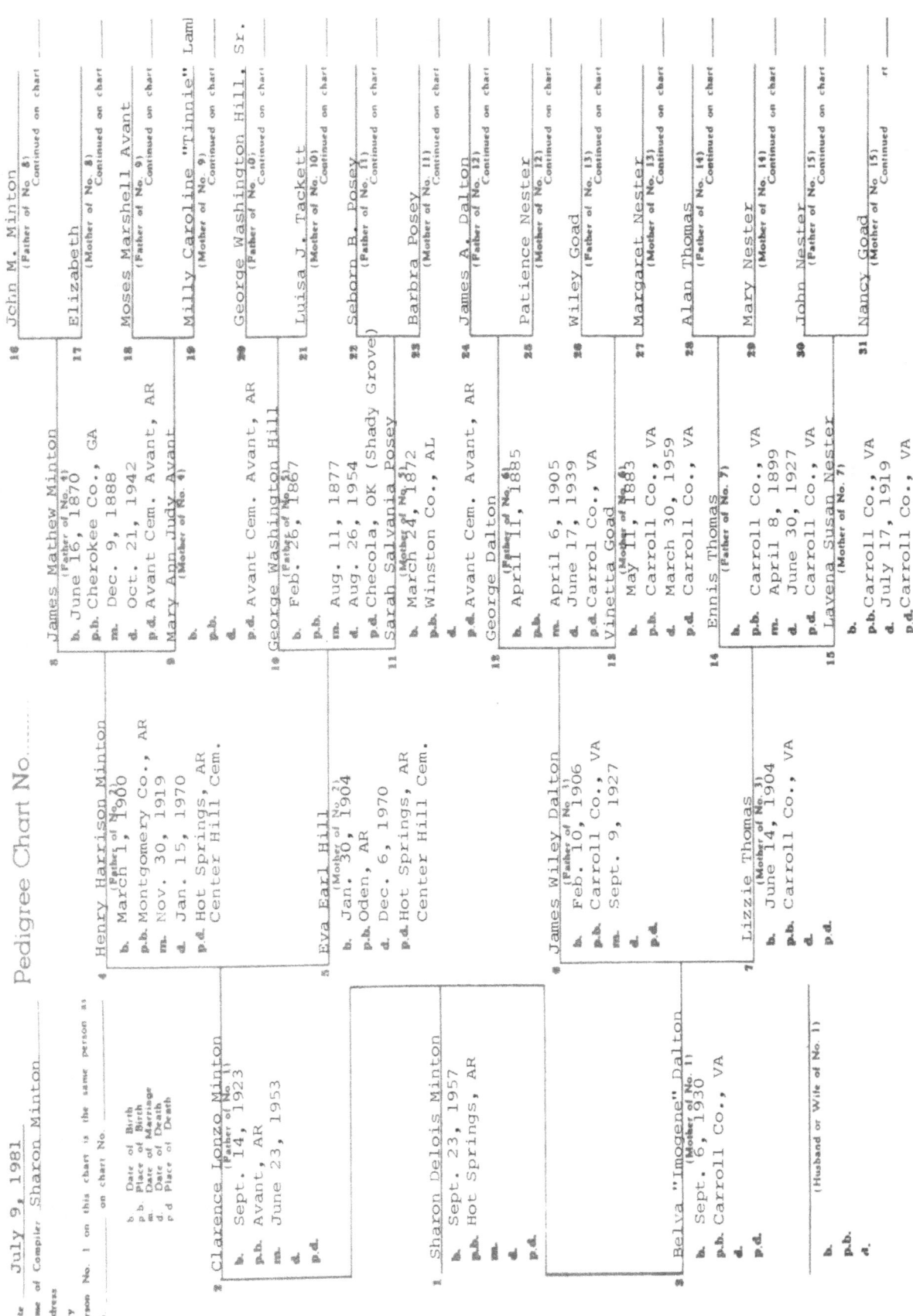

Pedigree Chart No. 1

Date 16 March 1981
Name of Compiler Mary S. Owen
Address
City
Person No. 1 on this chart is the same person as _____ on chart No. _____

b. Date of Birth
p.b. Place of Birth
m. Date of Marriage
d. Date of Death
p.d. Place of Death

**1 Ernest Teler Owen**
b. 23 May 1897
p.b. Mansfield, AR
m. 2 Feb 1933
d. 6 Aug 1981
p.d. Hot Springs, AR

**2 John Thomas Owen** (Father of No. 1)
b. 30 Sept 1859
p.b. Homer, GA
m. 6 Dec 1883
d. 24 Nov 1933
p.d. Mansfield, AR

**3 Mary Esther B. Claborn** (Mother of No. 1)
b. 10 Mar 1863
p.b. Weakley Co., TN
d. 16 Mar 1936
p.d. Mansfield, AR

Mary Frances Schilling (Husband or Wife of No. 1)
b. 8 Dec 1908
p.b. Draughon, AR
d.

**4 Francis Manley Owen** (Father of No. 2)
b. 9 Feb. 1833
p.b. Anderson Co., S.C.
m. 1) 8 Dec 1852  2) 7 Dec 1858
d. 15 April 1905
p.d. Mansfield, AR

**5 Mary Elizabeth Hutcherson** (Mother of No. 2)
b. 14 Oct 1835
p.b. Ft. Lamar, GA
d. 19 June 1915
p.d. Mansfield, AR

**6 William Calhoun Claborn** (Father of No. 3)
b. 4 Mar 1830
p.b. Weakley Co., TN
m. 12 Sept 1854
d. 3 July 1908
p.d. Mansfield, AR

**7 Mary Jane Blackley** (Mother of No. 3)
b. 4 June 1835
p.b. Weakley Co., TN
d. 5 Mar 1905
p.d. Mansfield, AR

**8 Elijah Owen** (Father of No. 4)
b. July 1804
p.b. Greenville Co., S.C.
m. ca 1831
d. 24 Oct. 1864
p.d. Banks Co., GA

**9 Elizabeth (Patsy) Kelly** (Mother of No. 4)
b. ca 1815
p.b. S.C.
d. ?
p.d. Banks Co., GA

**10 Joshua Hutcherson** (Father of No. 5)
b. 16 Feb. 1808
p.b. N.C.
m. ca 1833
d. 1 Aug 1890
p.d. Ft. Lamar, GA

**11 Flora McDonald** (Mother of No. 5)
b. 26 Jan 1813
p.b. Elbert Co., GA
d. after 1844
p.d. Ft. Lamar, GA

**12 Alfred Claborn** (Father of No. 6)
b. 26 Oct 1801
p.b. Bedford Co., VA
m. Before 1830
d. 1858
p.d. Weakley Co., TN

**13 Catherine Rhodes** (Mother of No. 6)
b. 1809
p.b. Bedford Co., VA
d. after 1870
p.d. Mansfield, AR

**14 James Blackley** (Father of No. 7)
b. 12 Apr 1809
p.b. Bedford Co., VA
m. 1) Huggins  2) Elizabeth Sanders
d.
p.d.

**15 Elizabeth Huggins** (Mother of No. 7)
b. 26 Nov 1812
p.b. Bedford Co., VA
d. Mar. 1851
p.d. Weakley Co., TN

**16 Obediah Owen** (Father of No. 8)
Continued on chart

**17 Martha A. (Patsy) Ford** (Mother of No. 8)
Continued on chart

**18** (Father of No. 9)
Continued on chart

**19** (Mother of No. 9)
Continued on chart

**20 James Hutcherson (R.S.)** (Father of No. 10)
Continued on chart

**21 Mary** (Mother of No. 10)
Continued on chart

**22 John McDonald** (Father of No. 11)
Continued on chart

**23 Margaret McCurry** (Mother of No. 11)
Continued on chart

**24 John Clayborne** (Father of No. 12)
Continued on chart

**25 Polly Middleton** (Mother of No. 12)
Continued on chart

**26** (Father of No. 13)
Continued on chart

**27** (Mother of No. 13)
Continued on chart

**28 William Blackley** (Father of No. 14)
Continued on chart

**29 Nancy Holden** (Mother of No. 14)
Continued on chart

**30 Thomas Huggins** (Father of No. 15)
Continued on chart

**31 Elvira** (Mother of No. 15)
Continued on chart

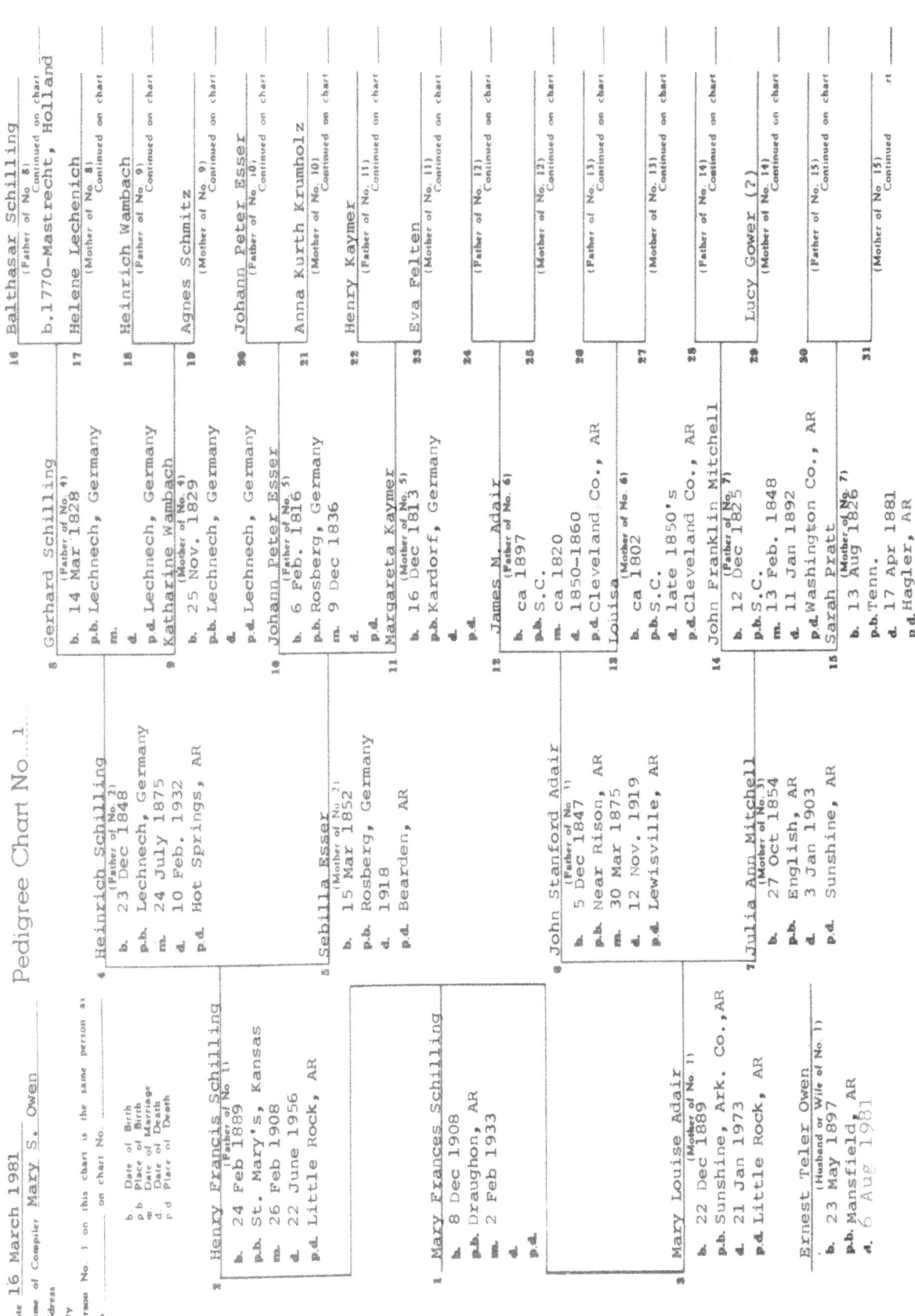

Pedigree Chart No. 1

Date 16 March 1981

Name of Compiler Mary S. Owen

Address

City

Person No. 1 on this chart is the same person as _____ on chart No. _____

b. Date of Birth
p.b Place of Birth
m. Date of Marriage
d. Date of Death
p.d Place of Death

1 Mary Frances Schilling
b. 8 Dec 1908
p.b. Draughon, AR
m. 2 Feb 1933
d.
p.d.

2 Henry Francis Schilling (Father of No. 1)
b. 24 Feb 1889
p.b. St. Mary's, Kansas
m. 26 Feb 1908
d. 22 June 1956
p.d. Little Rock, AR

3 Mary Louise Adair (Mother of No. 1)
b. 22 Dec 1889
p.b. Sunshine, Ark. Co., AR
d. 21 Jan 1973
p.d. Little Rock, AR

Ernest Teler Owen (Husband or Wife of No. 1)
b. 23 May 1897
p.b. Mansfield, AR
d. 6 Aug 1981

4 Heinrich Schilling (Father of No. 2)
b. 23 Dec 1848
p.b. Lechnech, Germany
m. 24 July 1875
d. 10 Feb. 1932
p.d. Hot Springs, AR

5 Sebilla Esser (Mother of No. 2)
b. 15 Mar 1852
p.b. Rosberg, Germany
d. 1918
p.d. Bearden, AR

6 John Stanford Adair (Father of No. 3)
b. 5 Dec 1847
p.b. Near Rison, AR
m. 30 Mar 1875
d. 12 Nov. 1919
p.d. Lewisville, AR

7 Julia Ann Mitchell (Mother of No. 3)
b. 27 Oct 1854
p.b. English, AR
d. 3 Jan 1903
p.d. Sunshine, AR

8 Gerhard Schilling (Father of No. 4)
b. 14 Mar 1828
p.b. Lechnech, Germany
m.
d.
p.d. Lechnech, Germany

9 Katharine Wambach (Mother of No. 4)
b. 25 Nov. 1829
p.b. Lechnech, Germany
d.

10 Johann Peter Esser (Father of No. 5)
b. 6 Feb. 1816
p.b. Rosberg, Germany
m. 9 Dec 1836
p.d.

11 Margareta Kaymer (Mother of No. 5)
b. 16 Dec 1813
p.b. Kardorf, Germany
d.
p.d.

12 James M. Adair (Father of No. 6)
b. ca 1897
p.b. S.C.
m. ca 1820
d. 1850-1860
p.d. Cleveland Co., AR

13 Louisa (Mother of No. 6)
b. ca 1802
p.b. S.C.
d. late 1850's
p.d. Cleveland Co., AR

14 John Franklin Mitchell (Father of No. 7)
b. 12 Dec 1825
p.b. S.C.
m. 13 Feb. 1848
d. 11 Jan 1892
p.d. Washington Co., AR

15 Sarah Pratt (Mother of No. 7)
b. 13 Aug 1826
p.b. Tenn.
d. 17 Apr 1881
p.d. Hagler, AR

16 Balthasar Schilling (Father of No. 8)
Continued on chart
b. 1770-Mastrecht, Holland

17 Helene Lechenich (Mother of No. 8)
Continued on chart

18 Heinrich Wambach (Father of No. 9)
Continued on chart

19 Agnes Schmitz (Mother of No. 9)
Continued on chart

20 Johann Peter Esser (Father of No. 10)
Continued on chart

21 Anna Kurth Krumholz (Mother of No. 10)
Continued on chart

22 Henry Kaymer (Father of No. 11)
Continued on chart

23 Eva Felten (Mother of No. 11)
Continued on chart

24 (Father of No. 12)
Continued on chart

25 (Mother of No. 12)
Continued on chart

26 (Father of No. 13)
Continued on chart

27 (Mother of No. 13)
Continued on chart

28 (Father of No. 14)
Continued on chart

29 Lucy Gower (2) (Mother of No. 14)
Continued on chart

30 (Father of No. 15)
Continued on chart

31 (Mother of No. 15)
Continued

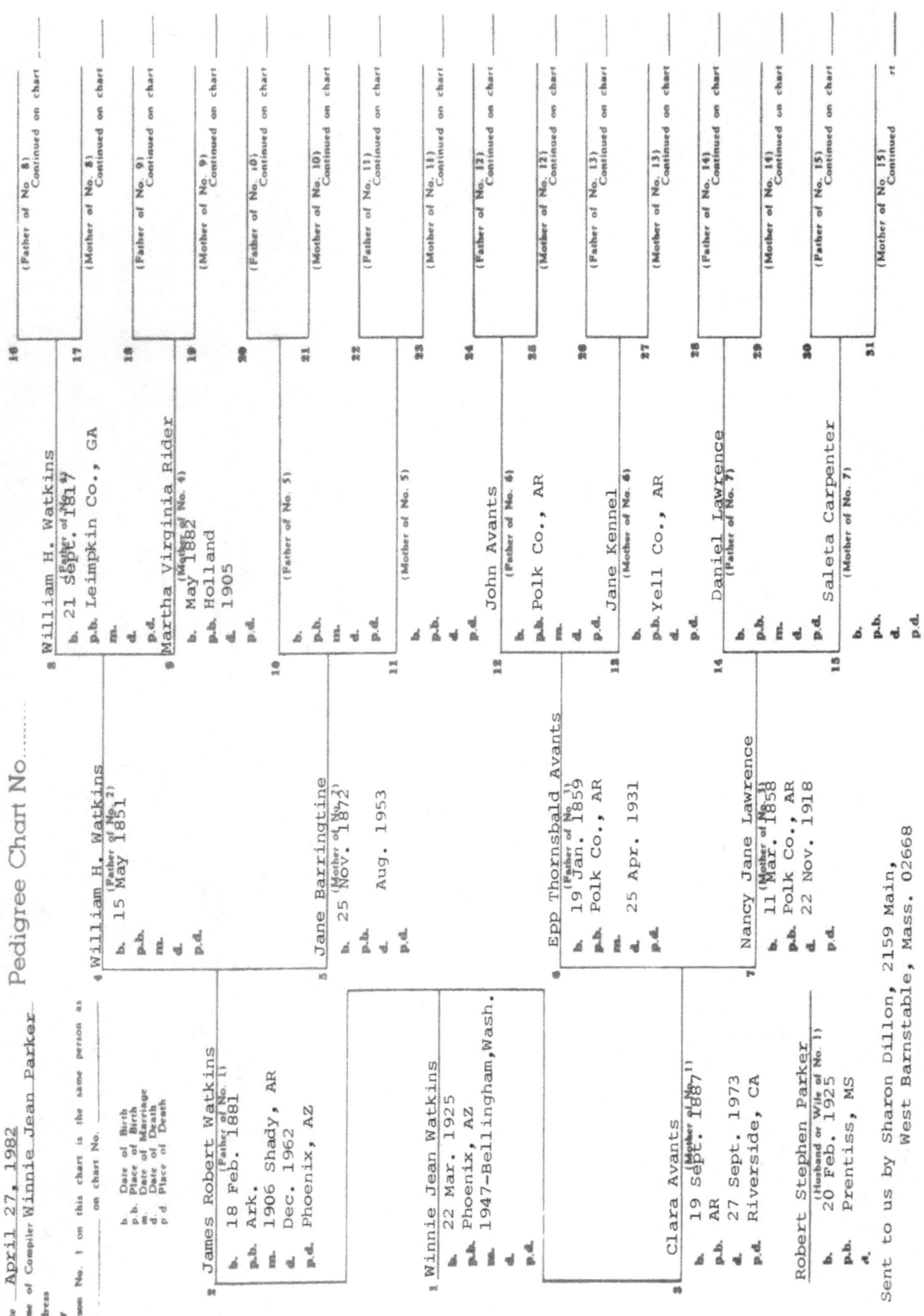

Date _April 27, 1982_          Pedigree Chart No. ........

Name of Compiler _Winnie Jean Parker_

Address

City

Person No. 1 on this chart is the same person as ............ on chart No. ............

No.

     b.   Date of Birth
     p.b.  Place of Birth
     m.   Date of Marriage
     d.   Date of Death
     p.d  Place of Death

**16** (Father of No. 8) Continued on chart

**17** (Mother of No. 8) Continued on chart

**18** (Father of No. 9) Continued on chart

**19** (Mother of No. 9) Continued on chart

**20** (Father of No. 10) Continued on chart

**21** (Mother of No. 10) Continued on chart

**22** (Father of No. 11) Continued on chart

**23** (Mother of No. 11) Continued on chart

**24** (Father of No. 12) Continued on chart

**25** (Mother of No. 12) Continued on chart

**26** (Father of No. 13) Continued on chart

**27** (Mother of No. 13) Continued on chart

**28** (Father of No. 14) Continued on chart

**29** (Mother of No. 14) Continued on chart

**30** (Father of No. 15) Continued on chart

**31** (Mother of No. 15) Continued

**8** William H. Watkins
  b. 21 Sept. 1817
  p.b. Leimpkin Co., GA
  m.
  d.
  p.d.
(Father of No. 4)

**9** Martha Virginia Rider
  b. May 1882
  p.b. Holland
  d. 1905
  p.d.
(Mother of No. 4)

**10** (Father of No. 5)
  b.
  p.b.
  m.
  d.
  p.d.

**11** (Mother of No. 5)
  b.
  p.b.
  d.
  p.d.

**12** John Avants
  b.
  p.b. Polk Co., AR
  m.
  d.
  p.d.
(Father of No. 6)

**13** Jane Kennel
  b.
  p.b. Yell Co., AR
  d.
  p.d.
(Mother of No. 6)

**14** Daniel Lawrence
  b.
  p.b.
  m.
  d.
  p.d.
(Father of No. 7)

**15** Saleta Carpenter
  b.
  p.b.
  d.
  p.d.
(Mother of No. 7)

**4** William H. Watkins
  b. 15 May 1851
  p.b.
  m.
  d.
  p.d.
(Father of No. 2)

**5** Jane Barringtine
  b. 25 Nov. 1872
  p.b.
  d. Aug. 1953
  p.d.
(Mother of No. 2)

**6** Epp Thornsbald Avants
  b. 19 Jan. 1859
  p.b. Polk Co., AR
  m.
  d. 25 Apr. 1931
  p.d.
(Father of No. 3)

**7** Nancy Jane Lawrence
  b. 11 Mar. 1858
  p.b. Polk Co., AR
  d. 22 Nov. 1918
  p.d.
(Mother of No. 3)

**2** James Robert Watkins
  b. 18 Feb. 1881
  p.b. Ark.
  m. 1906 Shady, AR
  d. Dec. 1962
  p.d. Phoenix, AZ
(Father of No. 1)

**3** Clara Avants
  b. 19 Sept. 1887
  p.b. AR
  d. 27 Sept. 1973
  p.d. Riverside, CA
(Mother of No. 1)

**1** Winnie Jean Watkins
  b. 22 Mar. 1925
  p.b. Phoenix, AZ
  m. 1947-Bellingham,Wash.
  d.
  p.d.

Robert Stephen Parker
  b. 20 Feb. 1925
  p.b. Prentiss, MS
  d.
(Husband or Wife of No. 1)

Sent to us by Sharon Dillon, 2159 Main,
             West Barnstable, Mass. 02668

# Pedigree Chart No.

Date 1981
Name of Compiler Jerry Ray Smith
Address
City
Person No. 1 on this chart is the same person #1
No _____ on chart No

b. Date of Birth
p.b. Place of Birth
m. Date of Marriage
d. Date of Death
p.d Place of Death

**1** Jerry Ray Smith
b. January 22, 1956
p.b. Okla. City, OK
m.
d.
p.d.

**2** James Jackson Smith
(Father of No. 1)
b.
p.b.
m.
d.
p.d.

**3** Letha Mary Ritter
(Mother of No. 1)
b. March 20, 1927
p.b. Milton, OK
d.
p.d.

(Husband or Wife of No. 1)
b.
p.b.
d.

**4** Samuel Moore Smith
(Father of No. 2)
b. May 1, 1883
p.b. Dawsonville, GA
m. April 22, 1824
d. October 5, 1940
p.d. Cartersville, OK

**5** Emmer Lee Ann Spradlin
(Mother of No. 2)
b. Aug. 26, 1888
p.b. Alpine, AR
d. Aug. 28, 1958
p.d. Cartersville, OK

**6** Thomas Franklin Ritter
(Father of No. 3)
b. May 12, 1883
p.b. Garland Co., AR
m.
d. Oct. 17, 1970
p.d. Ft. Smith, AR

**7** Anna Louisa Tenn. Spears
(Mother of No. 3)
b. Aug. 9, 1888
p.b. Garland Co., AR
d. Jan. 17, 1973
p.d. Poteau, OK

**8** Isaac David Smith
(Father of No. 4)
b. January 1815
p.b. Pickens, SC
m. ca. 1849
d. January 1902
p.d. Omaha, Texas

**9** Nancy Brooks
(Mother of No. 4)
b. April 1825 or 1827
p.b. Sandy Run, NC
d. January 1902
p.d. Omaha, Texas

**10** James B. Spradlin
(Father of No. 5)
b. ca. 1821
p.b. Georgia
m. Nov. 19, 1881
d. ca 1889
p.d. Alpine, AR

**11** Sarah Ann Pitts
(Mother of No. 5)
b. July 1850
p.b. Mississippi
d. July 1910
p.d. Keota, OK

**12** Ashley Franklin Ritter
(Father of No. 6)
b. 1853
p.b. Moore Co., NC
m. ca 1874
d. Oct. 18, 1925
p.d. Hot Springs, AR

**13** Mary Ann Merriott
(Mother of No. 6)
b. March 1847
p.b. Rhea Co., TN
d. Nov. 29, 1912
p.d. Little Rock, AR

**14** Nathaniel M. Spears
(Father of No. 7)
b. ca 1843
p.b. Montgomery, AL
m. July 1860
d. ca 1888
p.d. Garland Co., AR

**15** Margaret Ann Phillips
(Mother of No. 7)
b. May 1843
p.b. Wilson Co., TN
d. ca 1916
p.d. Muse, OK

**16** (Father of No. 8)
Continued on chart

**17** (Mother of No. 8)
Continued on chart

**18** Aaron Brooks
(Father of No. 9)
Continued on chart

**19** Elizabeth
(Mother of No. 9)
Continued on chart

**20** Irvin Spradlin (probably)
(Father of No. 10)
Continued on chart

**21** (Mother of No. 10)
Continued on chart

**22** Isaac Pitts
(Father of No. 11)
Continued on chart

**23** Mary A. Tucker
(Mother of No. 11)
Continued on chart

**24** George D. Ritter
(Father of No. 12)
Continued on chart

**25** Mildred Jackson
(Mother of No. 12)
Continued on chart

**26** John Henry Merriott
(Father of No. 13)
Continued on chart

**27** Jane Guerin
(Mother of No. 13)
Continued on chart

**28** John Spears
(Father of No. 14)
Continued on chart

**29** Elizabeth Mason
(Mother of No. 14)
Continued on chart

**30** Zachariah H. Phillips
(Father of No. 15)
Continued on chart

**31** Mary Pyland
(Mother of No. 15)
Continued

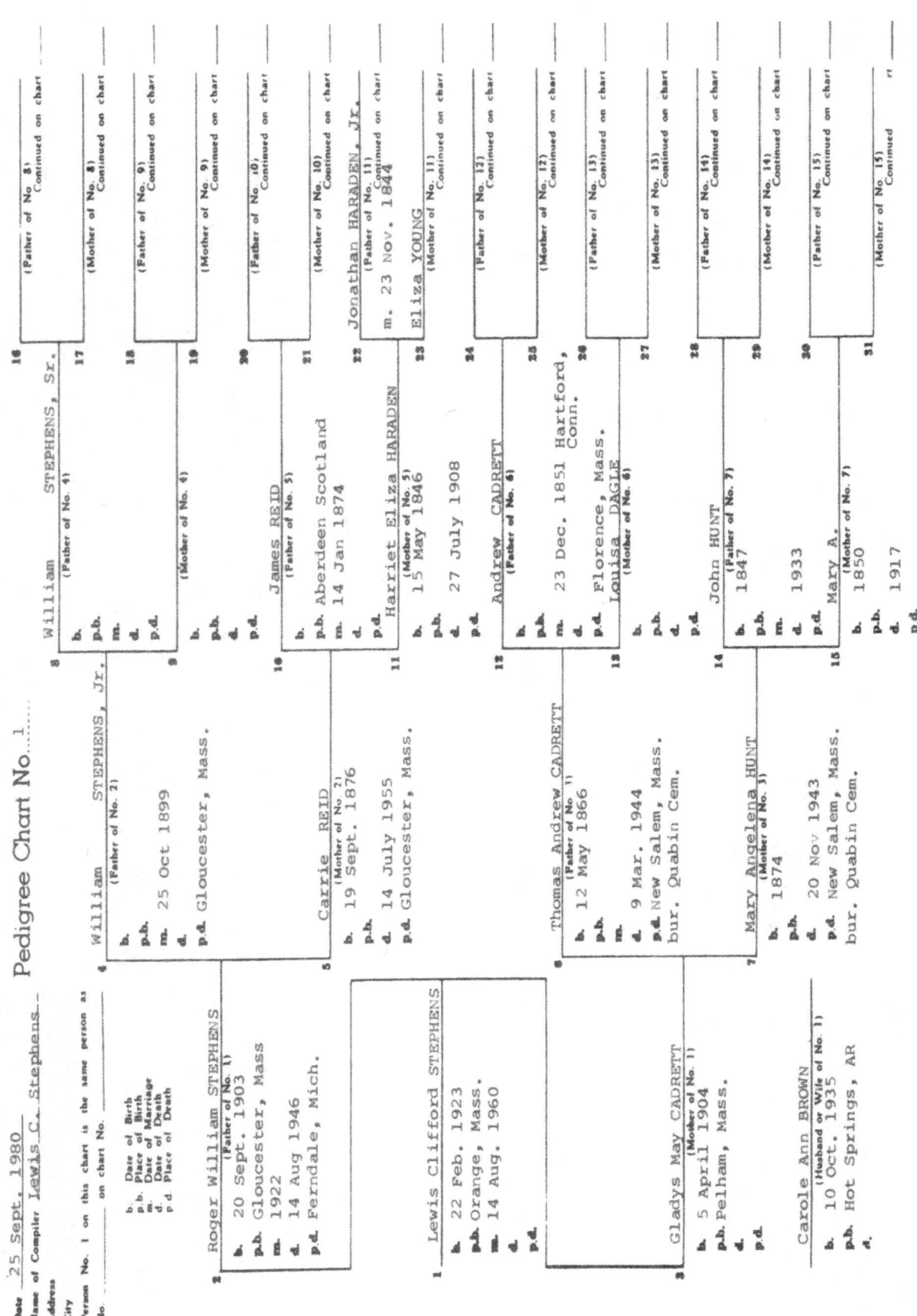

Pedigree Chart No. 1

Date 25 Sept. 1980
Name of Compiler Lewis C. Stephens
Address
City
Person No. 1 on this chart is the same person as _____ on chart No. _____

 b. Date of Birth
 p.b. Place of Birth
 m. Date of Marriage
 d. Date of Death
 p.d Place of Death

**1** Lewis Clifford STEPHENS
b. 22 Feb. 1923
p.b. Orange, Mass.
m. 14 Aug. 1960
d.
p.d.

**2** Roger William STEPHENS
(Father of No. 1)
b. 20 Sept. 1903
p.b. Gloucester, Mass
m. 1922
d. 14 Aug 1946
p.d. Ferndale, Mich.

**3** Gladys May CADRETT
(Mother of No. 1)
b. 5 April 1904
p.b. Pelham, Mass.
d.
p.d.

**4** William STEPHENS, Jr.
(Father of No. 2)
b.
p.b.
m. 25 Oct 1899
d.
p.d. Gloucester, Mass.

**5** Carrie REID
(Mother of No. 2)
b. 19 Sept. 1876
p.b.
d. 14 July 1955
p.d. Gloucester, Mass.

**6** Thomas Andrew CADRETT
(Father of No. 1)
b. 12 May 1866
p.b.
m.
d. 9 Mar. 1944
p.d. New Salem, Mass.
bur. Quabin Cem.

**7** Mary Angelena HUNT
(Mother of No. 3)
b. 1874
p.b.
d. 20 Nov 1943
p.d. New Salem, Mass.
bur. Quabin Cem.

Carole Ann BROWN
(Husband or Wife of No. 1)
b. 10 Oct. 1935
p.b. Hot Springs, AR
d.

**8** William STEPHENS, Sr.
(Father of No. 4)
b.
p.b.
m.
d.
p.d.

**9** (Mother of No. 4)
b.
p.b.
d.
p.d.

**10** James REID
(Father of No. 5)
b.
p.b. Aberdeen Scotland
m. 14 Jan 1874
d.
p.d.

**11** Harriet Eliza HARADEN
(Mother of No. 5)
b. 15 May 1846
d. 27 July 1908
p.d.

**12** Andrew CADRETT
(Father of No. 6)
b.
p.b.
m. 23 Dec. 1851 Hartford, Conn.
d.
p.d. Florence, Mass.

**13** Louisa DAGLE
(Mother of No. 6)
b.
p.b.
d.
p.d.

**14** John HUNT
(Father of No. 7)
b. 1847
p.b.
m.
d. 1933
p.d.

**15** Mary A.
(Mother of No. 7)
b. 1850
p.b.
d. 1917
p.d.

**16** (Father of No. 8) Continued on chart

**17** (Mother of No. 8) Continued on chart

**18** (Father of No. 9) Continued on chart

**19** (Mother of No. 9) Continued on chart

**20** (Father of No. 10) Continued on chart

**21** (Mother of No. 10) Continued on chart

**22** Jonathan HARADEN, Jr.
(Father of No. 11) Continued on chart
m. 23 Nov. 1844

**23** Eliza YOUNG
(Mother of No. 11) Continued on chart

**24** (Father of No. 12) Continued on chart

**25** (Mother of No. 12) Continued on chart

**26** (Father of No. 13) Continued on chart

**27** (Mother of No. 13) Continued on chart

**28** (Father of No. 14) Continued on chart

**29** (Mother of No. 14) Continued on chart

**30** (Father of No. 15) Continued on chart

**31** (Mother of No. 15) Continued on chart

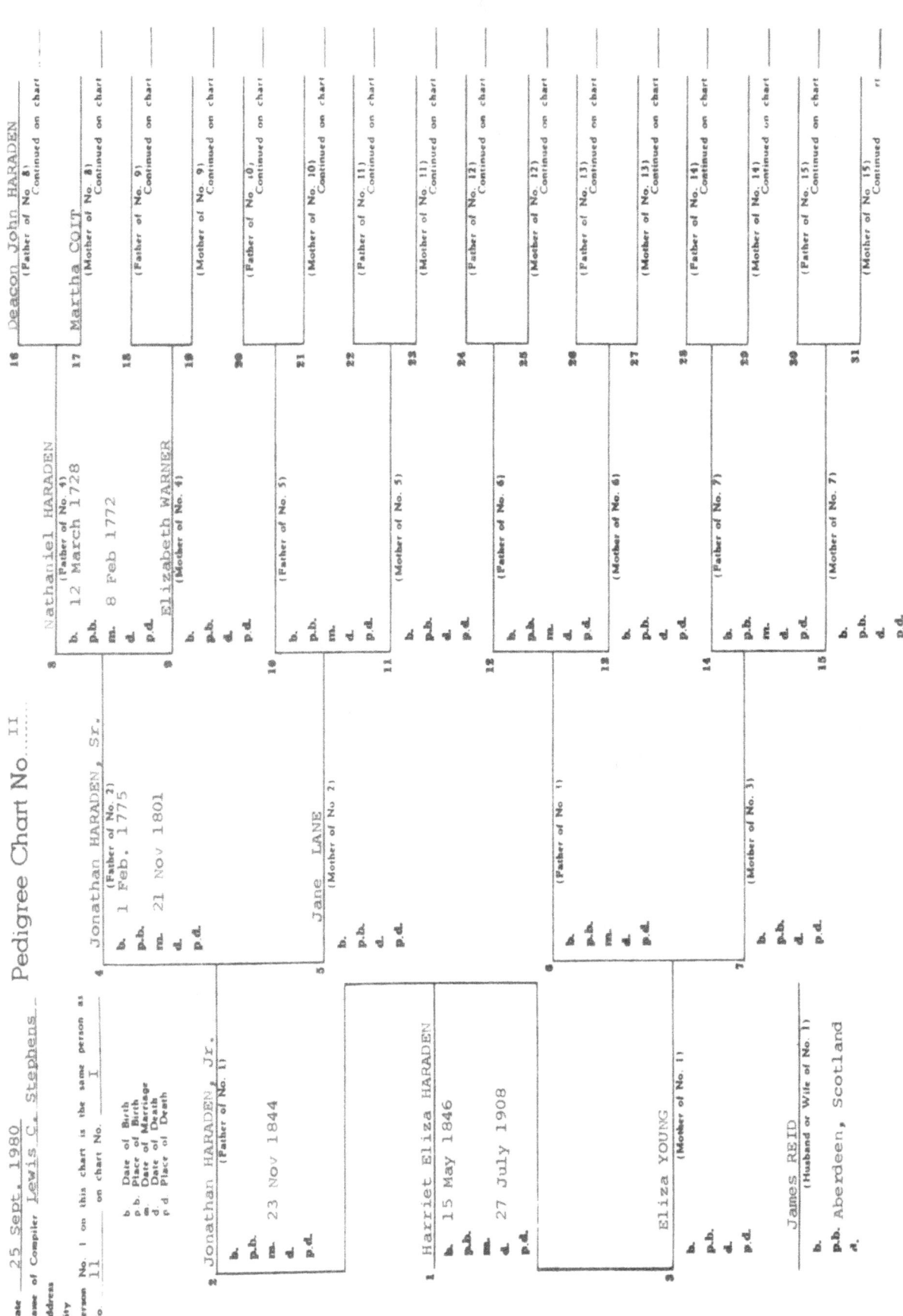

Pedigree Chart No. 11

Date 25 Sept. 1980
Name of Compiler Lewis C. Stephens
Address
City
Person No. 1 on this chart is the same person as
No. 11 on chart No. 1

b    Date of Birth
p.b  Place of Birth
d.   Date of Death
p.d  Place of Death

1 Harriet Eliza HARADEN
b. 15 May 1846
p.b.
m.
d. 27 July 1908
p.d.

2 Jonathan HARADEN, Jr.
(Father of No. 1)
b.
p.b.
m. 23 Nov 1844
d.
p.d.

3 Eliza YOUNG
(Mother of No. 1)
b.
p.b.
d.
p.d.

4 Jonathan HARADEN, Sr.
(Father of No. 2)
b. 1 Feb. 1775
p.b.
m. 21 Nov 1801
d.
p.d.

5 Jane LANE
(Mother of No 2)
b.
p.b.
d.
p.d.

6 (Father of No. 1)
b.
p.b.
m.
d.
p.d.

7 (Mother of No. 3)
b.
p.b.
d.
p.d.

James REID
(Husband or Wife of No. 1)
b.
p.b. Aberdeen, Scotland
d.

8 Nathaniel HARADEN
(Father of No. 4)
b. 12 March 1728
p.b.
m. 8 Feb 1772
d.
p.d.

9 Elizabeth WARNER
(Mother of No. 4)
b.
p.b.
d.
p.d.

10 (Father of No. 5)
b.
p.b.
m.
d.
p.d.

11 (Mother of No. 5)
b.
p.b.
d.
p.d.

12 (Father of No. 6)
b.
p.b.
m.
d.
p.d.

13 (Mother of No. 6)
b.
p.b.
d.
p.d.

14 (Father of No. 7)
b.
p.b.
m.
d.
p.d.

15 (Mother of No. 7)
b.
p.b.
d.
p.d.

16 Deacon John HARADEN
(Father of No. 8) Continued on chart

17 Martha COIT
(Mother of No. 8) Continued on chart

18 (Father of No. 9) Continued on chart

19 (Mother of No. 9) Continued on chart

20 (Father of No. 10, Continued on chart

21 (Mother of No. 10) Continued on chart

22 (Father of No. 11) Continued on chart

23 (Mother of No. 11) Continued on chart

24 (Father of No. 12) Continued on chart

25 (Mother of No. 12) Continued on chart

26 (Father of No. 13) Continued on chart

27 (Mother of No. 13) Continued on chart

28 (Father of No. 14) Continued on chart

29 (Mother of No. 14) Continued on chart

30 (Father of No. 15) Continued on chart

31 (Mother of No. 15) Continued

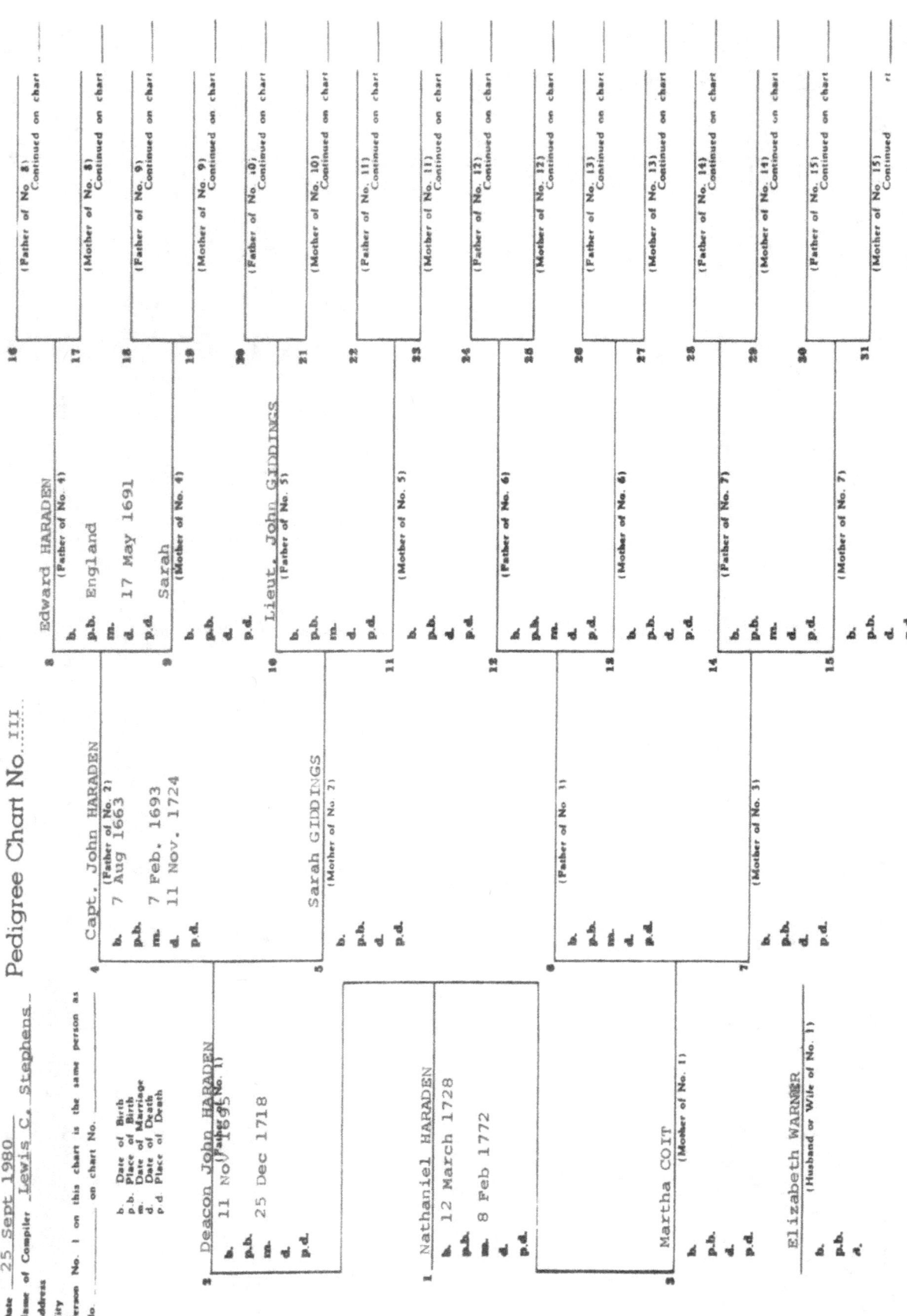

Pedigree Chart No. III

Date 25 Sept 1980
Name of Compiler Lewis C. Stephens
Address
City
Person No. 1 on this chart is the same person as _____ on chart No. _____

b. Date of Birth
p.b. Place of Birth
m. Date of Marriage
d. Date of Death
p.d Place of Death

1 Nathaniel HARADEN
b. 12 March 1728
p.b.
m. 8 Feb 1772
d.
p.d.

2 Deacon John HARADEN
(Father of No. 1)
b. 11 Nov. 1695
p.b. 25 Dec 1718
m.
d.
p.d.

3 Martha COIT
(Mother of No. 1)
b.
p.b.
d.
p.d.

Elizabeth WARNER
(Husband or Wife of No. 1)
b.
p.b.
d.

4 Capt. John HARADEN
(Father of No. 2)
b. 7 Aug 1663
p.b.
m. 7 Feb. 1693
d. 11 Nov. 1724
p.d.

5 Sarah GIDDINGS
(Mother of No. 2)
b.
p.b.
d.
p.d.

6 (Father of No. 3)
b.
p.b.
m.
d.
p.d.

7 (Mother of No. 3)
b.
p.b.
d.
p.d.

8 Edward HARADEN
(Father of No. 4)
b. England
p.b.
m. 17 May 1691
d. Sarah
p.d.

9 (Mother of No. 4)
b.
p.b.
d.
p.d.

10 Lieut. John GIDDINGS
(Father of No. 5)
b.
p.b.
m.
d.
p.d.

11 (Mother of No. 5)
b.
p.b.
d.
p.d.

12 (Father of No. 6)
b.
p.b.
m.
d.
p.d.

13 (Mother of No. 6)
b.
p.b.
d.
p.d.

14 (Father of No. 7)
b.
p.b.
m.
d.
p.d.

15 (Mother of No. 7)
b.
p.b.
d.
p.d.

16 (Father of No. 8) Continued on chart
17 (Mother of No. 8) Continued on chart
18 (Father of No. 9) Continued on chart
19 (Mother of No. 9) Continued on chart
20 (Father of No. 10) Continued on chart
21 (Mother of No. 10) Continued on chart
22 (Father of No. 11) Continued on chart
23 (Mother of No. 11) Continued on chart
24 (Father of No. 12) Continued on chart
25 (Mother of No. 12) Continued on chart
26 (Father of No. 13) Continued on chart
27 (Mother of No. 13) Continued on chart
28 (Father of No. 14) Continued on chart
29 (Mother of No. 14) Continued on chart
30 (Father of No. 15) Continued on chart
31 (Mother of No. 15) Continued on chart

# Pedigree Chart No. 1

Date: 25 Sept 1980
Name of Compiler: Lewis C. Stephens
Address
City
Person No 1 on this chart is the same person as _____ on chart No.

b   Date of Birth
p.b   Place of Birth
m.   Date of Marriage
d   Date of Death
p.d   Place of Death

**1 Carole Ann BROWN**
b. 10 Oct 1935
p.b. Hot Springs, AR
m. 14 Aug 1960
d.
p.d.

**Lewis Clifford Stephens** (Husband or Wife of No. 1)
b. 22 Feb 1923
p.b. Orange, Mass.
d.

**2 Lewis Edward BROWN** (Father of No. 1)
b. 20 April 1908
p.b. Hot Springs, AR
m.
d.
p.d.

**3 Margaret Louise HILL** (Mother of No. 1)
b. 29 July 1908
p.b. Hot Springs, AR
d.
p.d.

**4 James Jeffery BROWN** (Father of No. 2)
b. 21 April 1889
p.b.
m.
d. 24 Feb 1933
p.d. Hot Springs, AR
bur. Scott Cem.

**5 Burley M. LYNCH** (Mother of No. 2)
b. 27 May 1889
p.b.
d. 11 Apr 1974
p.d. Hot Springs, AR
bur. Scott Cem.

**6 Samuel Columbus HILL** (Father of No. 3)
b. 22 Dec 1861
p.b.
m. 3 Jan 1894
d. Jan/Feb. 1927
p.d. Hot Springs, AR
bur. Shady Grove Cem.

**7 Mary Orpha SHAW** (Mother of No. 3)
b. 28 June 1874
p.b. Cherokee Co., KS
d.
p.d.

**8 Edward D. BROWN** (Father of No. 4)
b.
p.b.
m.
d.
p.d.

**9 Sarah (Sally) SIMPSON** (Mother of No. 4)
b.
p.b.
d.
p.d.

**10 Louis Thomas LYNCH** (Father of No. 5)
b. 1847
p.b. Cairo, Ill.
m.
d. 2 Nov 1912
p.d.

**11 Rebecca Ann McGREW** (Mother of No. 5)
b. 1866
p.b.
d. 1931
p.d.

**12 Euphrates Dawson HILL** (Father of No. 6)
b.
p.b. Paducah, KY
m.
d. ca 1903/04
p.d. Hot Springs, AR

**13 Mary Jane WILLIAMSON** (Mother of No. 6)
b.
p.b. Springfield, MO
d. ca 1903
p.d. Hot Springs, AR

**14 John B. SHAW** (Father of No. 7)
b. 1 Aug 1845
p.b. 23 Aug 1866
m.
d. 3 Dec 1917
p.d. Hot Springs, AR

**15 Delphina BAIRD** (Mother of No. 7)
b. 7 Aug 1849
p.b.
d. 28 Feb 1930
p.d. Hot Springs, AR

|  |  |  | |
|---|---|---|---|
| 16 | Edward D. BROWN | (Father of No. 8) | Continued on chart |
| 17 | Sarah McKINNEY | (Mother of No. 8) | Continued on chart |
| 18 | Chester D. SIMPSON | (Father of No. 9) | Continued on chart |
| 19 | Elizabeth BALDWIN | (Mother of No. 9) | Continued on chart |
| 20 | | (Father of No. 10) | Continued on chart |
| 21 | | (Mother of No. 10) | Continued on chart |
| 22 | Daniel H. McGREW | (Father of No. 11) | Continued on chart |
| 23 | Elizabeth FULTON | (Mother of No. 11) | Continued on chart |
| 24 | | (Father of No. 12) | Continued on chart |
| 25 | | (Mother of No. 12) | Continued on chart |
| 26 | | (Father of No. 13) | Continued on chart |
| 27 | | (Mother of No. 13) | Continued on chart |
| 28 | | (Father of No. 14) | Continued on chart |
| 29 | | (Mother of No. 14) | Continued on chart |
| 30 | | (Father of No. 15) | Continued on chart |
| 31 | | (Mother of No. 15) | Continued |

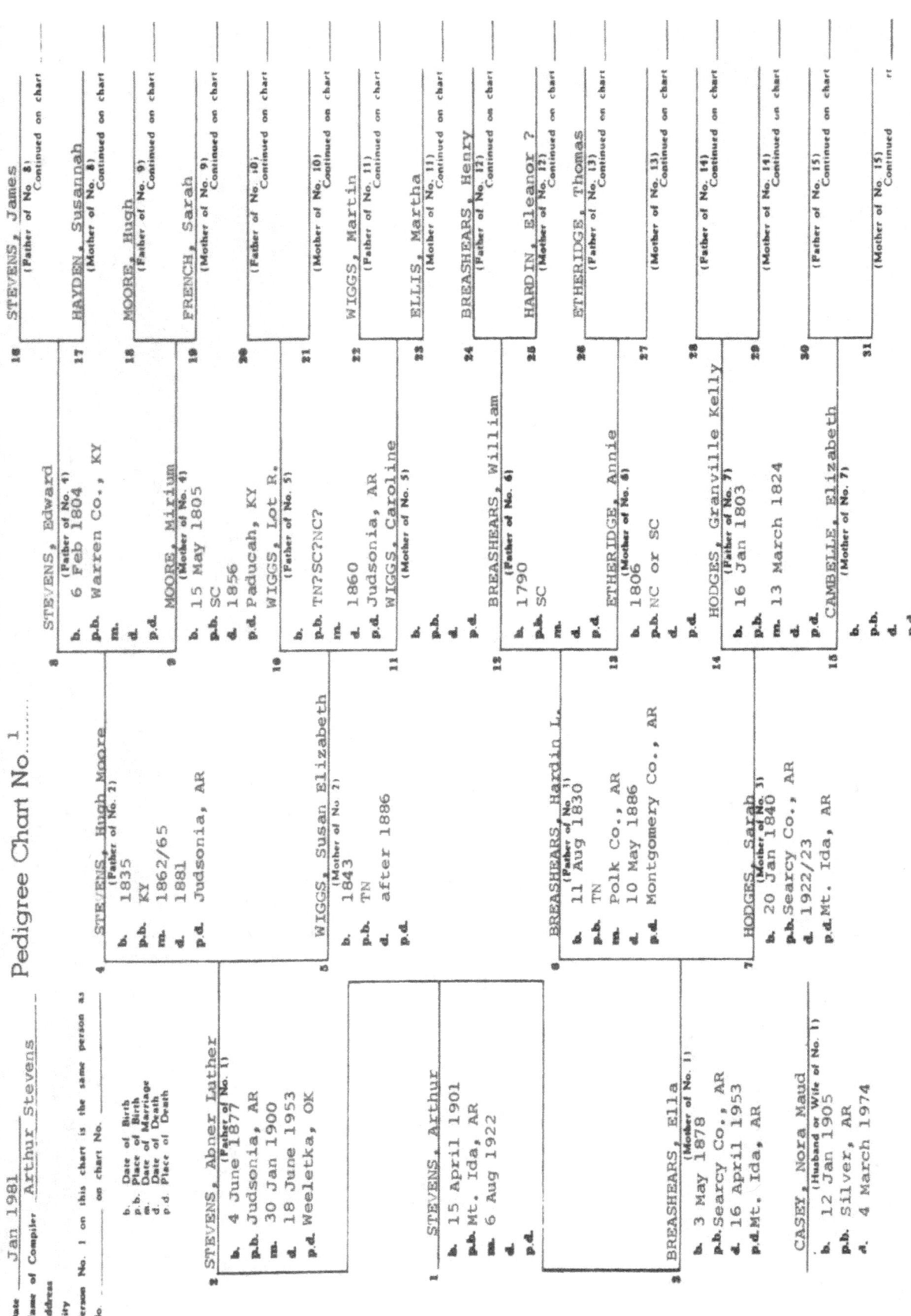

Pedigree Chart No. 1..........

Date _____ Jan 1981 _____
Name of Compiler _____ Arthur Stevens _____
Address
City
Person No. 1 on this chart is the same person as
No. _____ on chart No.

b.　Date of Birth
p.b.　Place of Birth
m.　Date of Marriage
d.　Date of Death
p.d.　Place of Death

1 STEVENS, Arthur
b.　15 April 1901
p.b. Mt. Ida, AR
m.　6 Aug 1922
d.
p.d.

2 STEVENS, Abner Luther
(Father of No. 1)
b.　4 June 1877
p.b. Judsonia, AR
m.　30 Jan 1900
d.　18 June 1953
p.d. Weeletka, OK

3 BREASHEARS, Ella
(Mother of No. 1)
b.　3 May 1878
p.b. Searcy Co., AR
d.　16 April 1953
p.d. Mt. Ida, AR

CASEY, Nora Maud
(Husband or Wife of No. 1)
b.　12 Jan 1905
p.b. Silver, AR
d.　4 March 1974

4 STEVENS, Hugh Moore
(Father of No. 2)
b.　1835
p.b.　KY
m.　1862/65
d.　1881
p.d. Judsonia, AR

5 WIGGS, Susan Elizabeth
(Mother of No. 2)
b.　1843
p.b.　TN
d.　after 1886
p.d.

6 BREASHEARS, Hardin L.
(Father of No. 3)
b.　11 Aug 1830
p.b.　TN
m.　Polk Co., AR
d.　10 May 1886
p.d. Montgomery Co., AR

7 HODGES, Sarah
(Mother of No. 3)
b.　20 Jan 1840
p.b. Searcy Co., AR
d.　1922/23
p.d. Mt. Ida, AR

8 STEVENS, Edward
(Father of No. 4)
b.　6 Feb 1804
p.b. Warren Co., KY
m.
d.
p.d.

9 MOORE, Mirium
(Mother of No. 4)
b.　15 May 1805
p.b.　SC
d.　1856
p.d. Paducah, KY

10 WIGGS, Lot R.
(Father of No. 5)
b.
p.b. TN?SC?NC?
m.
d.　1860
p.d. Judsonia, AR

11 WIGGS, Caroline
(Mother of No. 5)
b.
p.b.
d.
p.d.

12 BREASHEARS, William
(Father of No. 6)
b.　1790
p.b.　SC
m.
d.
p.d.

13 ETHERIDGE, Annie
(Mother of No. 6)
b.　1806
p.b. NC or SC
d.
p.d.

14 HODGES, Granville Kelly
(Father of No. 7)
b.　16 Jan 1803
p.b.
m.　13 March 1824
d.
p.d.

15 CAMBELLE, Elizabeth
(Mother of No. 7)
b.
p.b.
d.
p.d.

16 STEVENS, James
(Father of No. 8)　Continued on chart ____

17 HAYDEN, Susannah
(Mother of No. 8)　Continued on chart ____

18 MOORE, Hugh
(Father of No. 9)　Continued on chart ____

19 FRENCH, Sarah
(Mother of No. 9)　Continued on chart ____

20
(Father of No. 10)　Continued on chart ____

21
(Mother of No. 10)　Continued on chart ____

22 WIGGS, Martin
(Father of No. 11)　Continued on chart ____

23 ELLIS, Martha
(Mother of No. 11)　Continued on chart ____

24 BREASHEARS, Henry
(Father of No. 12)　Continued on chart ____

25 HARDIN, Eleanor ?
(Mother of No. 12)　Continued on chart ____

26 ETHERIDGE, Thomas
(Father of No. 13)　Continued on chart ____

27
(Mother of No. 13)　Continued on chart ____

28
(Father of No. 14)　Continued on chart ____

29
(Mother of No. 14)　Continued on chart ____

30
(Father of No. 15)　Continued on chart ____

31
(Mother of No. 15)　Continued ____

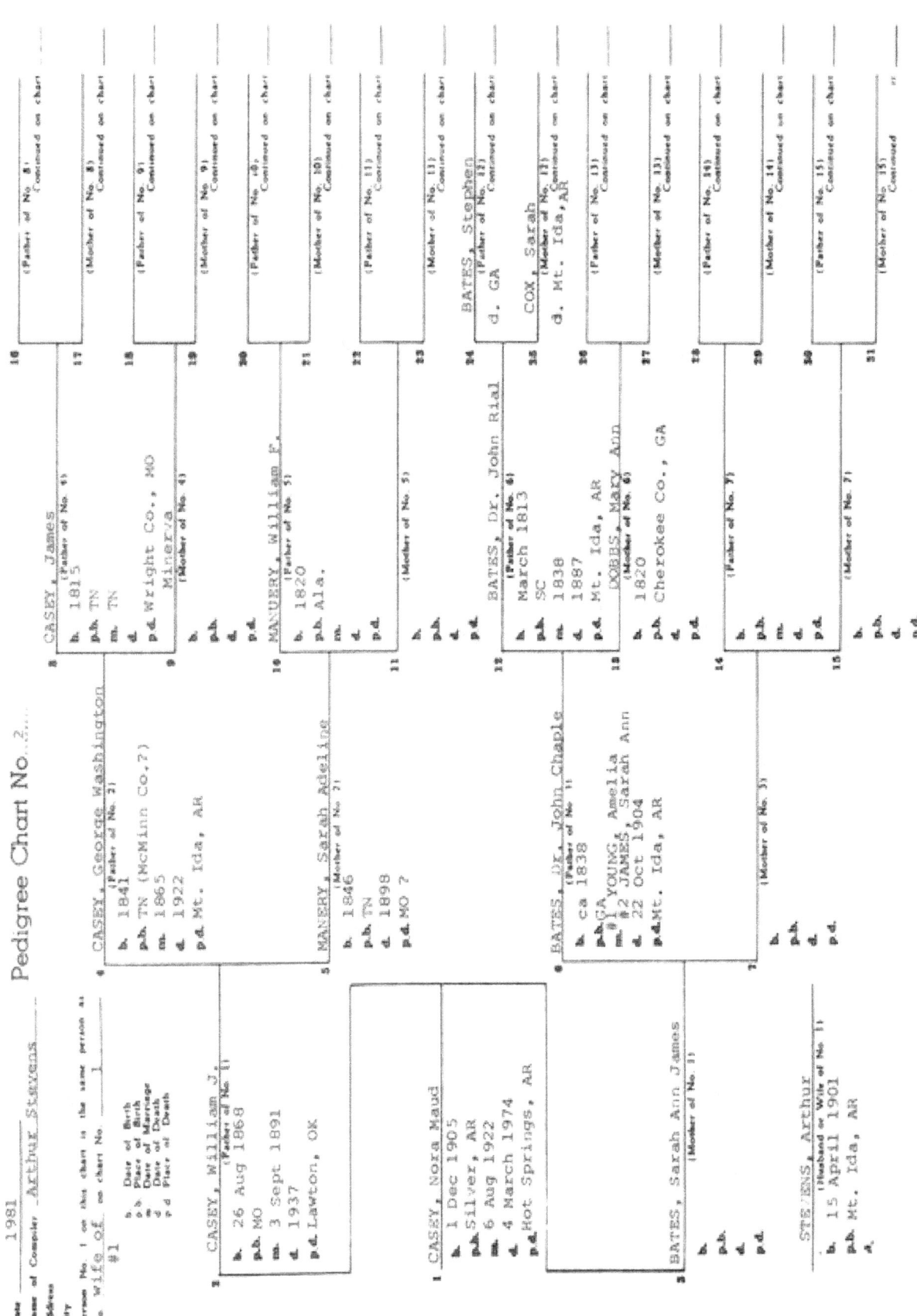

Pedigree Chart No. 2

# Pedigree Chart No. 1

Date 11-21-1982
Name of Compiler Glenda Suit
Address
City
Person No. 1 on this chart is the same person as
No. _____ on chart No.

```
b.   Date of Birth
p.b. Place of Birth
m.   Date of Marriage
d.   Date of Death
p.d  Place of Death
```

1 Victor Paul Suit
b. 11-20-1943
p.b. Bonnerdale, Ark.
m. 6-5-1976
d.
p.d.

2 Dairty Bly Suit (Father of No. 1)
b. 11-29-1909
p.b. Bonnerdale, Ark.
m. 9-14-1933
d.
p.d.

3 Lucy Mrytle Adams (Mother of No. 1)
b. 1-14-1913
p.b. Mazarn, Ark.
m.
d.
p.d.

Glenda Gail Munger (Wife of No. 1)
b. 2-14-1947
p.b. Colo. Springs, Colo.
d.

4 William Monroe Suit (Father of No. 2)
b. 7-16-1887
p.b. Garland Co., Ark.
m. 3-29-1907
d. 12-2-1950
p.d. Bonnerdale, Ark.

5 Lydia Frances Henson (Mother of No. 2)
b. 4-2-1890
p.b. Royal, Ark.
d. 3-10-1934
p.d. Royal, Ark.

6 Edmon Morgan Adams (Father of No. 3)
b. 7-8-1878
p.b. Monteagle, Tenn.
m. 6-7-1908
d. 3-12-1950
p.d. Bonnerdale, Ark.

7 Sarah Elizabeth Knox (Mother of No. 3)
b. 2-20-1888
p.b. Fayette Co., Ala.
d. 1-30-1975
p.d. Hot Springs, Ark.

8 Callie Suit (Father of No. 4)

9 Luevenia Burden (Mother of No. 4)
b. 9-?-1867
p.b. Mississippi
d.
p.d. Arkansas

10 John Henry Henson (Father of No. 5)
b. 3-15-1855
p.b. Garland Co., Ark.
m.
d. 4-6-1940
p.d. Hot Springs, Ark.

11 Louvisa Cunningham (Mother of No. 5)
b. 1-23-1856
p.b. Arkansas
d. 9-15-1900
p.d. Hot Springs, Ark.

12 John Quincy Adams (Father of No. 6)
b. 1820
p.b. N. Carolina
m. 2-9-1878
d. 1886
p.d. Grundy Co., Tenn.

13 Sarah Elizabeth Byers (Mother of No. 6)
b. 1-?-1840
p.b. Ala.
d. 7-12-1907
p.d. Hot Springs, Ark.

14 Hugh Clapton Knox (Father of No. 7)
b. 6-22-1863
p.b. Tallapoosa Co., Ala.
m. 2-3-1884
d. 4-30-1928
p.d. Hot Springs, Ark.

15 Mary Frances McCollum (Mother of No. 7)
b. 10-6-1862
p.b. Fayette Co., Ala.
d. 5-5-1943
p.d. Hot Springs, Ark.

16 (Father of No. 8)  Continued on chart _____

17 (Mother of No. 8)  Continued on chart _____

18 James F. Burden (Father of No. 9)  Continued on chart 2

19 Camelia Parsons (Mother of No. 9)  Continued on chart 2

20 (Father of No. 10)  Continued on chart _____

21 (Mother of No. 10)  Continued on chart _____

22 Robert M. Cunningham (Father of No. 11)  Continued on chart 3

23 Louvisa Garrett (Mother of No. 11)  Continued on chart 3

24 (Father of No. 12)  Continued on chart _____

25 (Mother of No. 12)  Continued on chart _____

26 (Father of No. 13)  Continued on chart _____

27 (Mother of No. 13)  Continued on chart _____

28 Samuel Knox (Father of No. 14)  Continued on chart _____

29 Sarah Jordan (Mother of No. 14)  Continued on chart _____

30 William McCollum (Father of No. 15)  Continued on chart _____

31 Susan Eason (Mother of No. 15)  Continued on chart _____

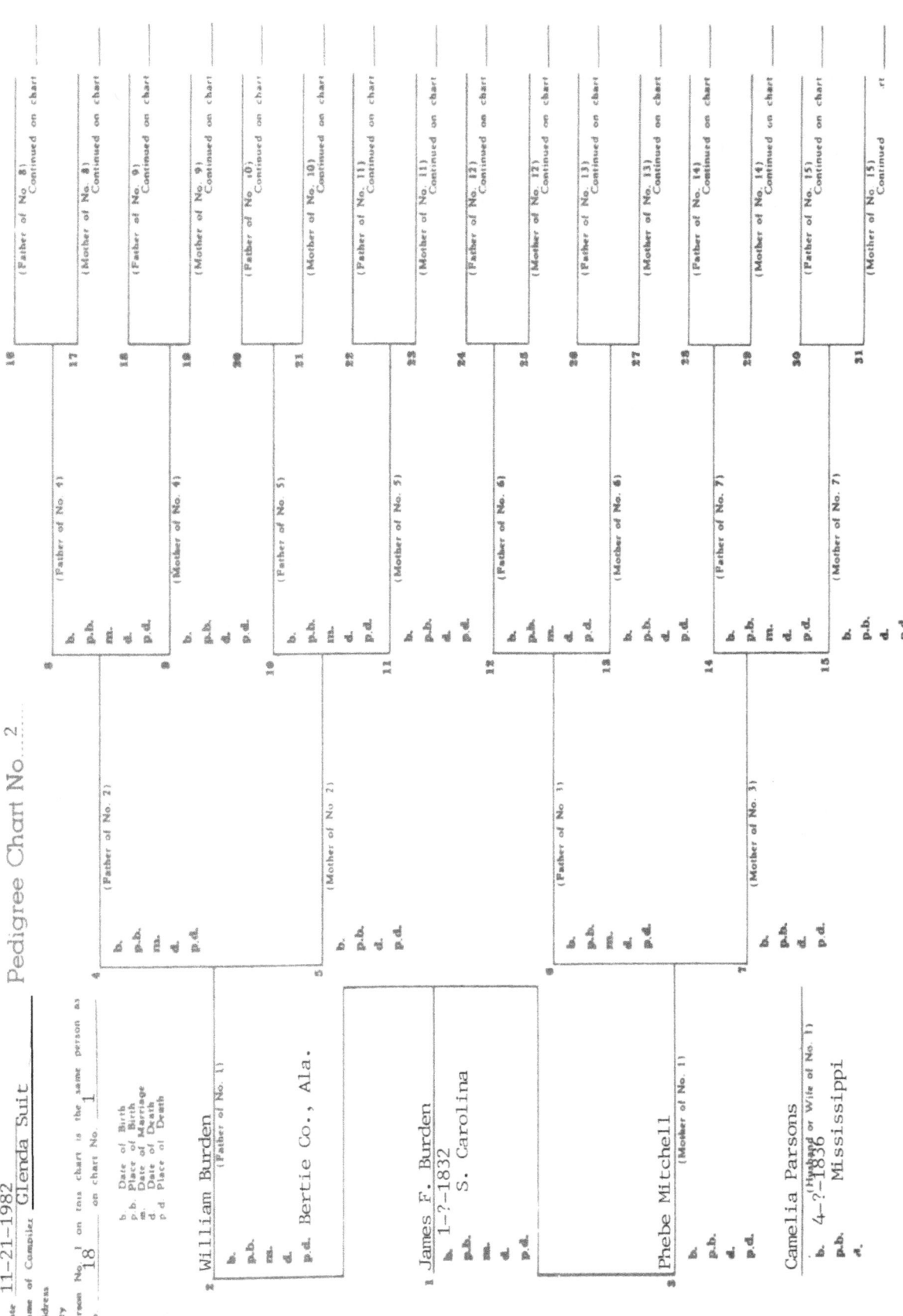

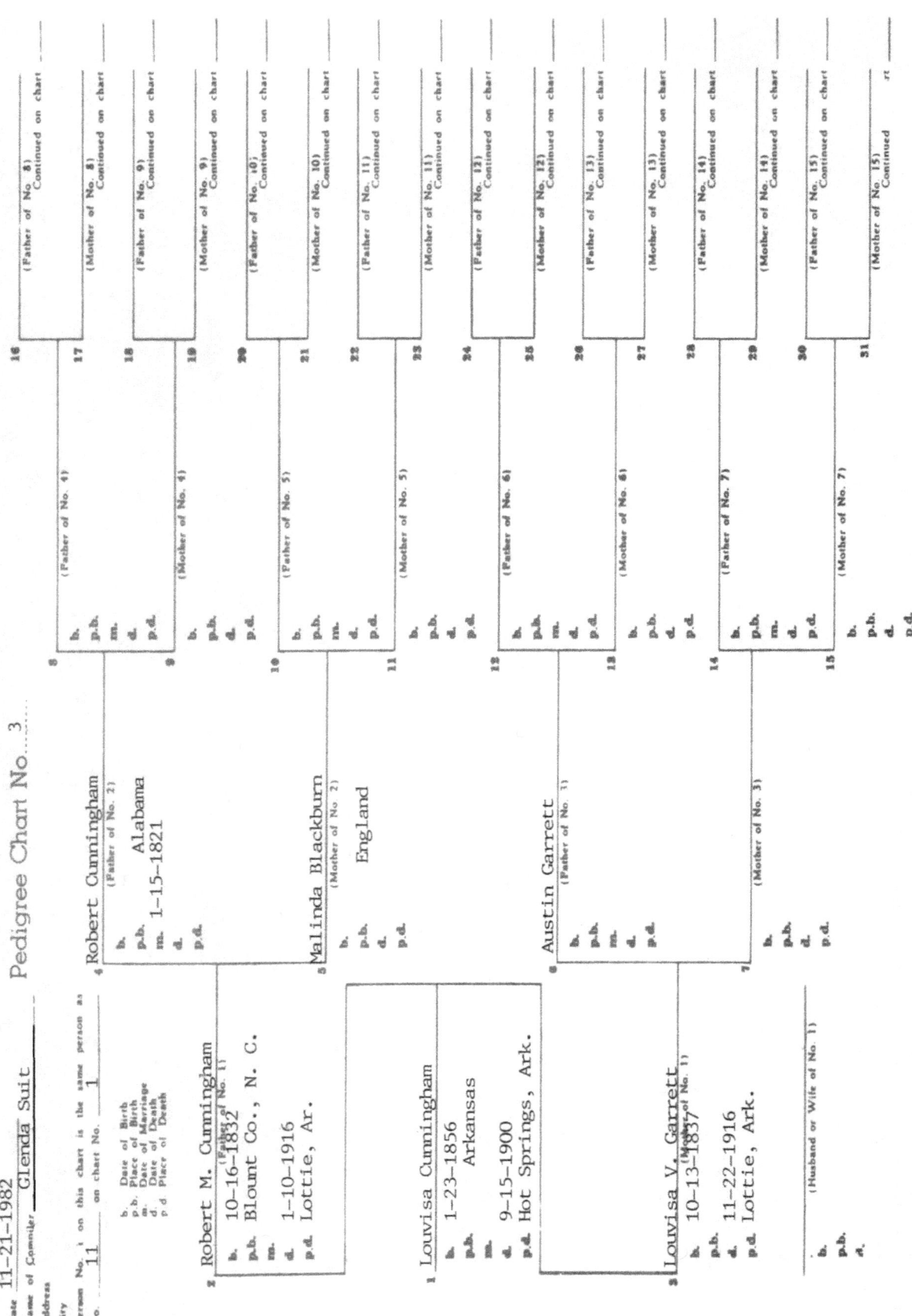

Pedigree Chart No. 3

Date 11-21-1982
Name of Compiler  Glenda Suit
Address
City
Person No. 1 on this chart is the same person as
No. 11 on chart No. 1

b.  Date of Birth
p.b. Place of Birth
m.  Date of Marriage
d.  Date of Death
p.d Place of Death

2 Robert M. Cunningham (Father of No. 1)
b. 10-16-1832
p.b. Blount Co., N. C.
m.
d. 1-10-1916
p.d. Lottie, Ar.

1 Louvisa Cunningham
b. 1-23-1856
p.b. Arkansas
m.
d. 9-15-1900
p.d. Hot Springs, Ark.

3 Louvisa V. Garrett (Mother of No. 1)
b. 10-13-1837
p.b.
d. 11-22-1916
p.d. Lottie, Ark.

(Husband or Wife of No. 1)
b.
p.b.
d.

4 Robert Cunningham (Father of No. 2)
b.
p.b. Alabama
m. 1-15-1821
d.
p.d.

5 Malinda Blackburn (Mother of No 2)
b.
p.b. England
d.
p.d.

6 Austin Garrett (Father of No. 3)
b.
p.b.
m.
d.
p.d.

7 (Mother of No. 3)
b.
p.b.
d.
p.d.

8 (Father of No. 4)
b.
p.b.
m.
d.
p.d.

9 (Mother of No. 4)
b.
p.b.
d.
p.d.

10 (Father of No. 5)
b.
p.b.
m.
d.
p.d.

11 (Mother of No. 5)
b.
p.b.
d.
p.d.

12 (Father of No. 6)
b.
p.b.
m.
d.
p.d.

13 (Mother of No. 6)
b.
p.b.
d.
p.d.

14 (Father of No. 7)
b.
p.b.
m.
d.
p.d.

15 (Mother of No. 7)
b.
p.b.
d.
p.d.

16 (Father of No. 8) Continued on chart
17 (Mother of No. 8) Continued on chart
18 (Father of No. 9) Continued on chart
19 (Mother of No. 9) Continued on chart
20 (Father of No. 10) Continued on chart
21 (Mother of No. 10) Continued on chart
22 (Father of No. 11) Continued on chart
23 (Mother of No. 11) Continued on chart
24 (Father of No. 12) Continued on chart
25 (Mother of No. 12) Continued on chart
26 (Father of No. 13) Continued on chart
27 (Mother of No. 13) Continued on chart
28 (Father of No. 14) Continued on chart
29 (Mother of No. 14) Continued on chart
30 (Father of No. 15) Continued on chart
31 (Mother of No. 15) Continued

## Pedigree Chart No. 4

Date 11-21-1982
Name of Compiler Glenda Suit
Address
City
Person No. 1 on this chart is the same person as No. 7 on chart No. 1

b. Date of Birth
p.b. Place of Birth
m. Date of Marriage
d. Date of Death
p.d. Place of Death

(Husband or Wife of No. 1)
b.
p.b.
d.

**1 Glenda Suit**

**2 Hugh Clapton Knox** (Father of No. 1)
b. 6-22-1863
p.b. Tallapoosa Co., Ala.
m. 2-3-1884
d. 4-30-1928
p.d. Hot Springs, Ark.

**3 Mary Frances McCollum** (Mother of No. 1)
b. 10-6-1862
p.b. Fayette Co., Ala.
d. 5-5-1943
p.d. Hot Springs, Ark.

**1 Sarah Elizabeth Knox**
b. 2-20-1888
p.b. Fayette Co., Ala.
m. 6-7-1908
d. 1-30-1975
p.d. Hot Springs, Ark.

**4 Samuel Knox** (Father of No. 2)
b. 11-27-1817
p.b. Danville, Ark.
m. 10-17-1838
d. 12-28-1899
p.d. Magazine, Ark.

**5 Sarah Jordon** (Mother of No. 2)
b. 1819
p.b. Georgia
d. 2-24-1891
p.d. Magazine, Ark.

**6 William McCollum** (Father of No. 1)
b. 1840
p.b. Fayette Co., Ala.
d. 1899
p.d. New River, Ala.

**7 Susan Eason** (Mother of No. 3)
b. 1843
p.b. Georgia
d. 9-?-1891
p.d.

**8 John Knox** (Father of No. 4)
b. 4-9-1773
p.b. Chester Co., S. C.
m. 9-26-1852
d.
p.d.

**9 Elizabeth Martin** (Mother of No. 4)
b. 5-21-1789
p.b. Ireland
d. 2-25-1866
p.d.

**10 Elijah Jordon** (Father of No. 5)
b.
p.b.
m.
d.
p.d.

**11** (Mother of No. 5)
b.
p.b.
d.

**12 William McCollum** (Father of No. 6)
b. 3-17-1804
p.b. S. Carolina
m.
d. 8-17-1887
p.d.

**13 Mary Philips** (Mother of No. 6)
b. 1802
p.b. Alabama
d. 1849
p.d.

**14 Harrison Eason** (Father of No. 7)
b. 1815
p.b. Morgan Co., Ga.
m.
d. 10-8-1889
p.d.

**15 Mary Kelly** (Mother of No. 7)
b. 1818
p.b. Fayette Co., Ala.
d. 3-5-1898
p.d.

**16 Rev. James Knox, Jr.** (Father of No. 8)
Continued on chart 5

**17 Janet Miller** (Mother of No. 8)
Continued on chart 5

**18 Rev. James Martin** (Father of No. 9)
Continued on chart

**19 Mary Graham** (Mother of No. 9)
Continued on chart

**20** (Father of No. 10)
Continued on chart

**21** (Mother of No. 10)
Continued on chart

**22** (Father of No. 11)
Continued on chart

**23** (Mother of No. 11)
Continued on chart

**24** (Father of No. 12)
Continued on chart

**25** (Mother of No. 12)
Continued on chart

**26** (Father of No. 13)
Continued on chart

**27** (Mother of No. 13)
Continued on chart

**28 Thomas Eason** (Father of No. 14)
b. 1792
Continued on chart

**29 Patsey Welch** (Mother of No. 14)
b. 1792
Continued on chart

**30** (Father of No. 15)
Continued on chart

**31** (Mother of No. 15)
Continued

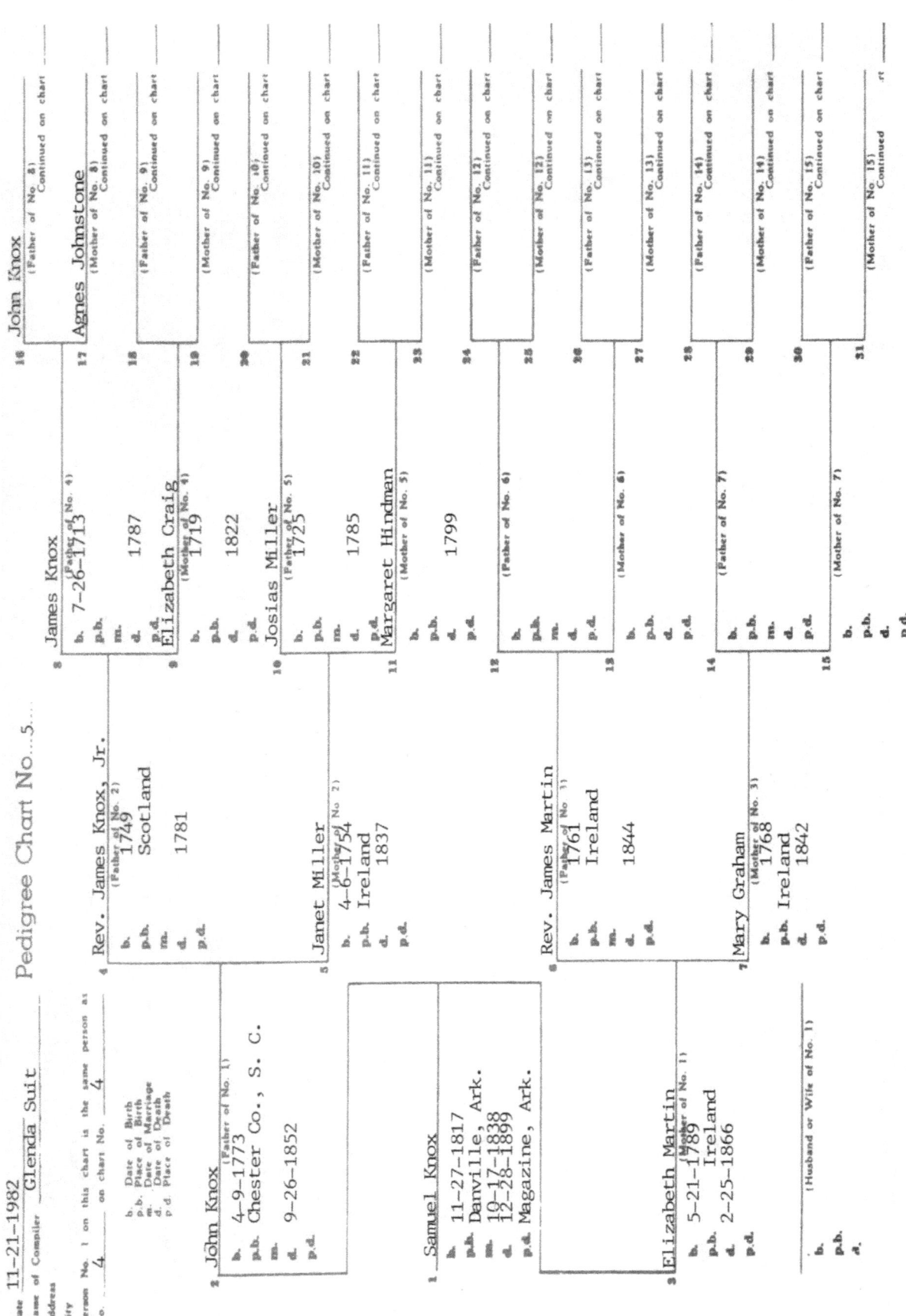

Pedigree Chart No. 5

Date 11-21-1982
Name of Compiler Glenda Suit
Address
City
Person No. 1 on this chart is the same person as No. 4 on chart No. 4

b. Date of Birth
p.b. Place of Birth
m. Date of Marriage
d. Date of Death
p.d. Place of Death

1 Samuel Knox
b. 11-27-1817
p.b. Danville, Ark.
m. 10-17-1838
d. 12-28-1899
p.d. Magazine, Ark.

2 John Knox (Father of No. 1)
b. 4-9-1773
p.b. Chester Co., S. C.
m.
d. 9-26-1852
p.d.

3 Elizabeth Martin (Mother of No. 1)
b. 5-21-1789
p.b. Ireland
d. 2-25-1866
p.d.

4 Rev. James Knox, Jr. (Father of No. 2)
b. 1749
p.b. Scotland
m.
d. 1781
p.d.

5 Janet Miller (Mother of No. 2)
b. 4-6-1754
p.b. Ireland
d. 1837
p.d.

6 Rev. James Martin (Father of No. 3)
b. 1761
p.b. Ireland
m.
d. 1844
p.d.

7 Mary Graham (Mother of No. 3)
b. 1768
p.b. Ireland
d. 1842
p.d.

8 James Knox (Father of No. 4)
b. 7-26-1713
p.b.
m.
d. 1787
p.d.

9 Elizabeth Craig (Mother of No. 4)
b. 1719
p.b.
d. 1822
p.d.

10 Josias Miller (Father of No. 5)
b. 1725
p.b.
m.
d. 1785
p.d.

11 Margaret Hindman (Mother of No. 5)
b.
p.b.
d. 1799
p.d.

12 (Father of No. 6)
b.
p.b.
m.
d.
p.d.

13 (Mother of No. 6)
b.
p.b.
d.
p.d.

14 (Father of No. 7)
b.
p.b.
m.
d.
p.d.

15 (Mother of No. 7)
b.
p.b.
d.
p.d.

16 John Knox (Father of No. 8) Continued on chart

17 Agnes Johnstone (Mother of No. 8) Continued on chart

18 (Father of No. 9) Continued on chart

19 (Mother of No. 9) Continued on chart

20 (Father of No. 10) Continued on chart

21 (Mother of No. 10) Continued on chart

22 (Father of No. 11) Continued on chart

23 (Mother of No. 11) Continued on chart

24 (Father of No. 12) Continued on chart

25 (Mother of No. 12) Continued on chart

26 (Father of No. 13) Continued on chart

27 (Mother of No. 13) Continued on chart

28 (Father of No. 14) Continued on chart

29 (Mother of No. 14) Continued on chart

30 (Father of No. 15) Continued on chart

31 (Mother of No. 15) Continued on chart

(Husband or Wife of No. 1)
b.
p.b.
d.

# Pedigree Chart No. _____

Date 1982
Name of Compiler Nadine Stevenson
Address
City
Person No. 1 on this chart is the same person as _____ on chart No. _____

b   Date of Birth
p.b   Place of Birth
m   Date of Marriage
d   Date of Death
p.d   Place of Death

**1 Bernice Nadine Sparks**
b. 9-6-1924
p.b. Knox City, TX
m. 28-6-1945
d.
p.d.

**2 William Pleas Sparks** (Father of No. 1)
b. 22-8-1900
p.b. Murfreesboro, AR
m. 26-7-1923 Benjamin, TX
d.
p.d.

**3 Cora Lou Pettiet** (Mother of No. 1)
b. 25-12-1905
p.b. Ellis Co., TX
d. 25-10-1977
p.d. Westminster, CA

**Robert L. Stevenson** (Husband or Wife of No. 1)
b. 6-3-1921
p.b. Jersey City, N.J.
d.

**4 Thomas Jefferson Sparks** (Father of No. 2)
b. 4-2-1870
p.b. GA
m. 1891 Murfreesboro, AR
d. 22-6-1960
p.d. O'Brien, TX

**5 Eulila Ellen Henderson** (Mother of No. 2)
b. 1-1-1873
p.b. Murfreesboro, AR
d. 17-6-1963
p.d.

**6 Oscar Phillips Pettiet** (Father of No. 3)
b. 19-2-1875
p.b. Rusk, TX
m. 19-1-1897 Erath Co. TX
d. 8-11-1959
p.d. Rochester, TX

**7 Nora Lee Head** (Mother of No. 3)
b. 27-10-1878
p.b. Alexander, TX
d. 27-10-1878 (WHOOPS ERROR)
p.d. Rule, TX

**8 Citizen Napoleon Bonaparte Sparks** (Father of No. 4)
b. Feb 1841
p.b. GA (Carroll Co.?)
m. 10-10-1868 Carl.Co.GA
d. 28-4-1931 Pike Co. AR
p.d. Murfreesboro, AR

**9 Elizabeth Williams** (Mother of No. 4)
b. Jan 1848
p.b. GA
d. 1931-33
p.d. Murfreesboro, AR

**10 William Pleas Henderson** (Father of No. 5)
b. 1836
p.b. AL
m. 1850-53
d. 1928-29
p.d. Murfreesboro, AR

**11 Francis Carlana Burkett** (Mother of No. 5)
b. 1840
p.b. AL
d. 1907-08
p.d. Murfreesboro, AR

**12 Jim Mack Pettiet** (Father of No. 6)
b. 1843
p.b. Louisiana
m.
d.
p.d.

**13 Emily A. Cook** (Mother of No. 6)
b. 1840
p.b. AL
d.
p.d.

**14 Benjamin Wesley Head** (Father of No. 7)
b. 23-11-1838
p.b. Dresden, TN
m. 16-4-1861
d. 11 or 12-7-1909
p.d. Erath Co., TX

**15 Sarah E. McWhorter** (Mother of No. 7)
b. 12-10-1844
p.b. TN
d. 8-4-1884
p.d. Erath Co., TX

**16 Uriah Sparks** (Father of No. 8)
b. 28-11-1797 N.C. — Continued on chart

**17 #2 Sarah Whatley** (Mother of No. 8)
b. ca 1801 — Continued on chart

**18** (Father of No. 9) — Continued on chart

**19** (Mother of No. 9) — Continued on chart

**20 Abner Henderson** (Father of No. 10)
b. 1799 N.C.
d. 1865 Murfreesboro, AR — Continued on chart

**21 Levica Alford** (Mother of No. 10)
b. 1807 AL
d. 1881 Murf., AR — Continued on chart

**22** (Father of No. 11) — Continued on chart

**23** (Mother of No. 11) — Continued on chart

**24** (Father of No. 12) — Continued on chart

**25** (Mother of No. 12) — Continued on chart

**26 George Cook** (Father of No. 13) — Continued on chart

**27 Eimer Sarah ?** (Mother of No. 13) — Continued on chart

**28 Edward J. Head** (Father of No. 14)
b. 1810-20 VA
m. 1872 — Continued on chart

**29 Elizabeth** (Mother of No. 14)
b. 1818 VA — Continued on chart

**30 T. C. McWhorter** (Father of No. 15)
b. 1805 S.C. or KY — Continued on chart

**31 Ann Clayton** (Mother of No. 15)
b. 1810 KY — Continued

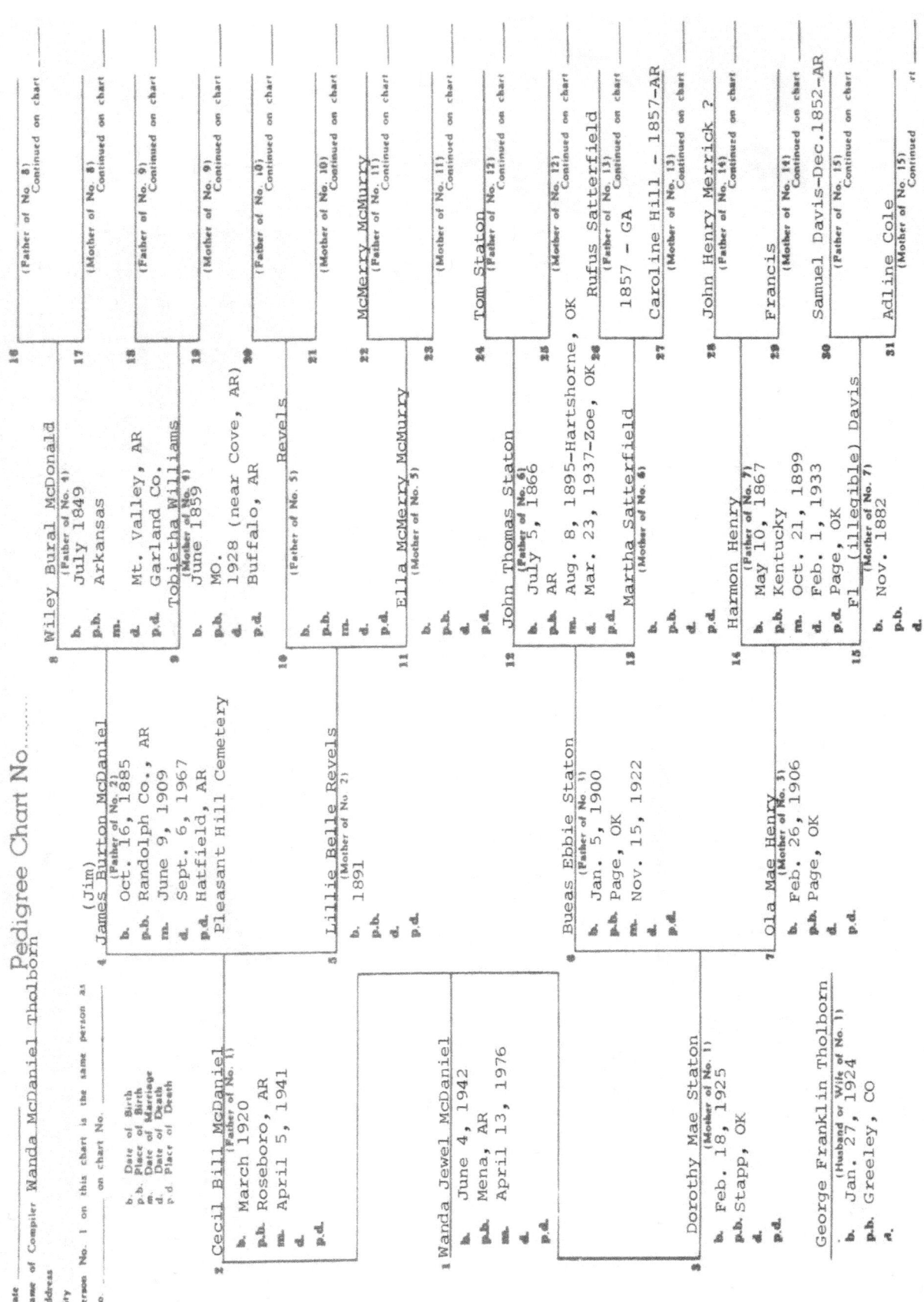

Date
Name of Compiler Wanda McDaniel Tholborn
Address
City
Person No. 1 on this chart is the same person as
No. _____ on chart No. _____

b. Date of Birth
p.b. Place of Birth
m. Date of Marriage
d. Date of Death
p.d Place of Death

1 Wanda Jewel McDaniel
b. June 4, 1942
p.b. Mena, AR
m. April 13, 1976
d.
p.d.

(Husband or Wife of No. 1)
George Franklin Tholborn
b. Jan. 27, 1924
p.b. Greeley, CO
m.

2 Cecil Bill McDaniel
(Father of No. 1)
b. March 1920
p.b. Roseboro, AR
m. April 5, 1941
d.
p.d.

3 Dorothy Mae Staton
(Mother of No. 1)
b. Feb. 18, 1925
p.b. Stapp, OK
d.
p.d.

4 James Burton McDaniel
(Jim)
(Father of No. 2)
b. Oct. 16, 1885
p.b. Randolph Co., AR
m. June 9, 1909
d. Sept. 6, 1967
p.d. Hatfield, AR
Pleasant Hill Cemetery

5 Lillie Belle Revels
(Mother of No 2)
b. 1891
p.b.
d.
p.d.

6 Bueas Ebbie Staton
(Father of No. 3)
b. Jan. 5, 1900
p.b. Page, OK
m. Nov. 15, 1922
d.
p.d.

7 Ola Mae Henry
(Mother of No. 3)
b. Feb. 26, 1906
p.b. Page, OK
d.
p.d.

8 Wiley Bural McDonald
(Father of No. 4)
b. July 1849
p.b. Arkansas
m.
d. Mt. Valley, AR
p.d. Garland Co.

9 Tobietha Williams
(Mother of No. 4)
b. June 1859
p.b. MO.
d. 1928 (near Cove, AR)
p.d. Buffalo, AR

10 Revels
(Father of No. 5)
b.
p.b.
m.
d.
p.d.

11 Ella McMerry McMurry
(Mother of No. 5)
b.
p.b.
d.
p.d.

12 John Thomas Staton
(Father of No. 6)
b. July 5, 1866
p.b. AR
m. Aug. 8, 1895-Hartshorne, OK
d. Mar. 23, 1937-Zoe, OK
p.d.

13 Martha Satterfield
(Mother of No. 6)
b.
p.b.
d.
p.d.

14 Harmon Henry
(Father of No. 7)
b. May 10, 1867
p.b. Kentucky
m. Oct. 21, 1899
d. Feb. 1, 1933
p.d. Page, OK

15 Fl (illegible) Davis
(Mother of No. 7)
b. Nov. 1882
p.b.
d.

16 _____ (Father of No. 8) Continued on chart

17 _____ (Mother of No. 8) Continued on chart

18 _____ (Father of No. 9) Continued on chart

19 _____ (Mother of No. 9) Continued on chart

20 _____ (Father of No. 10) Continued on chart

21 _____ (Mother of No. 10) Continued on chart

22 McMerry McMurry (Father of No. 11) Continued on chart

23 _____ (Mother of No. 11) Continued on chart

24 Tom Staton (Father of No. 12) Continued on chart

25 _____ (Mother of No. 12) Continued on chart

26 Rufus Satterfield 1857 – GA (Father of No. 13) Continued on chart

27 Caroline Hill – 1857-AR (Mother of No. 13) Continued on chart

28 John Henry Merrick ? (Father of No. 14) Continued on chart

29 Francis (Mother of No. 14) Continued on chart

30 Samuel Davis-Dec.1852-AR (Father of No. 15) Continued on chart

31 Adline Cole (Mother of No. 15) Continued on chart

Pedigree Chart No. _____

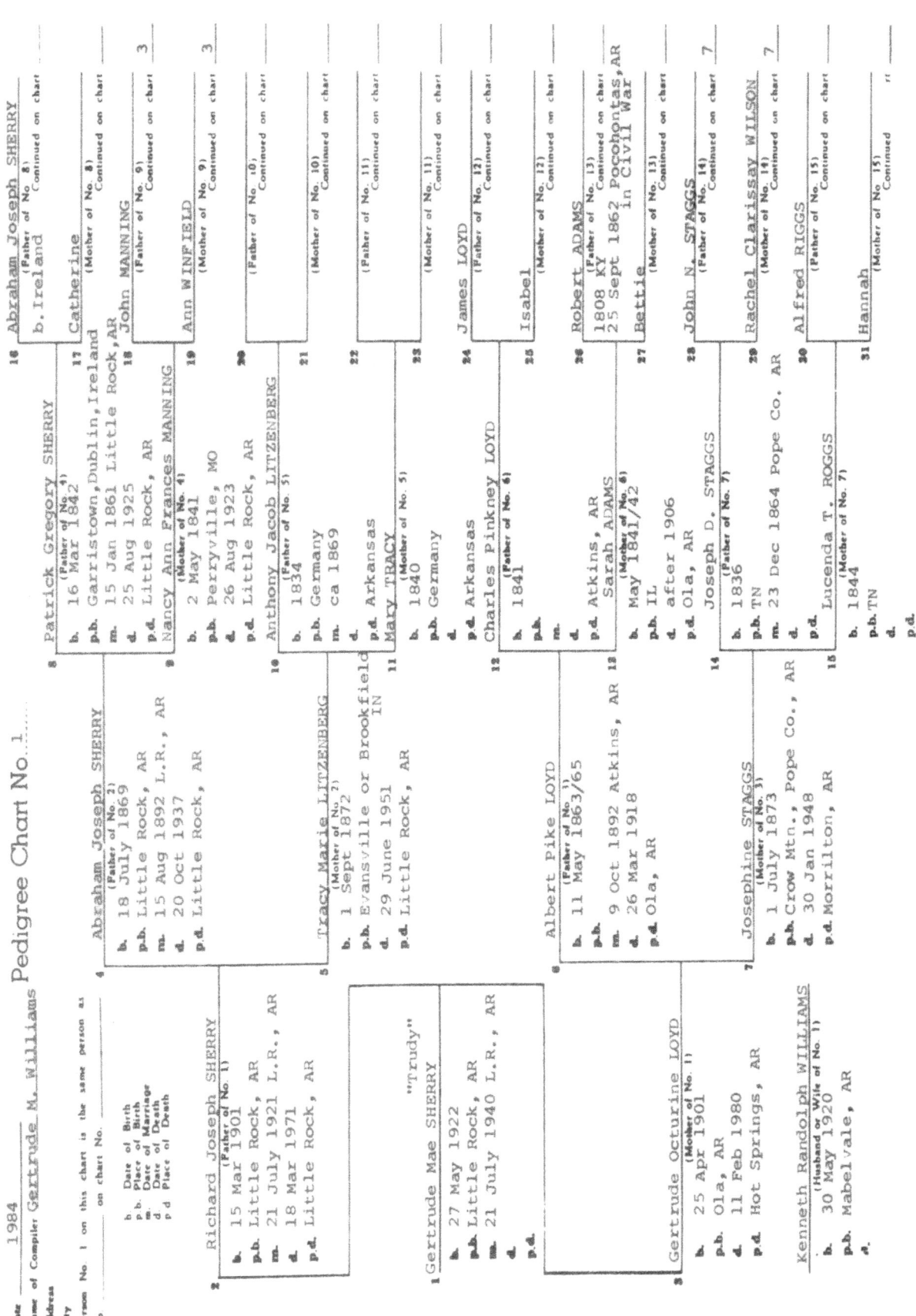

Pedigree Chart No. 1

Date _____ 1984

Name of Compiler __Gertrude M. Williams__

Address _____

City _____

Person No. 1 on this chart is the same person as
No. ____ on chart No. ____

b    Date of Birth
p.b  Place of Birth
m    Date of Marriage
d    Date of Death
p.d  Place of Death

**1** Gertrude Mae SHERRY
b.  27 May 1922
p.b. Little Rock, AR
m.  21 July 1940 L.R., AR
d.
p.d.

**2** Richard Joseph SHERRY (Father of No. 1)
b.  15 Mar 1901
p.b. Little Rock, AR
m.  21 July 1921 L.R., AR
d.  18 Mar 1971
p.d. Little Rock, AR

"Trudy"

**3** Gertrude Octurine LOYD (Mother of No. 1)
b.  25 Apr 1901
p.b. Ola, AR
d.  11 Feb 1980
p.d. Hot Springs, AR

Kenneth Randolph WILLIAMS (Husband or Wife of No. 1)
b.  30 May 1920
p.b. Mabelvale, AR
d.

**4** Abraham Joseph SHERRY (Father of No. 2)
b.  18 July 1869
p.b. Little Rock, AR
m.  15 Aug 1892 L.R., AR
d.  20 Oct 1937
p.d. Little Rock, AR

**5** Tracy Marie LITZENBERG (Mother of No. 2)
b.  1 Sept 1872
p.b. Evansville or Brookfield, IN
d.  29 June 1951
p.d. Little Rock, AR

**6** Albert Pike LOYD (Father of No. 3)
b.  11 May 1863/65
p.b.
m.  9 Oct 1892 Atkins, AR
d.  26 Mar 1918
p.d. Ola, AR

**7** Josephine STAGGS (Mother of No. 3)
b.  1 July 1873
p.b. Crow Mtn., Pope Co., AR
d.  30 Jan 1948
p.d. Morrilton, AR

**8** Patrick Gregory SHERRY (Father of No. 4)
b.  16 Mar 1842
p.b. Garristown, Dublin, Ireland
m.  15 Jan 1861 Little Rock, AR
d.  25 Aug 1925
p.d. Little Rock, AR

**9** Nancy Ann Frances MANNING (Mother of No. 4)
b.  2 May 1841
p.b. Perryville, MO
d.  26 Aug 1923
p.d. Little Rock, AR

**10** Anthony Jacob LITZENBERG (Father of No. 5)
b.  1834
p.b. Germany
m.  ca 1869
d.
p.d. Arkansas

**11** Mary TRACY (Mother of No. 5)
b.  1840
p.b. Germany
p.d. Arkansas

**12** Charles Pinkney LOYD (Father of No. 6)
b.  1841
p.b.
m.
d.
p.d. Atkins, AR
     Sarah ADAMS

**13** Sarah ADAMS (Mother of No. 6)
b.  May 1841/42
p.b. IL
d.  after 1906
p.d. Ola, AR
     Joseph D. STAGGS

**14** Joseph D. STAGGS (Father of No. 7)
b.  1836
p.b. TN
m.  23 Dec 1864 Pope Co. AR
d.
p.d.

**15** Lucenda T. ROGGS (Mother of No. 7)
b.  1844
p.b. TN
d.
p.d.

**16** Abraham Joseph SHERRY (Father of No. 8)  Continued on chart
b. Ireland

**17** Catherine (Mother of No. 8)  Continued on chart 3

**18** John MANNING (Father of No. 9)  Continued on chart 3

**19** Ann WINFIELD (Mother of No. 9)  Continued on chart 3

**20** (Father of No. 10)  Continued on chart

**21** (Mother of No. 10)  Continued on chart

**22** (Father of No. 11)  Continued on chart

**23** (Mother of No. 11)  Continued on chart

**24** James LOYD (Father of No. 12)  Continued on chart

**25** Isabel (Mother of No. 12)  Continued on chart

**26** Robert ADAMS (Father of No. 13)  Continued on chart
1808 KY
25 Sept 1862 Pocohontas, AR
in Civil War

**27** Bettie (Mother of No. 13)  Continued on chart

**28** John N. STAGGS (Father of No. 14)  Continued on chart 7

**29** Rachel Clarissay WILSON (Mother of No. 14)  Continued on chart 7

**30** Alfred RIGGS (Father of No. 15)  Continued on chart

**31** Hannah (Mother of No. 15)  Continued

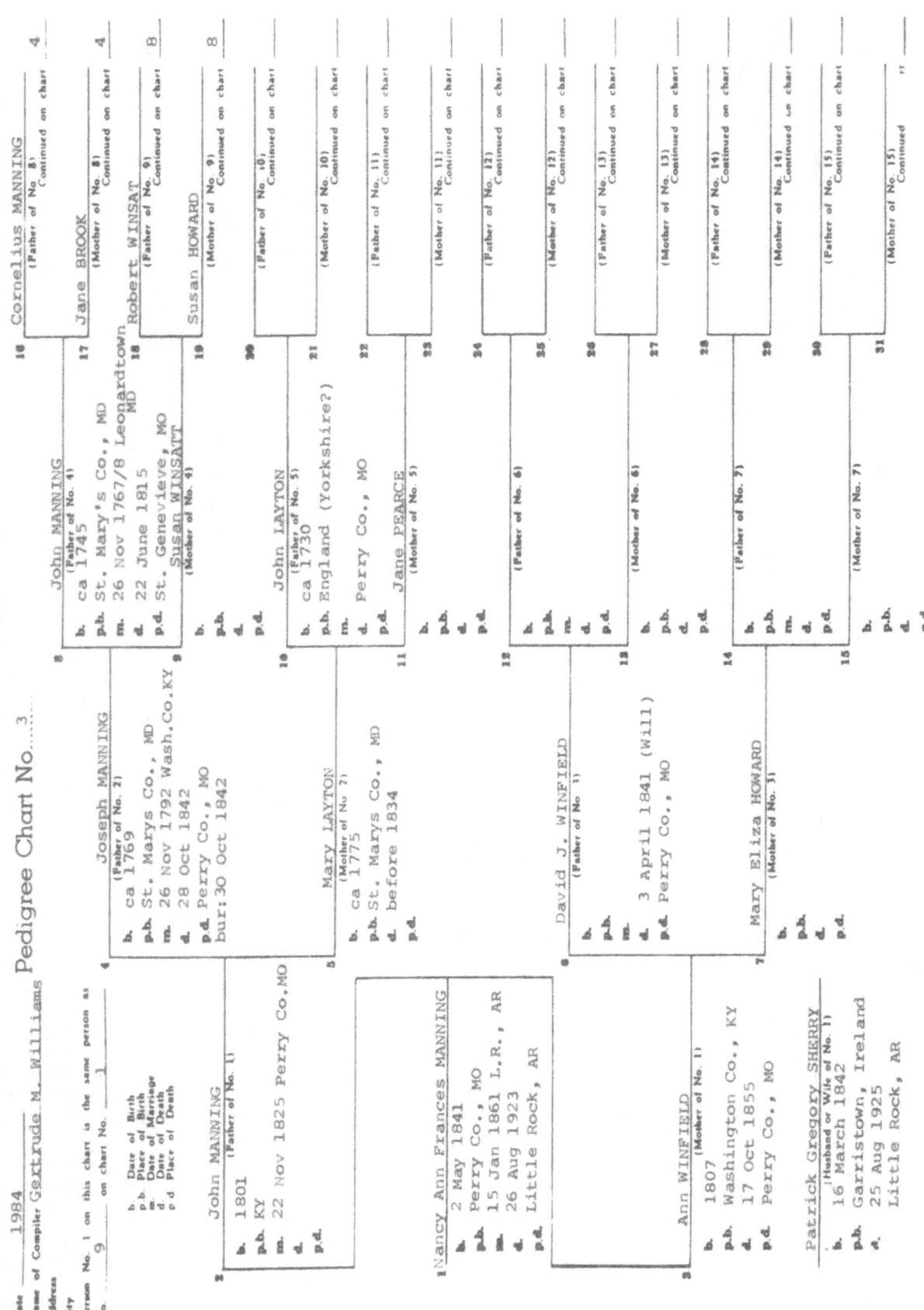

Pedigree Chart No. 3

Date 1984
Name of Compiler Gertrude M. Williams
Address
City
Person No. 1 on this chart is the same person as No. 9 on chart No. 1

b. Date of Birth
p.b. Place of Birth
m. Date of Marriage
p.d Place of Death

2 John MANNING (Father of No. 1)
b. 1801
p.b. KY
m. 22 Nov 1825 Perry Co.MO
d.
p.d.

1 Nancy Ann Frances MANNING
b. 2 May 1841
p.b. Perry Co., MO
m. 15 Jan 1861 L.R., AR
d. 26 Aug 1923
p.d. Little Rock, AR

3 Ann WINFIELD (Mother of No. 1)
b. 1807
p.b. Washington Co., KY
m. 17 Oct 1855
p.d. Perry Co., MO

Patrick Gregory SHERRY (Husband or Wife of No. 1)
b. 16 March 1842
p.b. Garristown, Ireland
d. 25 Aug 1925
Little Rock, AR

4 Joseph MANNING (Father of No. 2)
b. ca 1769
p.b. St. Marys Co., MD
m. 26 Nov 1792 Wash.Co.KY
d. 28 Oct 1842
p.d. Perry Co., MO
bur: 30 Oct 1842

5 Mary LAYTON (Mother of No 2)
b. ca 1775
p.b. St. Marys Co., MD
d. before 1834
p.d.

6 David J. WINFIELD (Father of No 1)
b.
p.b.
m.
d. 3 April 1841 (Will)
p.d. Perry Co., MO

7 Mary Eliza HOWARD (Mother of No 3)
b.
p.b.
d.
p.d.

8 John MANNING (Father of No. 4)
b. ca 1745
p.b. St. Mary's Co., MD
m. 26 Nov 1767/8 Leonardtown MD
d. 22 June 1815
p.d. St. Genevieve, MO

9 Susan WINSATT (Mother of No. 4)
b.
p.b.
d.
p.d.

10 John LAYTON (Father of No. 5)
b. ca 1730
p.b. England (Yorkshire?)
m.
d. Perry Co., MO
p.d.

11 Jane PEARCE (Mother of No. 5)
b.
p.b.
d.
p.d.

12 (Father of No. 6)
b.
p.b.
m.
d.
p.d.

13 (Mother of No. 6)
b.
p.b.
d.
p.d.

14 (Father of No. 7)
b.
p.b.
m.
d.
p.d.

15 (Mother of No. 7)
b.
p.b.
d.
p.d.

16 Cornelius MANNING (Father of No. 8) Continued on chart

17 Jane BROOK (Mother of No. 8) Continued on chart

18 Robert WINSAT (Father of No. 9) Continued on chart

19 Susan HOWARD (Mother of No. 9) Continued on chart

20 (Father of No. 10) Continued on chart

21 (Mother of No. 10) Continued on chart

22 (Father of No. 11) Continued on chart

23 (Mother of No. 11) Continued on chart

24 (Father of No. 12) Continued on chart

25 (Mother of No. 12) Continued on chart

26 (Father of No. 13) Continued on chart

27 (Mother of No. 13) Continued on chart

28 (Father of No. 14) Continued on chart

29 (Mother of No. 14) Continued on chart

30 (Father of No. 15) Continued on chart

31 (Mother of No. 15) Continued

4
4
8
8

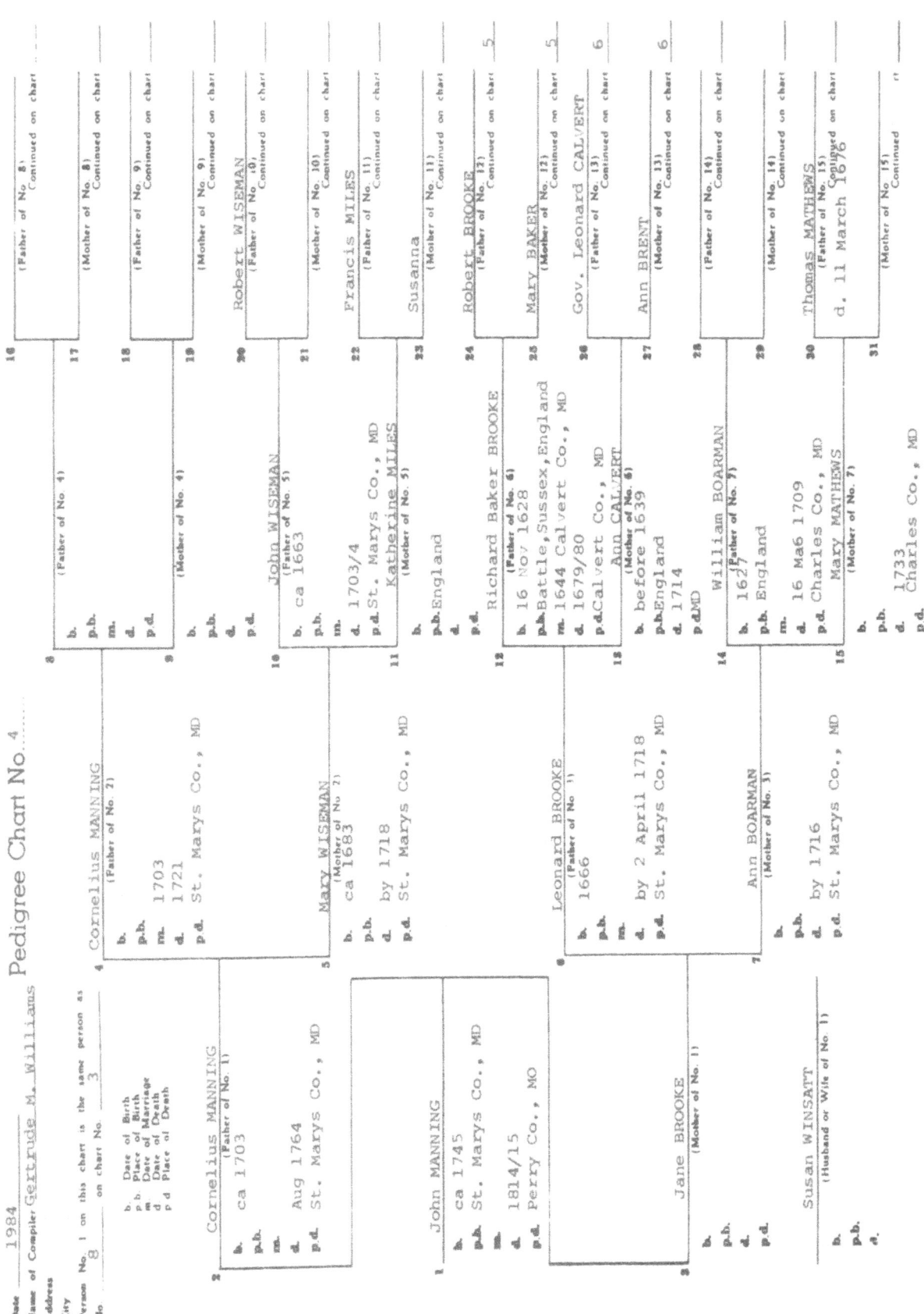

Pedigree Chart No. 4

Date 1984
Name of Compiler Gertrude M. Williams
Address
City
Person No. 1 on this chart is the same person as No. 8 on chart No. 3

b  Date of Birth
p.b  Place of Birth
m  Date of Marriage
d  Date of Death
p.d  Place of Death

1 John MANNING
b. ca 1745
p.b. St. Marys Co., MD
m. 1814/15
p.d. Perry Co., MO

2 Cornelius MANNING (Father of No. 1)
b. ca 1703
p.b. St. Marys Co., MD
m. Aug 1764
d.
p.d. St. Marys Co., MD

3 Jane BROOKE (Mother of No. 1)
b.
p.b.
d.
p.d.

(Husband or Wife of No. 1)
Susan WINSATT
b.
p.b.
d.

4 Cornelius MANNING (Father of No. 2)
b. 1703
p.b. 1721
m.
d.
p.d. St. Marys Co., MD

5 Mary WISEMAN (Mother of No. 2)
b. ca 1683
p.b.
d. by 1718
p.d. St. Marys Co., MD

6 Leonard BROOKE (Father of No. 3)
b. 1666
p.b.
m.
d. by 2 April 1718
p.d. St. Marys Co., MD

7 Ann BOARMAN (Mother of No. 3)
b. by 1716
p.b.
d.
p.d. St. Marys Co., MD

8 (Father of No. 4)
b.
p.b.
m.
d.
p.d.

9 (Mother of No. 4)
b.
p.b.
d.
p.d.

10 John WISEMAN (Father of No. 5)
b. ca 1663
p.b.
m.
d. 1703/4
p.d. St. Marys Co., MD

11 Katherine MILES (Mother of No. 5)
b.
p.b.
d.
p.d. St. Marys Co., MD

12 Richard Baker BROOKE (Father of No. 6)
b. 16 Nov 1628
p.b. Battle, Sussex, England
m. 1644 Calvert Co., MD
d. 1679/80
p.d. Calvert Co., MD

13 Ann CALVERT (Mother of No. 6)
b. before 1639
p.b. England
d. 1714
p.d. MD

14 William BOARMAN (Father of No. 7)
b. 1627
p.b. England
m.
d. 16 Ma6 1709
p.d. Charles Co., MD

15 Mary MATHEWS (Mother of No. 7)
b.
p.b.
d. 1733
p.d. Charles Co., MD

16 (Father of No. 8) Continued on chart

17 (Mother of No. 8) Continued on chart

18 (Father of No. 9) Continued on chart

19 (Mother of No. 9) Continued on chart

20 Robert WISEMAN (Father of No. 10) Continued on chart

21 (Mother of No. 10) Continued on chart

22 Francis MILES (Father of No. 11) Continued on chart

23 Susanna (Mother of No. 11) Continued on chart

24 Robert BROOKE (Father of No. 12) Continued on chart   5

25 Mary BAKER (Mother of No. 12) Continued on chart   5

26 Gov. Leonard CALVERT (Father of No. 13) Continued on chart   6

27 Ann BRENT (Mother of No. 13) Continued on chart   6

28 (Father of No. 14) Continued on chart

29 (Mother of No. 14) Continued on chart

30 Thomas MATHEWS (Father of No. 15) Continued on chart
d. 11 March 1676

31 (Mother of No. 15) Continued

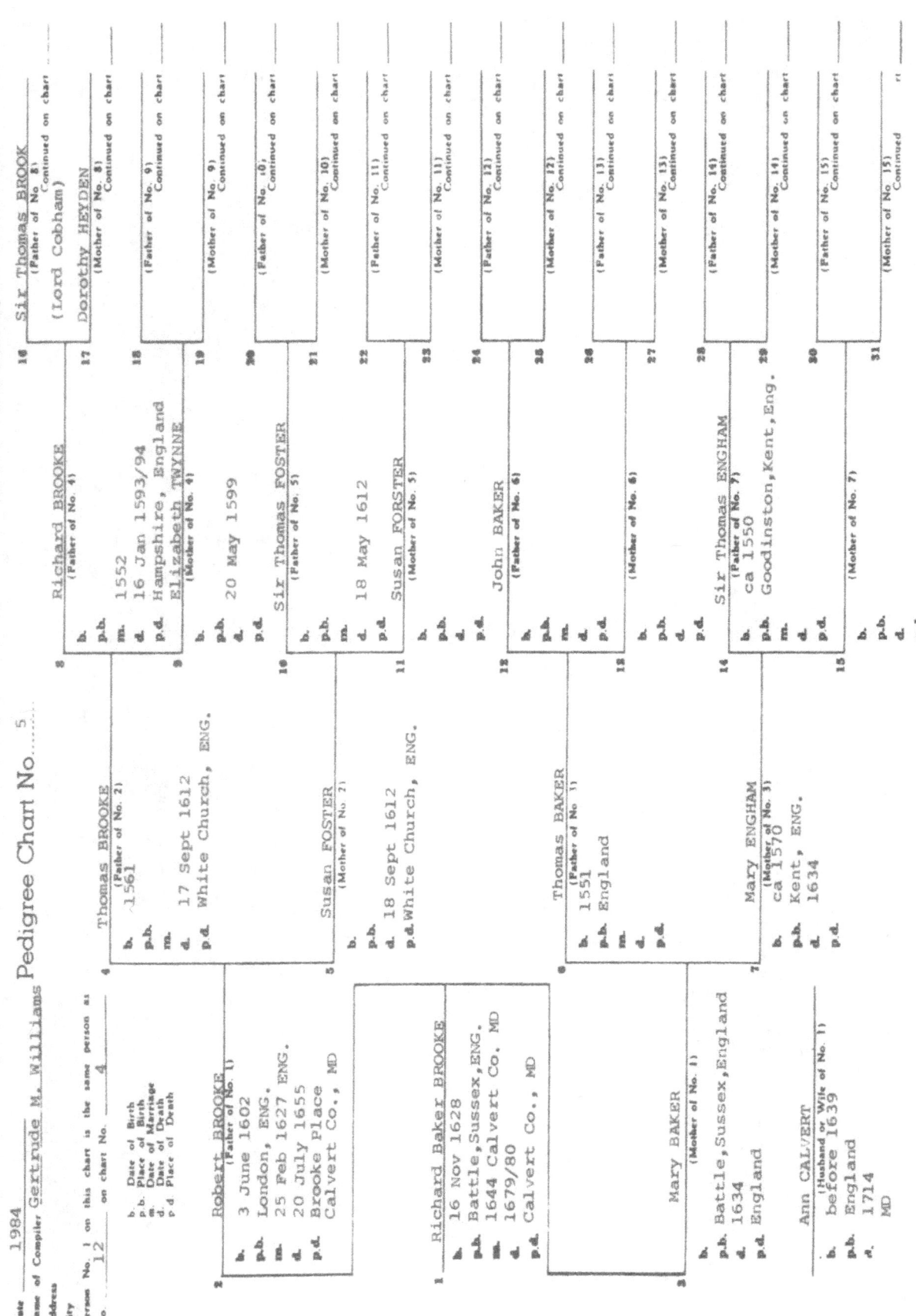

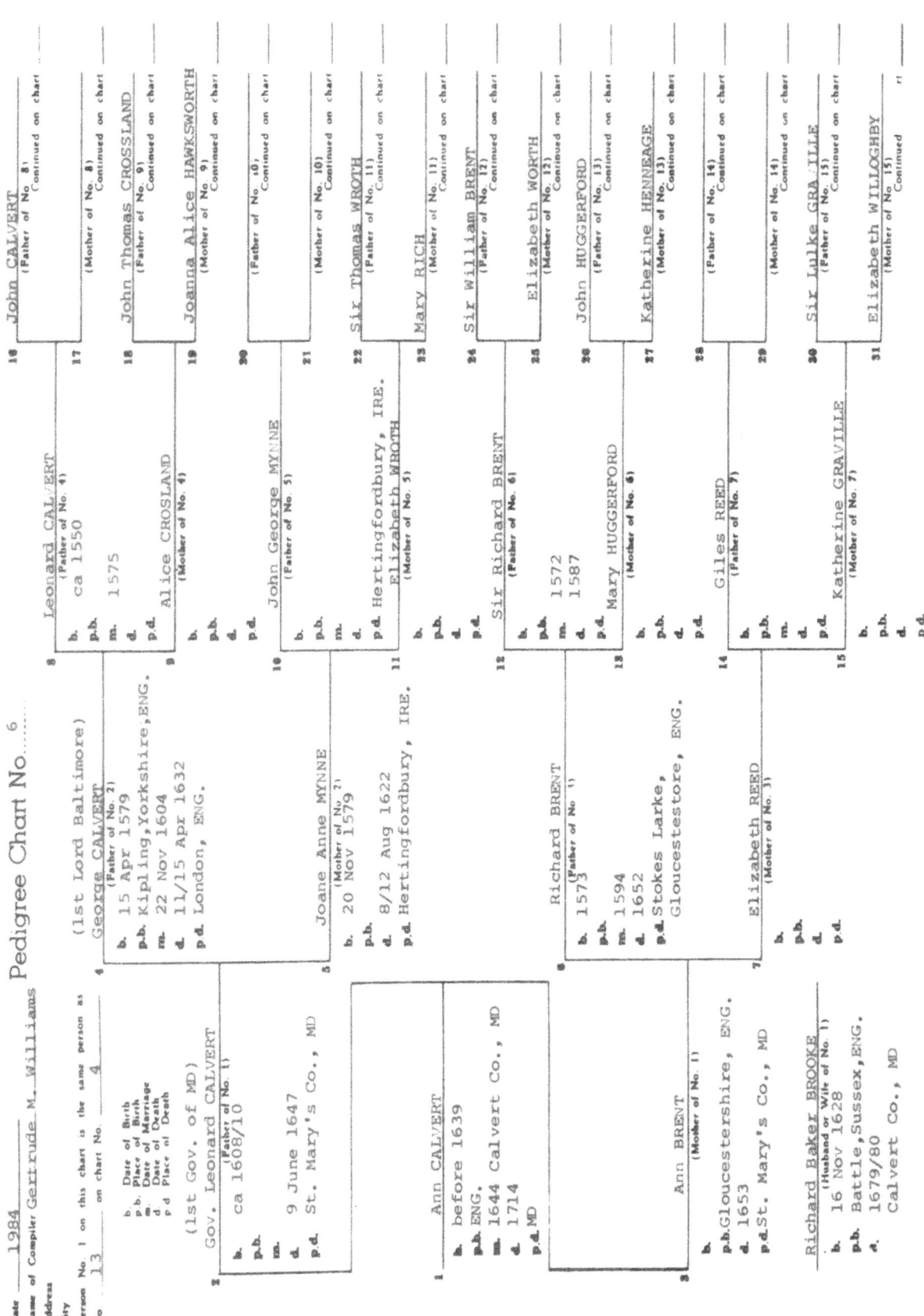

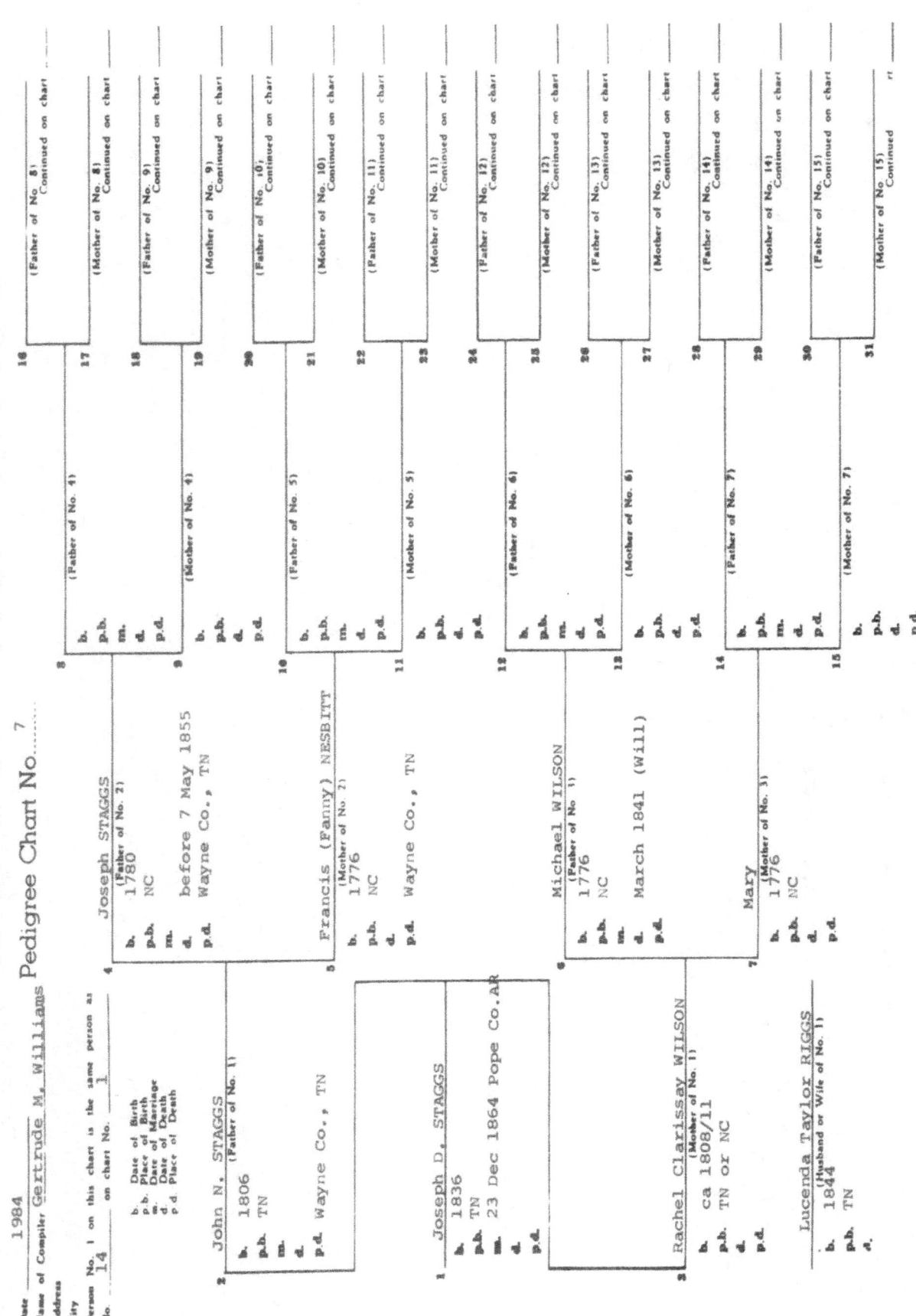

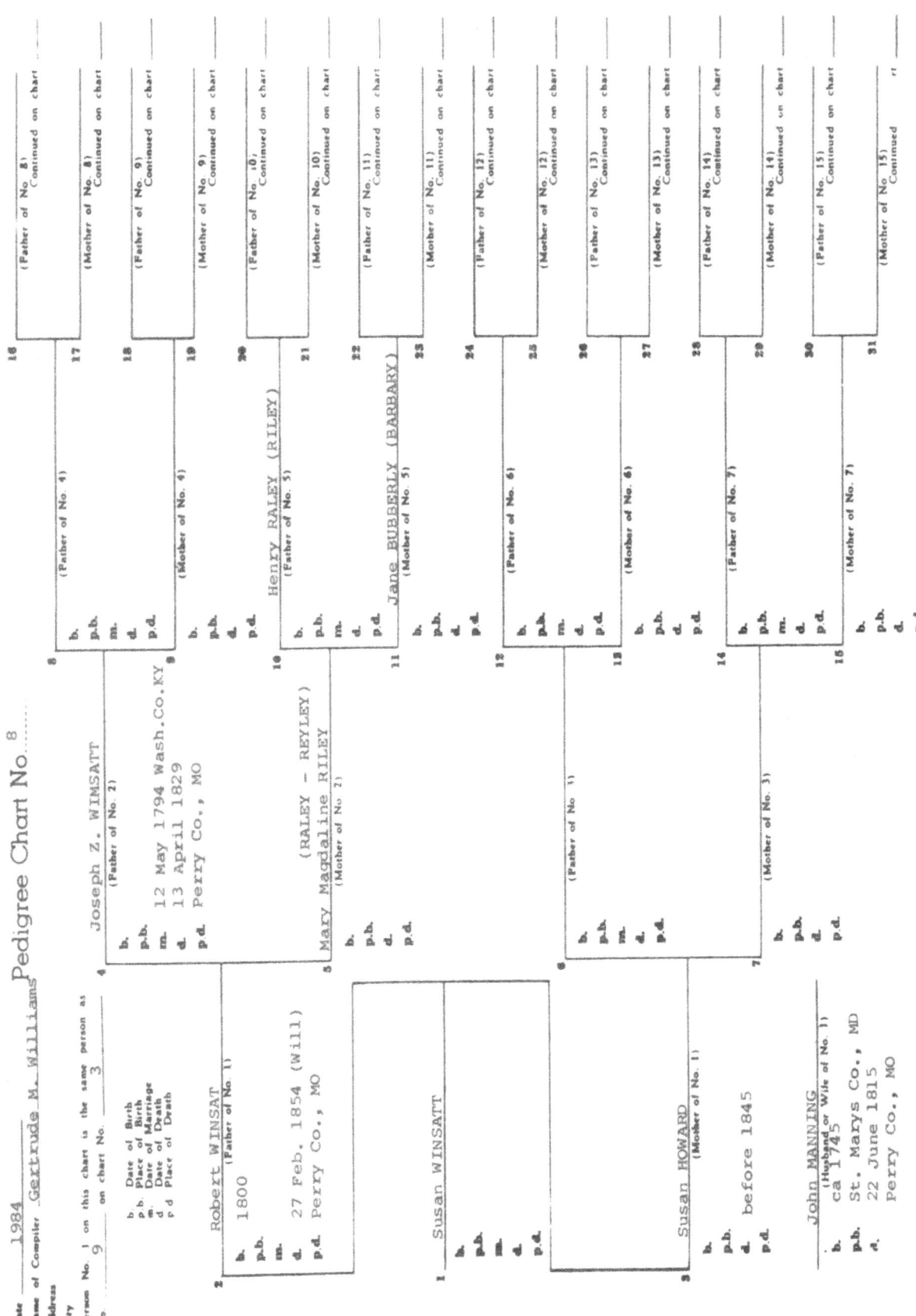

Pedigree Chart No. 8

Date _____ 1984

Name of Compiler _____ Gertrude M. Williams

Address _____

City _____

Person No. 1 on this chart is the same person as
No. 9 on chart No. 3

b. Date of Birth
p.b. Place of Birth
m. Date of Marriage
d. Date of Death
p.d Place of Death

2 Robert WINSAT (Father of No. 1)
b. 1800
p.b.
m.
d. 27 Feb. 1854 (Will)
p.d. Perry Co., MO

1 Susan WINSATT
b.
p.b.
m.
d.
p.d.

3 Susan HOWARD (Mother of No. 1)
b.
p.b.
d. before 1845
p.d.

John MANNING (Husband or Wife of No. 1)
b. ca 1745
p.b. St. Marys Co., MD
d. 22 June 1815
Perry Co., MO

4 Joseph Z. WIMSATT (Father of No. 2)
b.
p.b. 12 May 1794 Wash.Co.KY
m. 13 April 1829
d.
p.d Perry Co., MO

5 Mary Magdaline RILEY (RALEY - REYLEY) (Mother of No. 2)
b.
p.b.
d.
p.d.

6 (Father of No. 3)
b.
p.b.
m.
d.
p.d.

7 (Mother of No. 3)
b.
p.b.
d.
p.d.

8 (Father of No. 4)
b.
p.b.
m.
d.
p.d.

9 (Mother of No. 4)
b.
p.b.
d.
p.d.

10 Henry RALEY (RILEY) (Father of No. 5)
b.
p.b.
m.
d.
p.d.

11 Jane BUBBERLY (BARBARY) (Mother of No. 5)
b.
p.b.
d.
p.d.

12 (Father of No. 6)
b.
p.b.
m.
d.
p.d.

13 (Mother of No. 6)
b.
p.b.
d.
p.d.

14 (Father of No. 7)
b.
p.b.
m.
d.
p.d.

15 (Mother of No. 7)
b.
p.b.
d.
p.d.

16 (Father of No. 8) Continued on chart _____

17 (Mother of No. 8) Continued on chart _____

18 (Father of No. 9) Continued on chart _____

19 (Mother of No. 9) Continued on chart _____

20 (Father of No. 10) Continued on chart _____

21 (Mother of No. 10) Continued on chart _____

22 (Father of No. 11) Continued on chart _____

23 (Mother of No. 11) Continued on chart _____

24 (Father of No. 12) Continued on chart _____

25 (Mother of No. 12) Continued on chart _____

26 (Father of No. 13) Continued on chart _____

27 (Mother of No. 13) Continued on chart _____

28 (Father of No. 14) Continued on chart _____

29 (Mother of No. 14) Continued on chart _____

30 (Father of No. 15) Continued on chart _____

31 (Mother of No. 15) Continued _____

# Pedigree Chart No. 1

Date 20 Feb. 1981
Name of Compiler Letha M. Williams
Address
City
Person No. 1 on this chart is the same person as
No. SPOUSE on chart No. 2

b. Date of Birth
p.b. Place of Birth
m. Date of Marriage
d. Date of Death
p.d. Place of Death

**1** William Harve WILLIAMS
b. 3 Mar 1925
p.b. Hatfield, Polk, AR
m. 7 Sept 1948
d.
p.d.

**(Husband or Wife of No. 1)**
Letha Marie SMITH
b. 2 Feb 1932
p.b. Tuscola, Taylor, TX
d.

**2** (Father of No. 1)
Walter Penn WILLIAMS
b. 18 Feb 1898
p.b. Sheridan, Grant Co. AR
m. 24 Dec 1917 Polk Co. AR
d.
p.d.

**3** (Mother of No. 1)
Ava Belle PARHAM
b. 20 Nov 1897
p.b. Hatfield, Polk, AR
d.
p.d.

**4** (Father of No. 2)
Thomas WILLIAMS
b. 5 Aug 1805
p.b. "East" TN
m. 8 Mar 1852 AR
d. 15 Oct 1883
p.d. Big Fork, Polk, AR

m/1: Margeret BOZE
b. ca 1814 AL
m. 23 June 1831 AL
d. 6 Jan 1852 AR

**5** (Mother of No. 2)
Elizabeth BAGGS
b. 13 May 1830
p.b. Black Sprgs, Mont., AR
d. ca 1902 Center Point, AR
p.d. Howard Co., AR

**6** (Father of No. 3)
Charles Marion PARHAM
b. 9 Feb 1871
p.b. Hatfield, Polk, AR
m. 27 Dec 1892
d. 2 Aug 1906
p.d. Hatfield, Polk, AR

**7** (Mother of No. 3)
Leva Ann DAVIS
b. 14 Feb 1875
p.b. Banner, Calhoun, MS
d. 26 Aug 1954
p.d. Hatfield, Polk, AR

**8** (Father of No. 4)
Thomas WILLIAMS, Sr.
b. 1756
p.b. Chester Co., PA
m. 3 Aug 1800 TN
d. 5 Nov 1847
p.d. Jackson Co., AL

**9** (Mother of No. 4)
Rachel LONGACRE
b. 29 Jan 1759
p.b. Philadelphia, PA
d. after 1857
p.d. DeKalb Co., AL (?)

**10** (Father of No. 5)
John BAGGS
b. 11 Feb 1806
p.b. KY
m.
d. Jan 1869
p.d. near Mount Ida, AR

**11** (Mother of No. 5)
Agnes
b. 6 Jan 1807
p.b. KY
d.
p.d. AR

**12** (Father of No. 6)
Wyatt Rudolph PARHAM
b. ca 1852
p.b. Gordo, Pickins, AL
m./1 ca 1870 m/2 1906
d. September 1919
p.d. near Mena, Polk, AR

**13** (Mother of No. 6)
Rebecca LINER
b. ca 1846
p.b. AL
d.
p.d.

**14** (Father of No. 7)
John Quittman DAVIS
b. 5 Nov 1850
p.b. Lafayette Co., MS
m. 3 Dec 1870
d. 14 Nov 1890
p.d. near Hatfield, AR

**15** (Mother of No. 7)
Josephine Victoria HENDERSON
b. 25 Oct 1852
p.b. Lafayette Co., MS
d. 27 Feb 1915
p.d. near Hatfield, AR

**16** (Father of No. 8)
Continued on chart

**17** (Mother of No. 8)
Continued on chart

**18** (Father of No. 9)
Continued on chart

**19** (Mother of No. 9)
Continued on chart

**20** (Father of No. 10)
Continued on chart

**21** (Mother of No. 10)
Continued on chart

**22** (Father of No. 11)
Continued on chart

**23** (Mother of No. 11)
Continued on chart

**24** (Father of No. 12)
John PARHAM
Continued on chart  1/E

**25** (Mother of No. 12)
Susan
Continued on chart  1/E

**26** (Father of No. 13)
Charles Marion LINER
1818 AL
1866 AR
Continued on chart  1/E

**27** (Mother of No. 13)
Mary Adeline
1820 AR
1906 AR
Continued on chart

**28** (Father of No. 14)
William Green DAVIS
Continued on chart  1/G

**29** (Mother of No. 14)
Julia Ann MAULDIN
Continued on chart  1/G

**30** (Father of No. 15)
Samuel HENDERSON
Continued on chart  1/H

**31** (Mother of No. 15)
Cynthia PARKS
Continued on chart  1/H

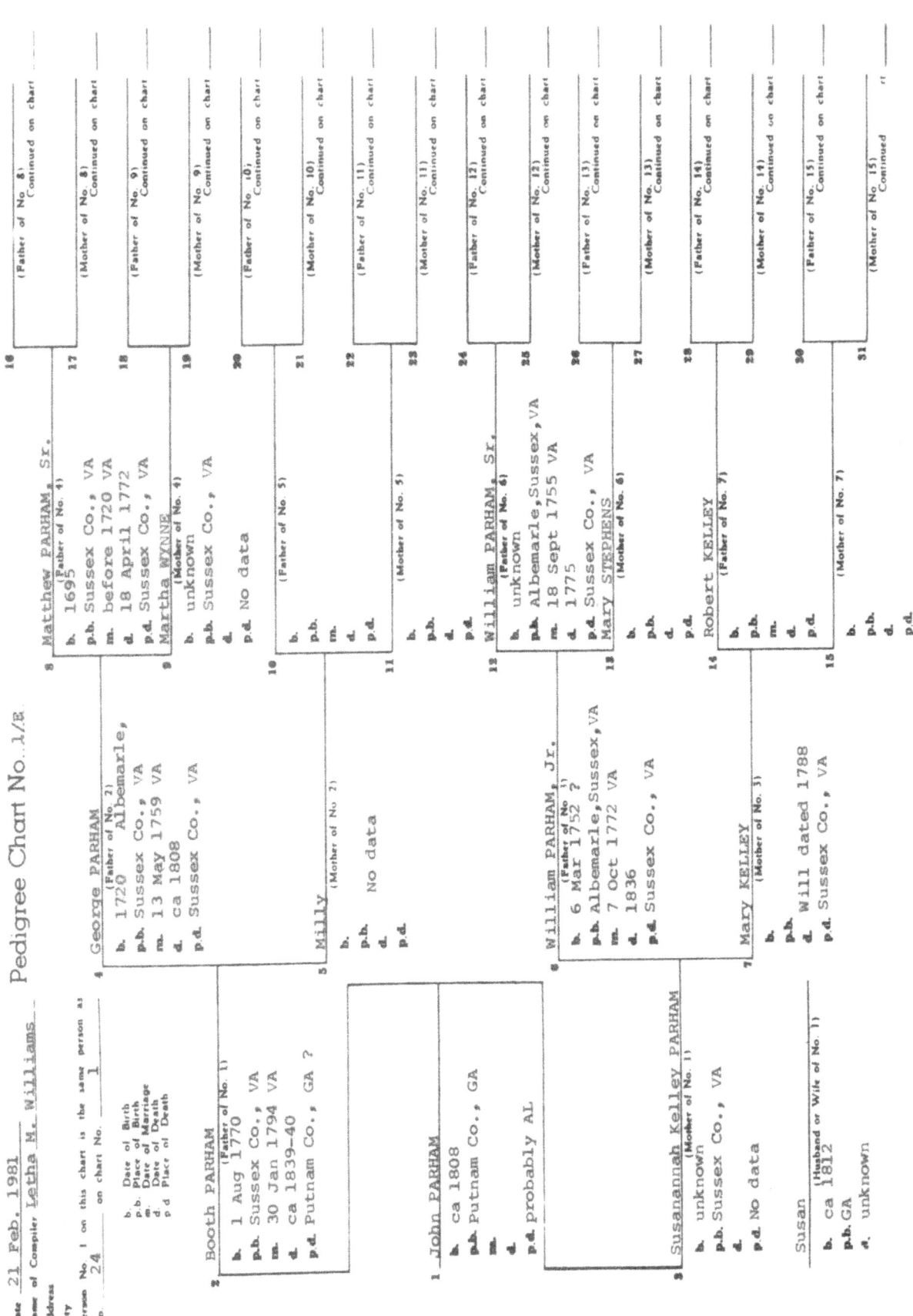

Date 21 Feb. 1981    Pedigree Chart No. 1/E

Name of Compiler Letha M. Williams

Address

City

Person No. 1 on this chart is the same person as

No. 24 on chart No. 1

b. Date of Birth
p.b. Place of Birth
m. Date of Marriage
d. Date of Death
p.d Place of Death

1 John PARHAM
b. ca 1808
p.b. Putnam Co., GA
m.
d.
p.d. probably AL

2 Booth PARHAM (Father of No. 1)
b. 1 Aug 1770
p.b. Sussex Co., VA
m. 30 Jan 1794 VA
d. ca 1839-40
p.d. Putnam Co., GA ?

3 Susanannah Kelley PARHAM (Mother of No. 1)
b. unknown
p.b. Sussex Co., VA
d.
p.d. No data

4 George PARHAM (Father of No. 2)
b. 1720 Albemarle,
p.b. Sussex Co., VA
m. 13 May 1759 VA
d. ca 1808
p.d Sussex Co., VA

5 Milly (Mother of No. 2)
b.
p.b. No data
d.
p.d.

6 William PARHAM, Jr. (Father of No. 3)
b. 6 Mar 1752 ?
p.b. Albemarle, Sussex, VA
m. 7 Oct 1772 VA
d. 1836
p.d. Sussex Co., VA

7 Mary KELLEY (Mother of No. 3)
b.
p.b. Will dated 1788
d.
p.d. Sussex Co., VA

Susan (Husband or Wife of No. 1)
b. ca 1812
p.b. GA
d. unknown

8 Matthew PARHAM, Sr. (Father of No. 4)
b. 1695
p.b. Sussex Co., VA
m. before 1720 VA
d. 18 April 1772
p.d. Sussex Co., VA

9 Martha WYNNE (Mother of No. 4)
b. unknown
p.b. Sussex Co., VA
d.
p.d. No data

10 (Father of No. 5)
b.
p.b.
m.
d.
p.d.

11 (Mother of No. 5)
b.
p.b.
d.
p.d.

12 William PARHAM, Sr. (Father of No. 6)
b. unknown
p.b. Albemarle, Sussex, VA
m. 18 Sept 1755 VA
d. 1775
p.d. Sussex Co., VA

13 Mary STEPHENS (Mother of No. 6)
b.
p.b.
d.
p.d.

14 Robert KELLEY (Father of No. 7)
b.
p.b.
m.
d.
p.d.

15 (Mother of No. 7)
b.
p.b.
d.
p.d.

16 (Father of No. 8) Continued on chart

17 (Mother of No. 8) Continued on chart

18 (Father of No. 9) Continued on chart

19 (Mother of No. 9) Continued on chart

20 (Father of No. 10) Continued on chart

21 (Mother of No. 10) Continued on chart

22 (Father of No. 11) Continued on chart

23 (Mother of No. 11) Continued on chart

24 (Father of No. 12) Continued on chart

25 (Mother of No. 12) Continued on chart

26 (Father of No. 13) Continued on chart

27 (Mother of No. 13) Continued on chart

28 (Father of No. 14) Continued on chart

29 (Mother of No. 14) Continued on chart

30 (Father of No. 15) Continued on chart

31 (Mother of No. 15) Continued

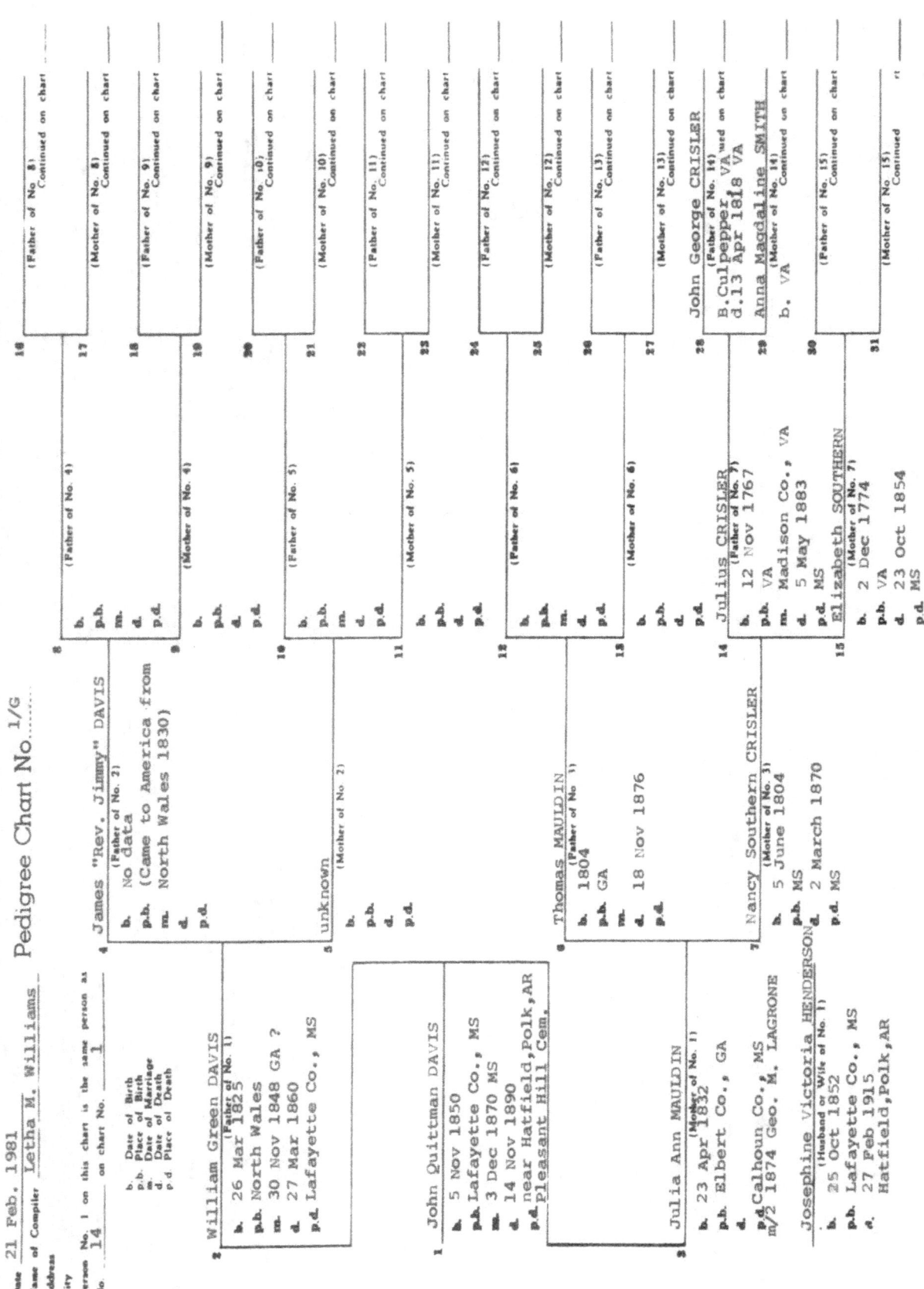

Pedigree Chart No. 1/H

Date 22 Feb. 1981
Name of Compiler Letha M. Williams
Address
City
Person No. 1 on this chart is the same person as _____ on chart No.
No.

b. Date of Birth
p.b. Place of Birth
m. Date of Marriage
d. Date of Death
p.d. Place of Death

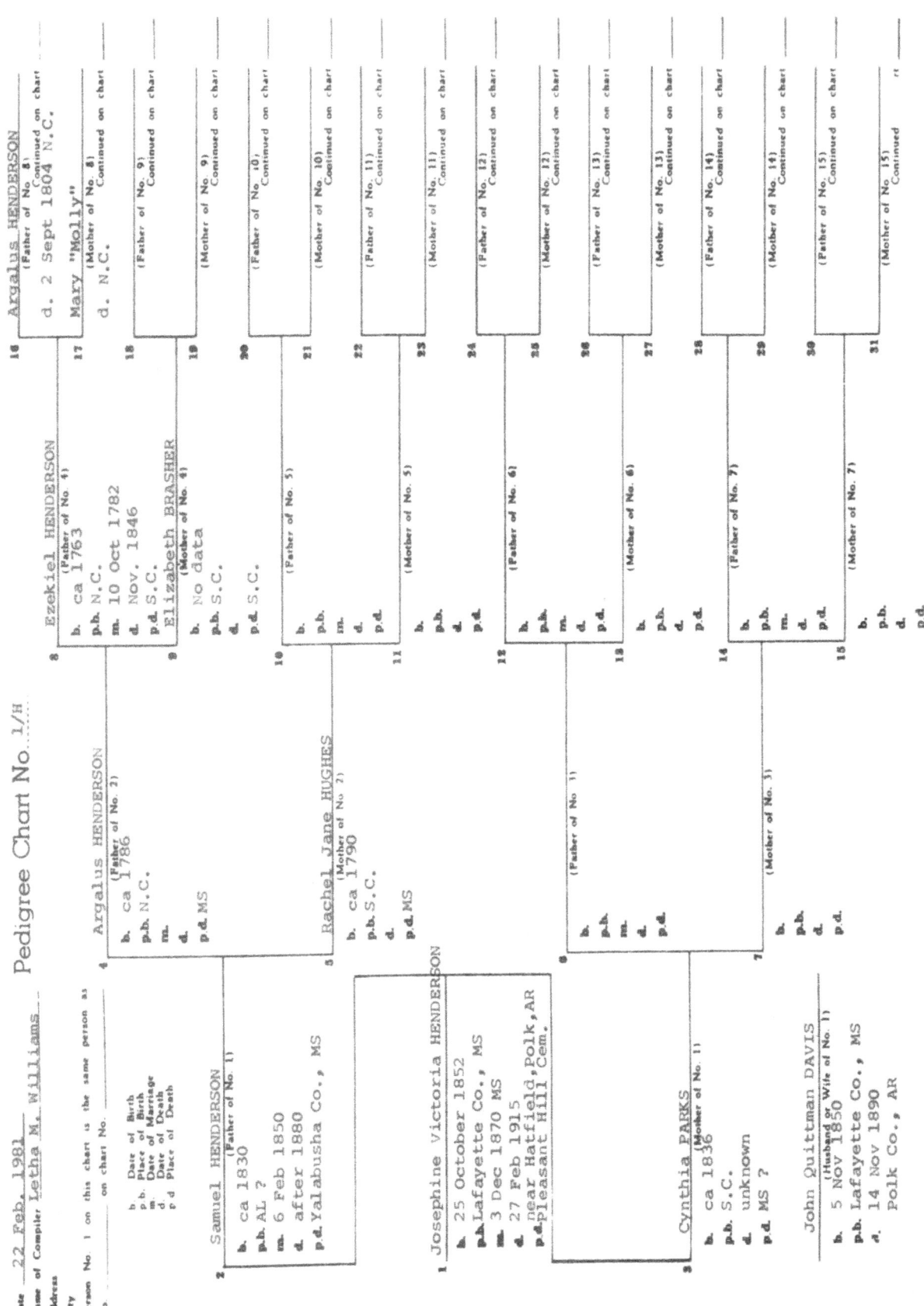

**1** Josephine Victoria HENDERSON
b. 25 October 1852
p.b. Lafayette Co., MS
m. 3 Dec 1870 MS
d. 27 Feb 1915
p.d. near Hatfield, Polk, AR
Pleasant Hill Cem.

**2** Samuel HENDERSON (Father of No. 1)
b. ca 1830
p.b. AL ?
m. 6 Feb 1850
d. after 1880
p.d. Yalabusha Co., MS

**3** Cynthia PARKS (Mother of No. 1)
b. ca 1836
p.b. S.C.
d. unknown
p.d. MS ?

John Quittman DAVIS (Husband or Wife of No. 1)
b. 5 Nov 1850
p.b. Lafayette Co., MS
d. 14 Nov 1890
Polk Co., AR

**4** Argalus HENDERSON (Father of No. 2)
b. ca 1786
p.b. N.C.
m.
d.
p.d. MS

**5** Rachel Jane HUGHES (Mother of No. 2)
b. ca 1790
p.b. S.C.
d.
p.d. MS

**6** (Father of No. 3)
b.
p.b.
m.
d.
p.d.

**7** (Mother of No. 3)
b.
p.b.
d.
p.d.

**8** Ezekiel HENDERSON (Father of No. 4)
b. ca 1763
p.b. N.C.
m. 10 Oct 1782
d. Nov. 1846
p.d. S.C.

**9** Elizabeth BRASHER (Mother of No. 4)
b. No data
p.b. S.C.
d.
p.d. S.C.

**10** (Father of No. 5)
b.
p.b.
m.
d.
p.d.

**11** (Mother of No. 5)
b.
p.b.
d.
p.d.

**12** (Father of No. 6)
b.
p.b.
m.
d.
p.d.

**13** (Mother of No. 6)
b.
p.b.
d.
p.d.

**14** (Father of No. 7)
b.
p.b.
m.
d.
p.d.

**15** (Mother of No. 7)
b.
p.b.
d.
p.d.

**16** Argalus HENDERSON (Father of No. 8)
d. 2 Sept 1804 N.C.
Continued on chart

**17** Mary "Molly" (Mother of No. 8)
d. N.C.
Continued on chart

**18** (Father of No. 9)
Continued on chart

**19** (Mother of No. 9)
Continued on chart

**20** (Father of No. 10)
Continued on chart

**21** (Mother of No. 10)
Continued on chart

**22** (Father of No. 11)
Continued on chart

**23** (Mother of No. 11)
Continued on chart

**24** (Father of No. 12)
Continued on chart

**25** (Mother of No. 12)
Continued on chart

**26** (Father of No. 13)
Continued on chart

**27** (Mother of No. 13)
Continued on chart

**28** (Father of No. 14)
Continued on chart

**29** (Mother of No. 14)
Continued on chart

**30** (Father of No. 15)
Continued on chart

**31** (Mother of No. 15)
Continued

## Pedigree Chart No. 2

Date: 20 Feb, 1981
Name of Compiler: Letha M. Williams
Address:
City:
Person No. 1 on this chart is the same person as
No. Spouse on chart No. 1

b. Date of Birth
p.b. Place of Birth
m. Date of Marriage
d. Date of Death
p.d. Place of Death

**1** Letha Marie SMITH
b. 2 Feb 1932
p.b. Tuscola, Taylor, TX
m. 7 Sept 1948 Hatfield, AR
d.
p.d.

**2** Byron Braxton SMITH, Sr.
(Father of No. 1)
b. 15 July 1908
p.b. Evant, Coryelle, TX
m. 18 Jan 1927 McCamey, TX
d.
p.d.

**3** Anna Etheline HALL
(Mother of No. 1)
b. 31 Aug 1909
p.b. Whiteland, McCulloch, TX
d.
p.d.

(Husband or Wife of No. 1)
William Harve WILLIAMS
b. 3 Mar 1925
p.b. Hatfield, Polk Co., AR
d.

**4** Dee David SMITH, MD
(Father of No. 2)
b. 31 May 1880
p.b. Grosbeck, Limestone, TX
m. 8 July 1899 Austin, TX
d. 19 June 1946
p.d. Temple, Bell, TX
bur. Brownwood, Brown, TX

**5** Artie Missie WOMBLE
(Mother of No. 2)
b. 6 Apr 1882
p.b. Florence, Williamson, TX
d. 28 Nov 1961
p.d. Brownwood, Brown, TX

(#24 & #27 are bro. and sister)

**6** John Ellis HALL
(Father of No. 3)
b. 9 May 1883
p.b. Wood, Coryelle, TX
m. 24 Dec 1905 TX
d. 9 May 1973
p.d. Palestine, Anderson, TX
bur. Brady, McCulloch, TX

**7** Martealia Ann HAYNES
(Mother of No. 3)
b. 25 Sept 1889
p.b. Terryville, Terril, TX
d. 18 July 1974
p.d. Palestine, Anderson, TX
bur. Brady, McCulloch, TX

**8** John Milton SMITH
(Father of No. 4)
b. 27 Nov 1857
p.b. LA ?
m. 24 Dec 1876 TX
d. 20 Nov 1917
p.d. Evant, Coryelle, TX

**9** Elizabeth Jane THAMES
(Mother of No. 4)
b. 18 July 1855
p.b. Meridian, Lauderdale, MS
d. 7 May 1935
p.d. Evant, Coryelle, TX

**10** William Louis WOMBLE
(Father of No. 5)
b. 28 Sept 1861
p.b. Atlanta, Stewart, GA
m. 16 Dec 1879 TN
d. 13 Dec 1942
p.d. Paint Rock, Concho, TX

**11** Louisa Jane GURLEY
(Mother of No. 5)
b. 23 Mar 1859
p.b. Lexington, Henderson, TN
d. 11 Nov 1935
p.d. Paint Rock, Concho, TX

**12** William Benjamin HALL
(Father of No. 6)
b. 8 Jan 1854
p.b. Marion Co., AR
m. 23 Jan 1876 TX
d. 21 June 1918
p.d. Carrol Colony, TX

**13** Mahala WOOD (DUNCAN)
(Mother of No. 6)
b. 5 Mar 1857
p.b. MO
d. 10 Sept 1935/6 ?
p.d. Brady, McCulloch, TX

**14** John Bythell HAYNES "Bice"
(Father of No. 7)
b. 4 June 1862
p.b. East Feleciana, LA
m.
d.
p.d. Brady, McCulloch, TX

**15** Georgeann TANKSLEY
(Mother of No. 7)
b. 29 Apr 1860 ?
p.b. DeWitt Co., TX
d. 2 Feb 1936
p.d. Brady, McCulloch, TX

**16** John Milton SMITH, Jr.
(Father of No. 8) Continued on chart No. 8
b. MS ?
d. TX

**17** CLEAVELAND (FOSTER)
(Mother of No. 8) Continued on chart No. 8
b. MS
d. TX

**18** Joseph William THAMES
(Father of No. 9) Continued on chart No. 9    2/B

**19** Hariette WILKES (McLEVAINE)
(Mother of No. 9) Continued on chart

**20** Henry James WOMBLE
(Father of No. 10) Continued on chart    2/C

**21** Sarah Ann Elizabeth HORTON
(Mother of No. 10) Continued on chart    2/C

**22** John Anthony GURLEY
(Father of No. 11) Continued on chart    2/D

**23** Parila Adeline CARTER
(Mother of No. 11) Continued on chart    2/D

**24** Abner HALL
(Father of No. 12) Continued on chart    2/E

**25** Sarah Ann DEUVALL
(Mother of No. 12) Continued on chart    2/E

**26** WOOD
(Father of No. 13) Continued on chart    2/F
b. MO
d. Civil War

**27** Susan Mahala HALL "Sude"
(Mother of No. 13) Continued on chart    2/F

**28** John Bythell HAYNES, Sr.
(Father of No. 14) Continued on chart    2/G

**29** Sarah Jane HARBOUR
(Mother of No. 14) Continued on chart    2/G

**30** Benjamin L. TANK(ER)SLEY
(Father of No. 15) Continued on chart    2/H

**31** Mary "Polly" BILLINGS
(Mother of No. 15) Continued    2/H

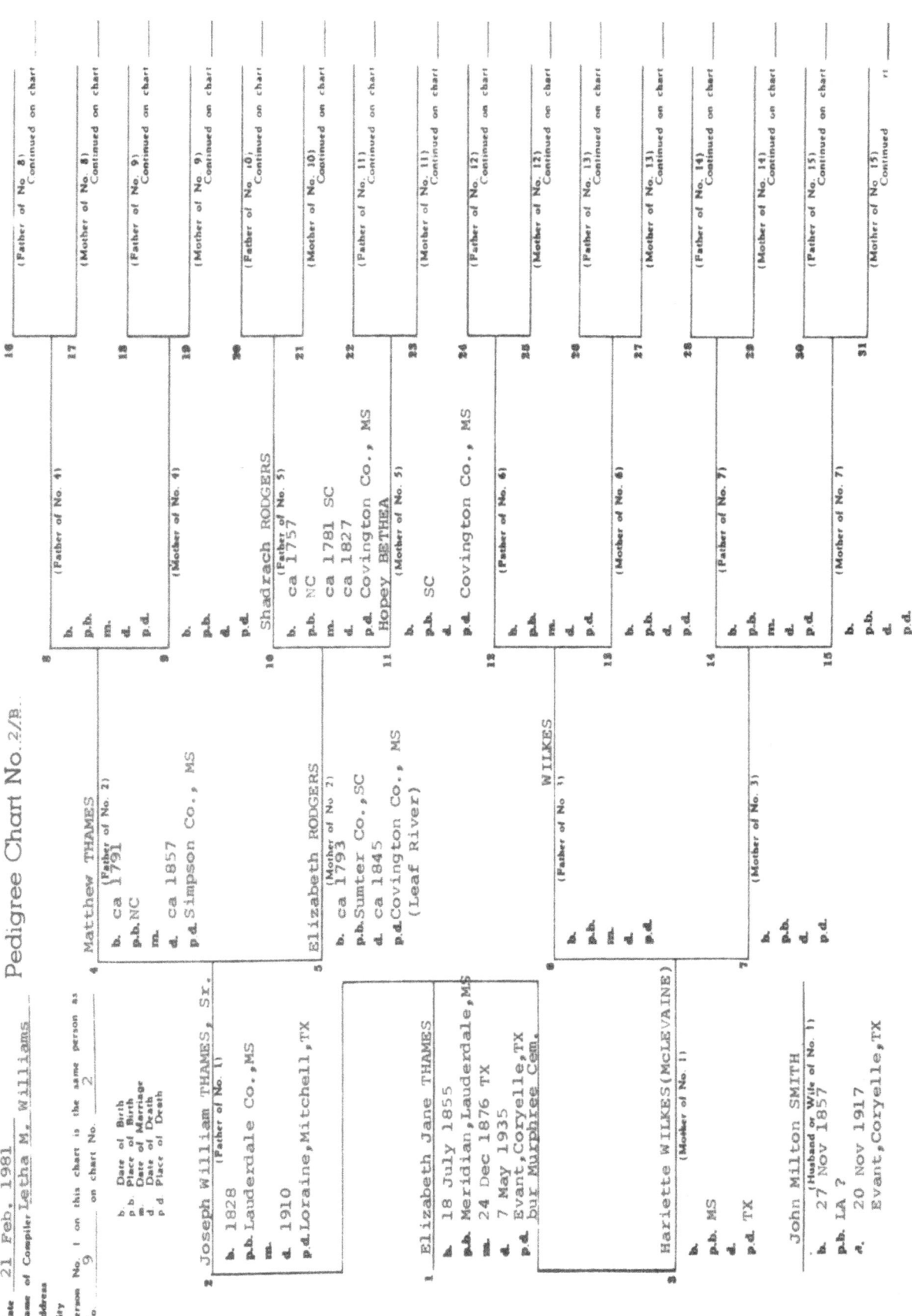

Pedigree Chart No. 2/B

Date 21 Feb. 1981
Name of Compiler Letha M. Williams
Address
City
Person No. 1 on this chart is the same person as No. 9 on chart No. 2

b. Date of Birth
p.b. Place of Birth
m. Date of Marriage
d. Date of Death
p.d Place of Death

1 Elizabeth Jane THAMES

b. 18 July 1855
p.b. Meridian,Lauderdale,MS
m. 24 Dec 1876 TX
d. 7 May 1935
p.d. Evant,Coryelle,TX
bur Murphree Cem.

2 Joseph William THAMES, Sr. (Father of No. 1)

b. 1828
p.b. Lauderdale Co.,MS
m.
d. 1910
p.d. Loraine,Mitchell,TX

3 Hariette WILKES(McLEVAINE) (Mother of No. 1)

b.
p.b. MS
d.
p.d. TX

John Milton SMITH (Husband or Wife of No. 1)

b. 27 Nov 1857
p.b. LA ?
d. 20 Nov 1917
d. Evant,Coryelle,TX

4 Matthew THAMES (Father of No. 2)

b. ca 1791
p.b. NC
m.
d. ca 1857
p.d. Simpson Co., MS

5 Elizabeth RODGERS (Mother of No 2)

b. ca 1793
p.b. Sumter Co.,SC
d. ca 1845
p.d. Covington Co., MS
(Leaf River)

6 WILKES (Father of No 1)

b.
p.b.
m.
d.
p.d.

7 (Mother of No. 3)

b.
p.b.
d.
p.d.

8 (Father of No. 4)

b.
p.b.
m.
d.
p.d.

9 (Mother of No. 4)

b.
p.b.
d.
p.d.

10 Shadrach RODGERS (Father of No. 5)

b. ca 1757
p.b. NC
m. ca 1781 SC
d. ca 1827
p.d. Covington Co., MS

11 Hopey BETHEA (Mother of No. 5)

b. SC
p.b. SC
d.
p.d. Covington Co., MS

12 (Father of No. 6)

b.
p.b.
m.
d.
p.d.

13 (Mother of No. 6)

b.
p.b.
d.
p.d.

14 (Father of No. 7)

b.
p.b.
m.
d.
p.d.

15 (Mother of No. 7)

b.
p.b.
d.
p.d.

16 (Father of No. 8) Continued on chart ____

17 (Mother of No. 8) Continued on chart ____

18 (Father of No. 9) Continued on chart ____

19 (Mother of No 9) Continued on chart ____

20 (Father of No 10) Continued on chart ____

21 (Mother of No. 10) Continued on chart ____

22 (Father of No 11) Continued on chart ____

23 (Mother of No 11) Continued on chart ____

24 (Father of No 12) Continued on chart ____

25 (Mother of No 12) Continued on chart ____

26 (Father of No 13) Continued on chart ____

27 (Mother of No 13) Continued on chart ____

28 (Father of No 14) Continued on chart ____

29 (Mother of No 14) Continued on chart ____

30 (Father of No 15) Continued on chart ____

31 (Mother of No. 15) Continued

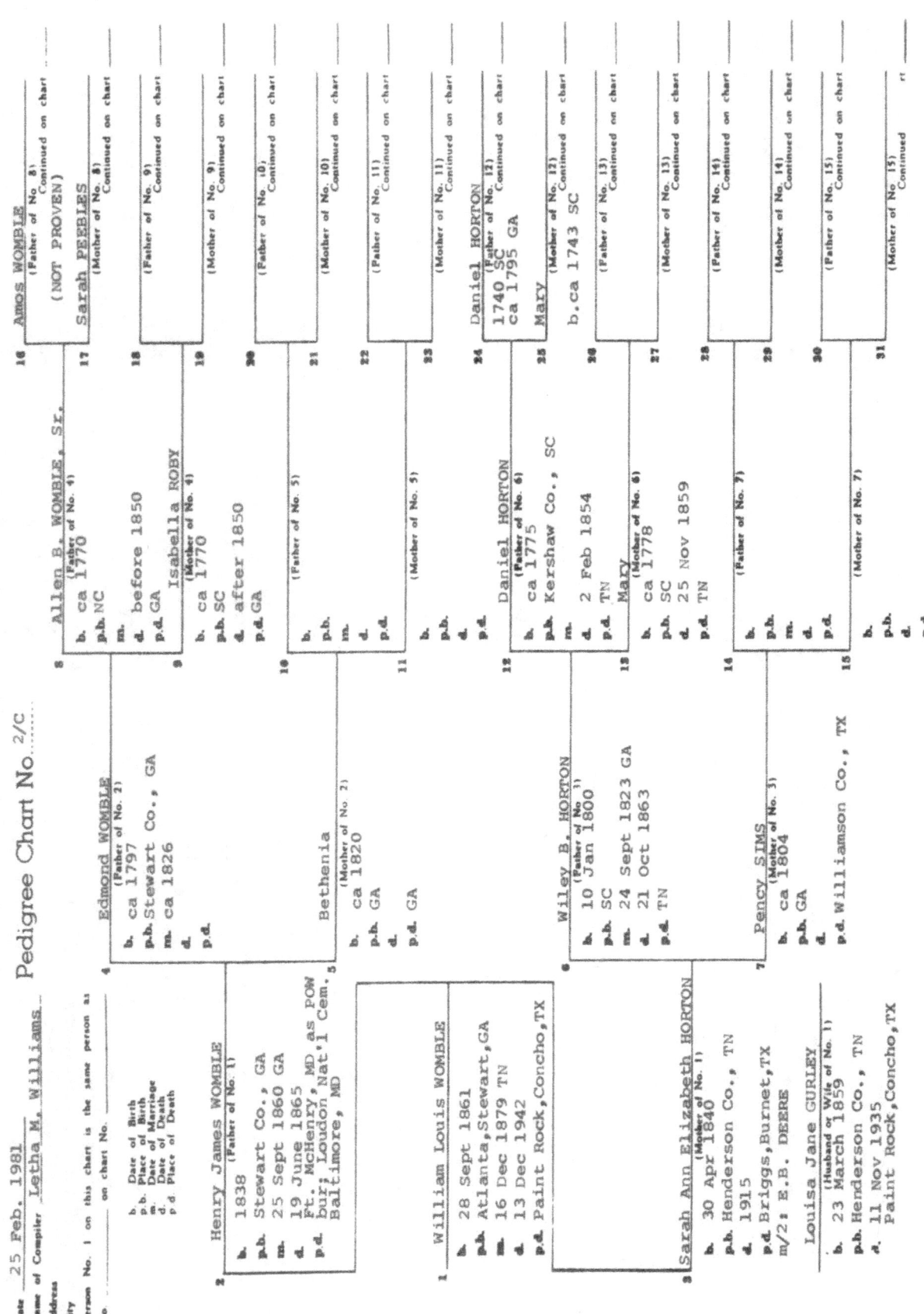

Pedigree Chart No. 2/C

Date  25 Feb. 1981
Name of Compiler  Letha M. Williams
Address
City
Person No. 1 on this chart is the same person as
No. _____ on chart No. _____

    b.   Date of Birth
    p.b. Place of Birth
    m.   Date of Marriage
    d.   Date of Death
    p.d. Place of Death

1  William Louis WOMBLE
    b.   28 Sept 1861
    p.b. Atlanta,Stewart,GA
    m.   16 Dec 1879 TN
    d.   13 Dec 1942
    p.d. Paint Rock,Concho,TX

2  Henry James WOMBLE (Father of No. 1)
    b.   1838
    p.b. Stewart Co., GA
    m.   25 Sept 1860 GA
    d.   19 June 1865
    p.d. Ft. McHenry, MD as POW
         bur; Loudon Nat'l Cem.,
         Baltimore, MD

3  Sarah Ann Elizabeth HORTON (Mother of No. 1)
    b.   30 Apr 1840
    p.b. Henderson Co., TN
    d.   1915
    p.d. Briggs,Burnet,TX
         m/2: E.B. DEERE

4  Edmond WOMBLE (Father of No. 2)
    b.   ca 1797
    p.b. Stewart Co., GA
    m.   ca 1826
    d.
    p.d.

5  Bethenia (Mother of No. 2)
    b.   ca 1820
    p.b. GA
    d.
    p.d. GA

6  Wiley B. HORTON (Father of No. 3)
    b.   10 Jan 1800
    p.b. SC
    m.   24 Sept 1823 GA
    d.   21 Oct 1863
    p.d. TN

7  Pency SIMS (Mother of No. 3)
    b.   ca 1804
    p.b. GA
    d.
    p.d. Williamson Co., TX

Louisa Jane GURLEY (Husband or Wife of No. 1)
    b.   23 March 1859
    p.b. Henderson Co., TN
    d.   11 Nov 1935
         Paint Rock,Concho,TX

8  Allen B. WOMBLE, Sr. (Father of No. 4)
    b.   ca 1770
    p.b. NC
    m.
    d.   before 1850
    p.d. GA

9  Isabella ROBY (Mother of No. 4)
    b.   ca 1770
    p.b. SC
    d.   after 1850
    p.d. GA

10  (Father of No. 5)
    b.
    p.b.
    m.
    d.
    p.d.

11  (Mother of No. 5)
    b.
    p.b.
    d.
    p.d.

12  Daniel HORTON (Father of No. 6)
    b.   ca 1775
    p.b. Kershaw Co., SC
    m.
    d.   2 Feb 1854
    p.d. TN

13  Mary (Mother of No. 6)
    b.   ca 1778
    p.b. SC
    d.   25 Nov 1859
    p.d. TN

14  (Father of No. 7)
    b.
    p.b.
    m.
    d.
    p.d.

15  (Mother of No. 7)
    b.
    p.b.
    d.
    p.d.

16  Amos WOMBLE (Father of No. 8)
         (NOT PROVEN)

17  Sarah PEEBLES (Mother of No. 8)

18  (Father of No. 9) Continued on chart

19  (Mother of No. 9) Continued on chart

20  (Father of No. 10) Continued on chart

21  (Mother of No. 10) Continued on chart

22  (Father of No. 11) Continued on chart

23  (Mother of No. 11) Continued on chart

24  Daniel HORTON (Father of No. 12)
         1740 SC
         ca 1795 GA

25  Mary (Mother of No. 12)
         b.ca 1743 SC

26  (Father of No. 13) Continued on chart

27  (Mother of No. 13) Continued on chart

28  (Father of No. 14) Continued on chart

29  (Mother of No. 14) Continued on chart

30  (Father of No. 15) Continued on chart

31  (Mother of No. 15) Continued on chart

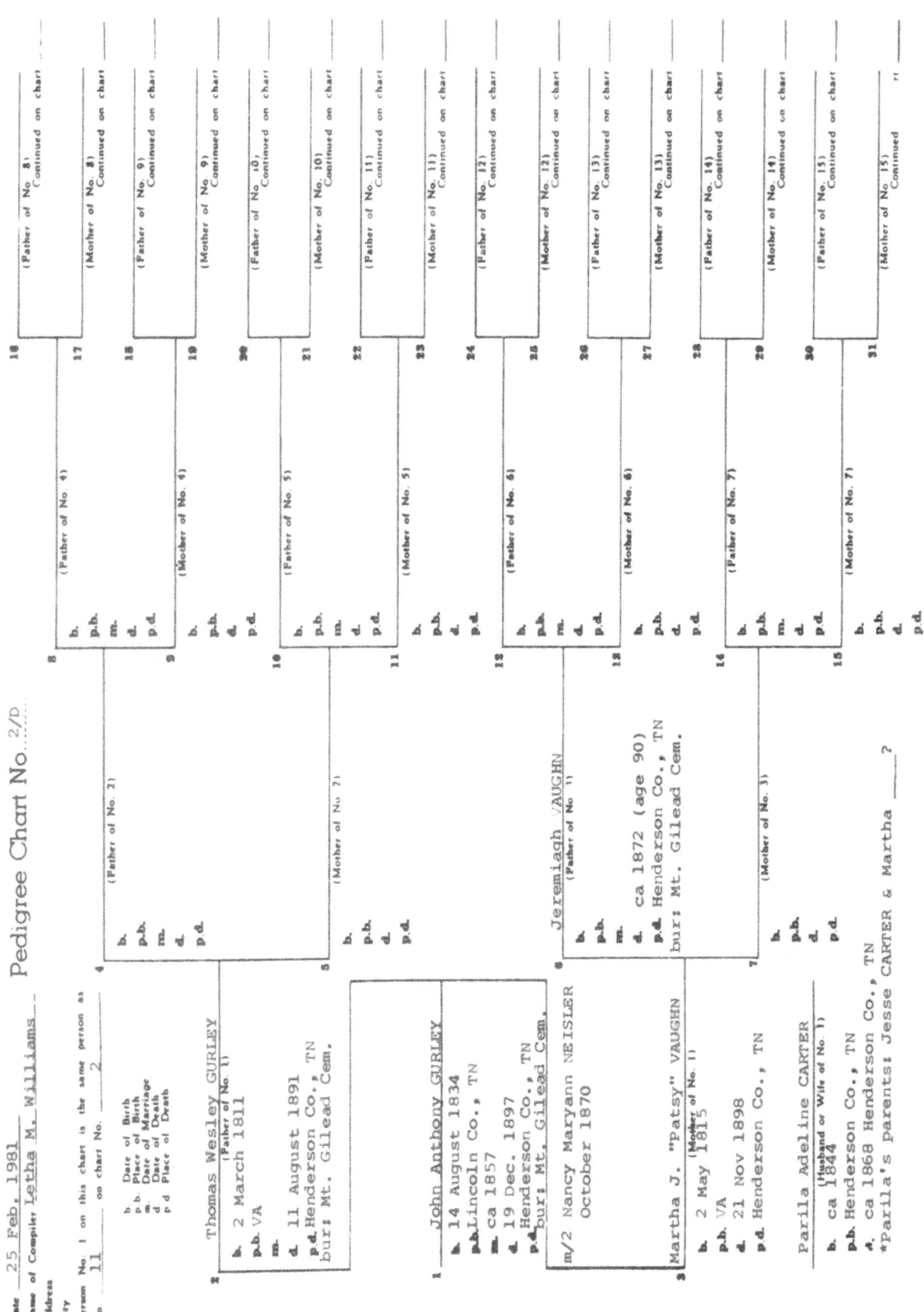

Pedigree Chart No. 2/D

Date 25 Feb. 1981
Name of Compiler Letha M. Williams
Address
City
Person No. 1 on this chart is the same person as
No. 11 on chart No. 2

b. Date of Birth
p.b. Place of Birth
m. Date of Marriage
d. Date of Death
p.d Place of Death

2 Thomas Wesley GURLEY (Father of No. 1)
b. 2 March 1811
p.b. VA
m.
d. 11 August 1891
p.d. Henderson Co., TN
bur: Mt. Gilead Cem.

1 John Anthony GURLEY (Father of No. 1)
b. 14 August 1834
p.b. Lincoln Co., TN
m. ca 1857
d. 19 Dec. 1897
p.d. Henderson Co., TN
bur: Mt. Gilead Cem.

m/2 Nancy Maryann NEISLER
October 1870

3 Martha J. "Patsy" VAUGHN (Mother of No. 1)
b. 2 May 1815
p.b. VA
d. 21 Nov 1898
p.d. Henderson Co., TN

6 Jeremiagh VAUGHN (Father of No. 1)
b.
p.b.
m.
d. ca 1872 (age 90)
p.d. Henderson Co., TN
bur: Mt. Gilead Cem.

7 (Mother of No. 3)
b.
p.b.
d.
p.d.

Parila Adeline CARTER
(Husband or Wife of No. 1)
b. ca 1844
p.b. Henderson Co., TN
d. ca 1868 Henderson Co., TN
*Parila's parents: Jesse CARTER & Martha _____ ?

4 (Father of No. 2)
b.
p.b.
m.
d.
p.d.

5 (Mother of No. 2)
b.
p.b.
d.
p.d.

8 (Father of No. 4)
b.
p.b.
m.
d.
p.d.

9 (Mother of No. 4)
b.
p.b.
d.
p.d.

10 (Father of No. 5)
b.
p.b.
m.
d.
p.d.

11 (Mother of No. 5)
b.
p.b.
d.
p.d.

12 (Father of No. 6)
b.
p.b.
m.
d.
p.d.

13 (Mother of No. 6)
b.
p.b.
d.
p.d.

14 (Father of No. 7)
b.
p.b.
m.
d.
p.d.

15 (Mother of No. 7)
b.
p.b.
d.
p.d.

16 (Father of No. 8) Continued on chart

17 (Mother of No. 8) Continued on chart

18 (Father of No. 9) Continued on chart

19 (Mother of No. 9) Continued on chart

20 (Father of No 10) Continued on chart

21 (Mother of No. 10) Continued on chart

22 (Father of No. 11) Continued on chart

23 (Mother of No. 11) Continued on chart

24 (Father of No. 12) Continued on chart

25 (Mother of No. 12) Continued on chart

26 (Father of No. 13) Continued on chart

27 (Mother of No. 13) Continued on chart

28 (Father of No. 14) Continued on chart

29 (Mother of No. 14) Continued on chart

30 (Father of No. 15) Continued on chart

31 (Mother of No. 15) Continued

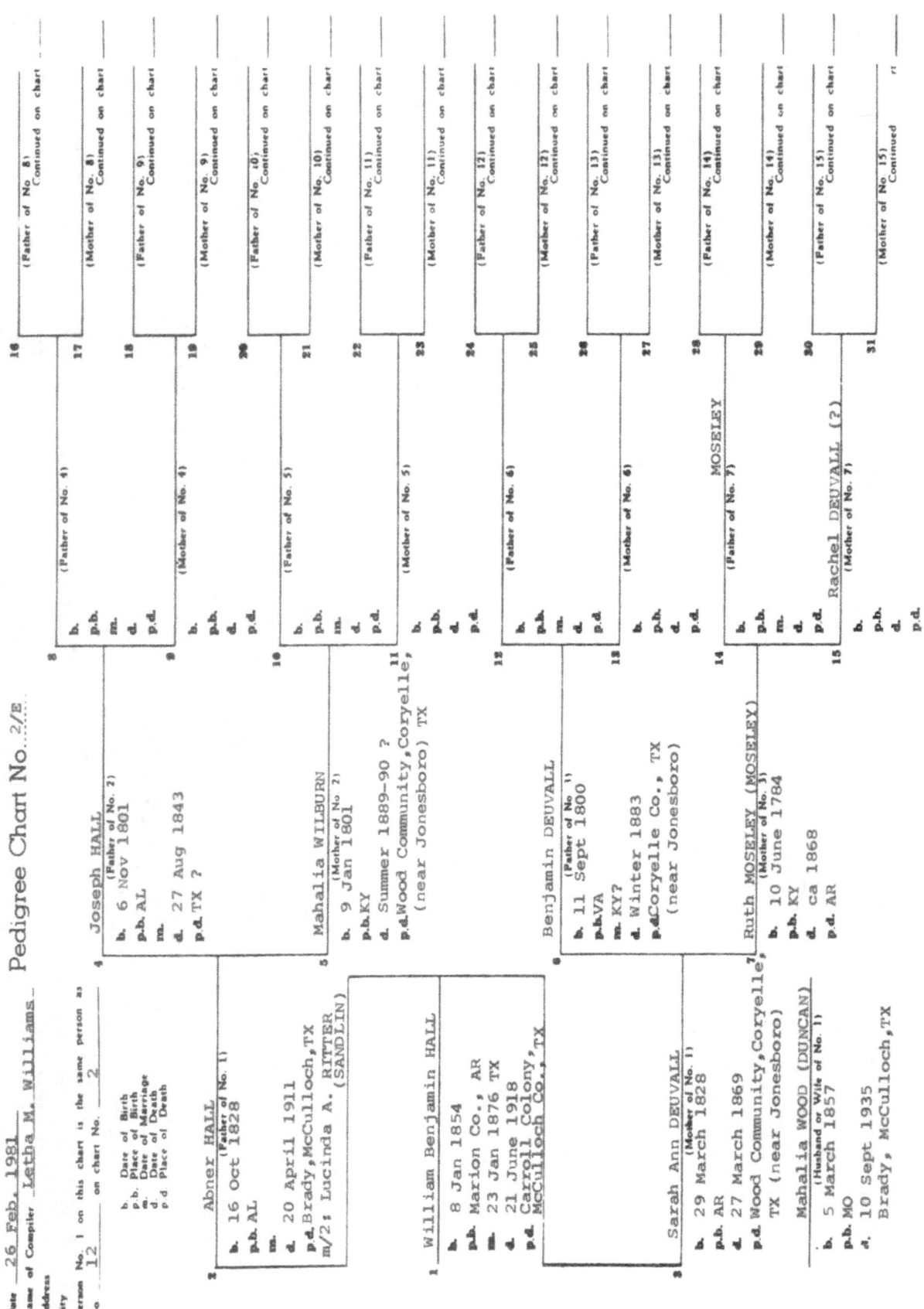

Pedigree Chart No. 2/E

Date 26 Feb. 1981
Name of Compiler Letha M. Williams
Address
City
Person No. 1 on this chart is the same person as No. 12 on chart No. 2

b. Date of Birth
p.b. Place of Birth
m. Date of Marriage
d. Date of Death
p.d Place of Death

1 William Benjamin HALL
b. 8 Jan 1854
p.b. Marion Co., AR
m. 23 Jan 1876 TX
d. 21 June 1918
p.d. Carroll Colony, McCulloch Co., TX

2 Abner HALL (Father of No. 1)
b. 16 Oct 1828
p.b. AL
m.
d. 20 April 1911
p.d. Brady, McCulloch, TX
m/2: Lucinda A. RITTER (SANDLIN)

3 Sarah Ann DEUVALL (Mother of No. 1)
b. 29 March 1828
p.b. AR
d. 27 March 1869
p.d. Wood Community, Coryelle, TX (near Jonesboro)

Mahalia WOOD (DUNCAN) (Husband or Wife of No. 1)
b. 5 March 1857
p.b. MO
d. 10 Sept 1935
Brady, McCulloch, TX

4 Joseph HALL (Father of No. 2)
b. 6 Nov 1801
p.b. AL
m.
d. 27 Aug 1843
p.d. TX ?

5 Mahalia WILBURN (Mother of No. 2)
b. 9 Jan 1801
p.b. KY
d. Summer 1889-90 ?
p.d. Wood Community, Coryelle, TX (near Jonesboro)

6 Benjamin DEUVALL (Father of No. 1)
b. 11 Sept 1800
p.b. VA
m. KY?
d. Winter 1883
p.d. Coryelle Co., TX (near Jonesboro)

7 Ruth MOSELEY (MOSELEY) (Mother of No. 3)
b. 10 June 1784
p.b. KY
d. ca 1868
p.d. AR

8 (Father of No. 4)
b.
p.b.
m.
p.d.

9 (Mother of No. 4)
b.
p.b.
d.
p.d.

10 (Father of No. 5)
b.
p.b.
m.
d.
p.d.

11 (Mother of No. 5)
b.
p.b.
d.
p.d.

12 (Father of No. 6)
b.
p.b.
m.
d.
p.d.

13 (Mother of No. 6)
b.
p.b.
d.
p.d.

14 MOSELEY (Father of No. 7)
b.
p.b.
m.
d.
p.d.

15 Rachel DEUVALL (?) (Mother of No. 7)
b.
p.b.
d.
p.d.

16 (Father of No. 8) Continued on chart

17 (Mother of No. 8) Continued on chart

18 (Father of No. 9) Continued on chart

19 (Mother of No. 9) Continued on chart

20 (Father of No. 10) Continued on chart

21 (Mother of No. 10) Continued on chart

22 (Father of No. 11) Continued on chart

23 (Mother of No. 11) Continued on chart

24 (Father of No. 12) Continued on chart

25 (Mother of No. 12) Continued on chart

26 (Father of No. 13) Continued on chart

27 (Mother of No. 13) Continued on chart

28 (Father of No. 14) Continued on chart

29 (Mother of No. 14) Continued on chart

30 (Father of No. 15) Continued on chart

31 (Mother of No. 15) Continued on chart

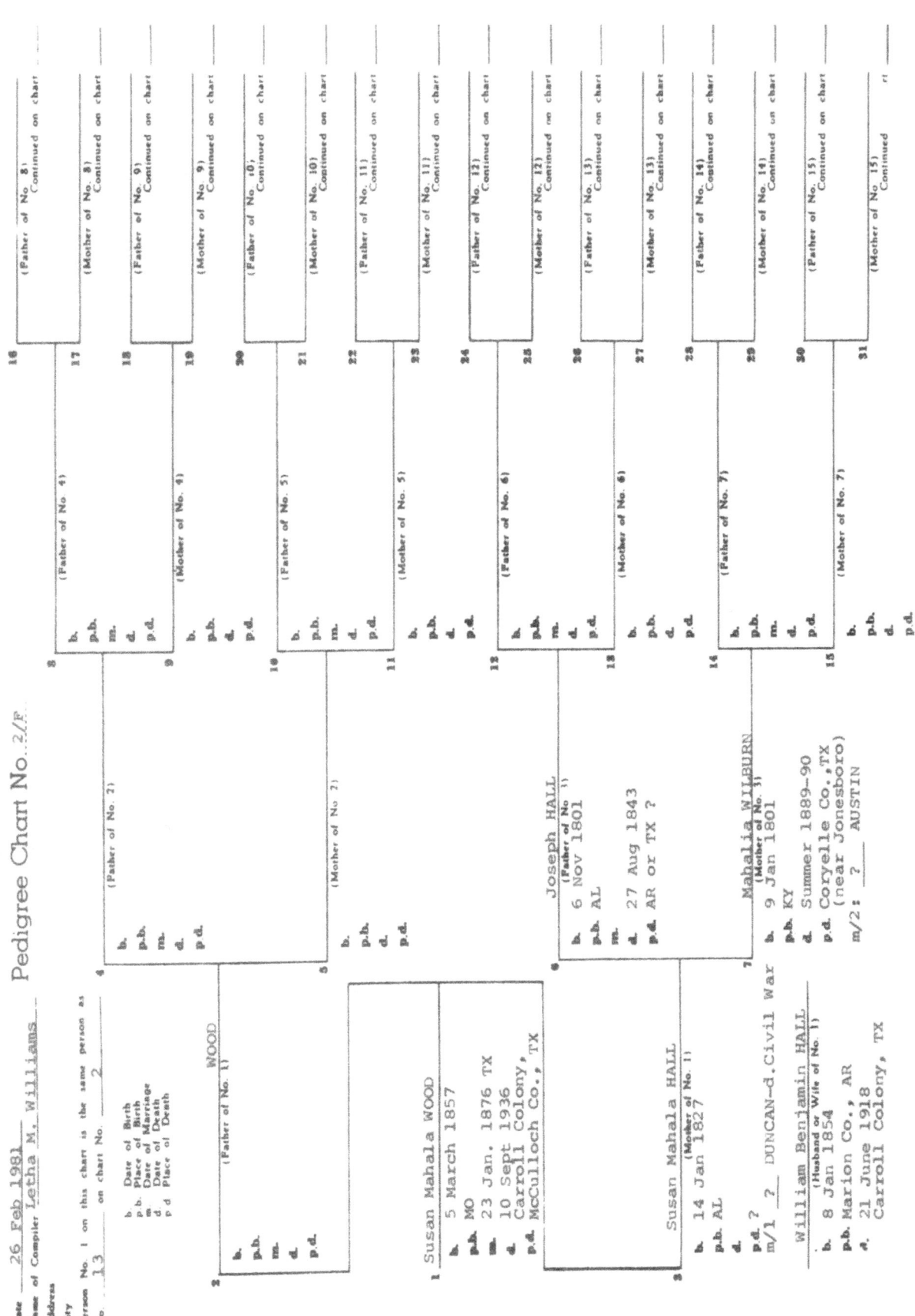

Pedigree Chart No. 2/F

Date 26 Feb 1981

Name of Compiler Letha M. Williams

Address

City

Person No. 1 on this chart is the same person as
No. 13 on chart No. 2

b.  Date of Birth
p.b. Place of Birth
m.  Date of Marriage
d.  Date of Death
p.d Place of Death

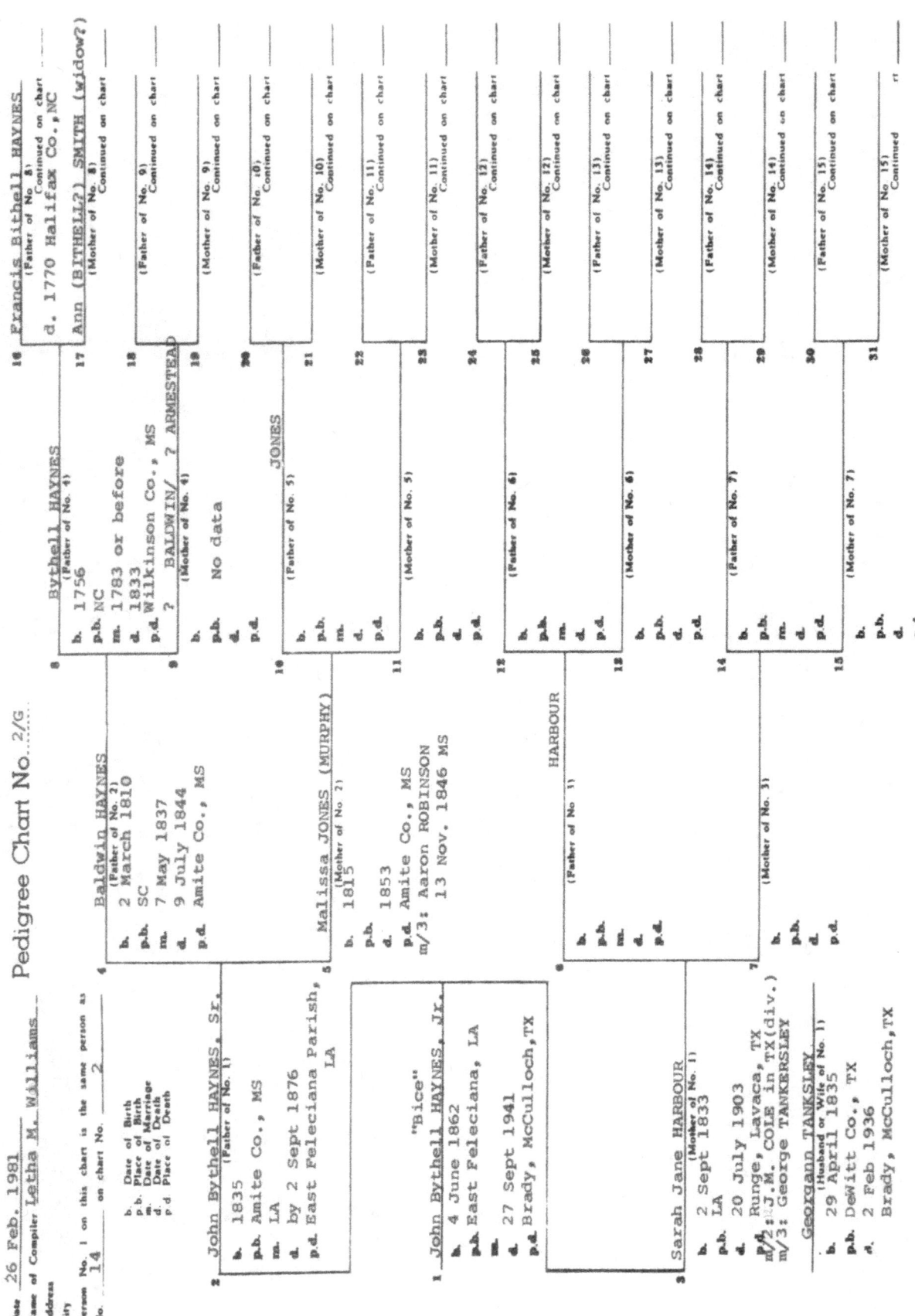

Date 26 Feb. 1981    Pedigree Chart No. 2/G

Name of Compiler Letha M. Williams

Address

City

Person No. 1 on this chart is the same person as No. 14 on chart No. 2

b. Date of Birth
p.b. Place of Birth
m. Date of Marriage
d. Date of Death
p.d Place of Death

1 John Bythell HAYNES, Jr.
(Father of No. 1)
b. 4 June 1862
p.b. East Feleciana, LA
m.
d. 27 Sept 1941
p.d. Brady, McCulloch, TX

3 Sarah Jane HARBOUR
(Mother of No. 1)
b. 2 Sept 1833
p.b. LA
d. 20 July 1903
m/2: J.M. COLE in TX(div.) Runge, Lavaca, TX
m/3: George TANKERSLEY

Georgann TANKSLEY
(Husband or Wife of No. 1)
b. 29 April 1835
p.b. DeWitt Co., TX
d. 2 Feb 1936
Brady, McCulloch, TX

2 John Bythell HAYNES, Sr.
(Father of No. 1)
b. 1835
p.b. Amite Co., MS
m. LA
d. by 2 Sept 1876
p.d. East Feleciana Parish, LA

"Bice"

5 Malissa JONES (MURPHY)
(Mother of No 2)
b. 1815
p.b.
d. 1853
p.d. Amite Co., MS
m/3: Aaron ROBINSON 13 Nov. 1846 MS

6 (Father of No. 3)
b.
p.b.
m.
d.
p.d.

HARBOUR

7 (Mother of No. 3)
b.
p.b.
d.
p.d.

4 Baldwin HAYNES
(Father of No. 2)
b. 2 March 1810
p.b. SC
m. 7 May 1837
d. 9 July 1844
p.d. Amite Co., MS

8 Bythell HAYNES
(Father of No. 4)
b. 1756
p.b. NC
m. 1783 or before
d. 1833
p.d. Wilkinson Co., MS

9 BALDWIN/ ? ARMESTEAD
(Mother of No. 4)
b.
p.b. No data
d.
p.d.

10 JONES
(Father of No. 5)
b.
p.b.
m.
d.
p.d.

11 (Mother of No. 5)
b.
p.b.
d.
p.d.

12 (Father of No. 6)
b.
p.b.
m.
d.
p.d.

13 (Mother of No. 6)
b.
p.b.
d.
p.d.

14 (Father of No. 7)
b.
p.b.
m.
d.
p.d.

15 (Mother of No. 7)
b.
p.b.
d.
p.d.

16 Francis Bithell HAYNES
(Father of No. 8)
Continued on chart
d. 1770 Halifax Co., NC

17 Ann (BITHELL?) SMITH (widow?)
(Mother of No. 8)
Continued on chart

18 (Father of No. 9)
Continued on chart

19 (Mother of No. 9)
Continued on chart

20 (Father of No. 10)
Continued on chart

21 (Mother of No. 10)
Continued on chart

22 (Father of No. 11)
Continued on chart

23 (Mother of No. 11)
Continued on chart

24 (Father of No. 12)
Continued on chart

25 (Mother of No. 12)
Continued on chart

26 (Father of No. 13)
Continued on chart

27 (Mother of No. 13)
Continued on chart

28 (Father of No. 14)
Continued on chart

29 (Mother of No. 14)
Continued on chart

30 (Father of No. 15)
Continued on chart

31 (Mother of No. 15)
Continued

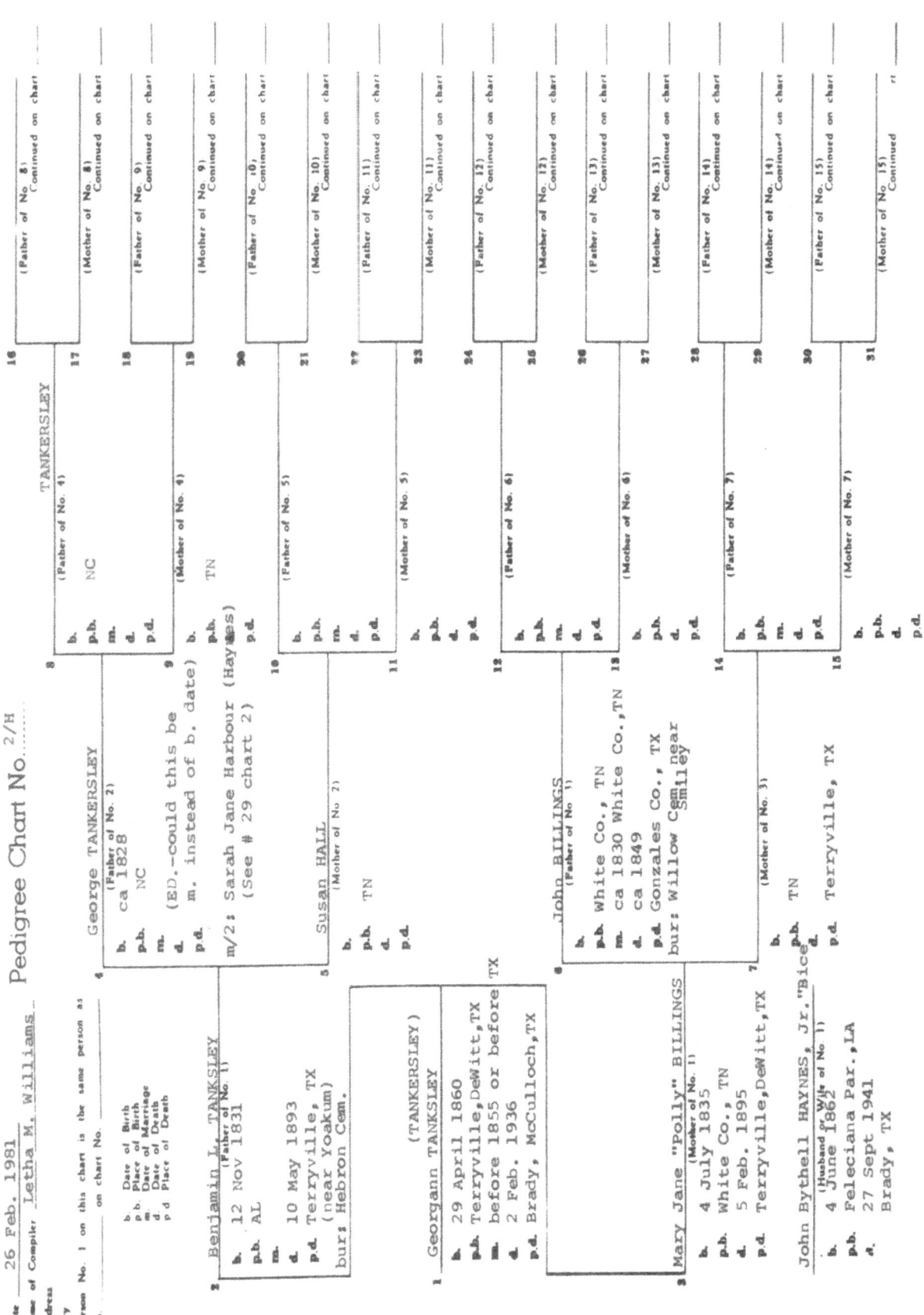

Pedigree Chart No. 2/H

Date 26 Feb. 1981
Name of Compiler Letha M. Williams
Address
City
Person No. 1 on this chart is the same person as
No. on chart No.

b. Date of Birth
p.b. Place of Birth
m. Date of Marriage
d. Date of Death
p.d Place of Death

16 (Father of No. 8)
    Continued on chart
17 (Mother of No. 8)
    Continued on chart
18 (Father of No. 9)
    Continued on chart
19 (Mother of No. 9)
    Continued on chart
20 (Father of No. 10)
    Continued on chart
21 (Mother of No. 10)
    Continued on chart
22 (Father of No. 11)
    Continued on chart
23 (Mother of No. 11)
    Continued on chart
24 (Father of No. 12)
    Continued on chart
25 (Mother of No. 12)
    Continued on chart
26 (Father of No. 13)
    Continued on chart
27 (Mother of No. 13)
    Continued on chart
28 (Father of No. 14)
    Continued on chart
29 (Mother of No. 14)
    Continued on chart
30 (Father of No. 15)
    Continued on chart
31 (Mother of No. 15)
    Continued

8 (Father of No. 4)
  TANKERSLEY
  b.
  p.b. NC
  m.
  d.
  p.d.
9 (Mother of No. 4)
  b.
  p.b. TN
  d.
  p.d.
10 (Father of No. 5)
  b.
  p.b.
  m.
  d.
  p.d.
11 (Mother of No. 5)
  b.
  p.b.
  d.
  p.d.
12 (Father of No. 6)
  b.
  p.b.
  m.
  d.
  p.d.
13 (Mother of No. 6)
  b.
  p.b.
  d.
  p.d.
14 (Father of No. 7)
  b.
  p.b.
  m.
  d.
  p.d.
15 (Mother of No. 7)
  b.
  p.b.
  d.
  p.d.

4 George TANKERSLEY
  (Father of No. 2)
  b. ca 1828
  p.b. NC
  m. (ED.—could this be
      m. instead of b. date)
  d.
  p.d.
  m/2: Sarah Jane Harbour (Haynes)
       (See # 29 chart 2)

5 Susan HALL
  (Mother of No. 2)
  b.
  p.b. TN
  d.
  p.d.

6 John BILLINGS
  (Father of No. 3)
  b.
  p.b. White Co., TN
  m. ca 1830 White Co., TN
  d. ca 1849
  p.d. Gonzales Co., TX
  bur: Willow Cem near Smiley

7 (Mother of No. 3)
  b.
  p.b. TN
  d.
  p.d. Terryville, TX

2 Benjamin L. TANKSLEY
  (Father of No. 1)
  b. 12 Nov 1831
  p.b. AL
  m.
  d. 10 May 1893
  p.d. Terryville, TX
       (near Yoakum)
  bur: Hebron Cem.

3 Mary Jane "Polly" BILLINGS
  (Mother of No. 1)
  b. 4 July 1835
  p.b. White Co., TN
  d. 5 Feb. 1895
  p.d. Terryville, DeWitt, TX

1 Georgann TANKSLEY
  (TANKERSLEY)
  b. 29 April 1860
  p.b. Terryville, DeWitt, TX
  m. before 1855 or before TX
  d. 2 Feb. 1936
  p.d. Brady, McCulloch, TX

John Bythell HAYNES, Jr. "Bice"
  (Husband or Wife of No. 1)
  b. 4 June 1862
  p.b. Feleciana Par., LA
  d. 27 Sept 1941
     Brady, TX
  p.d. Terryville, TX

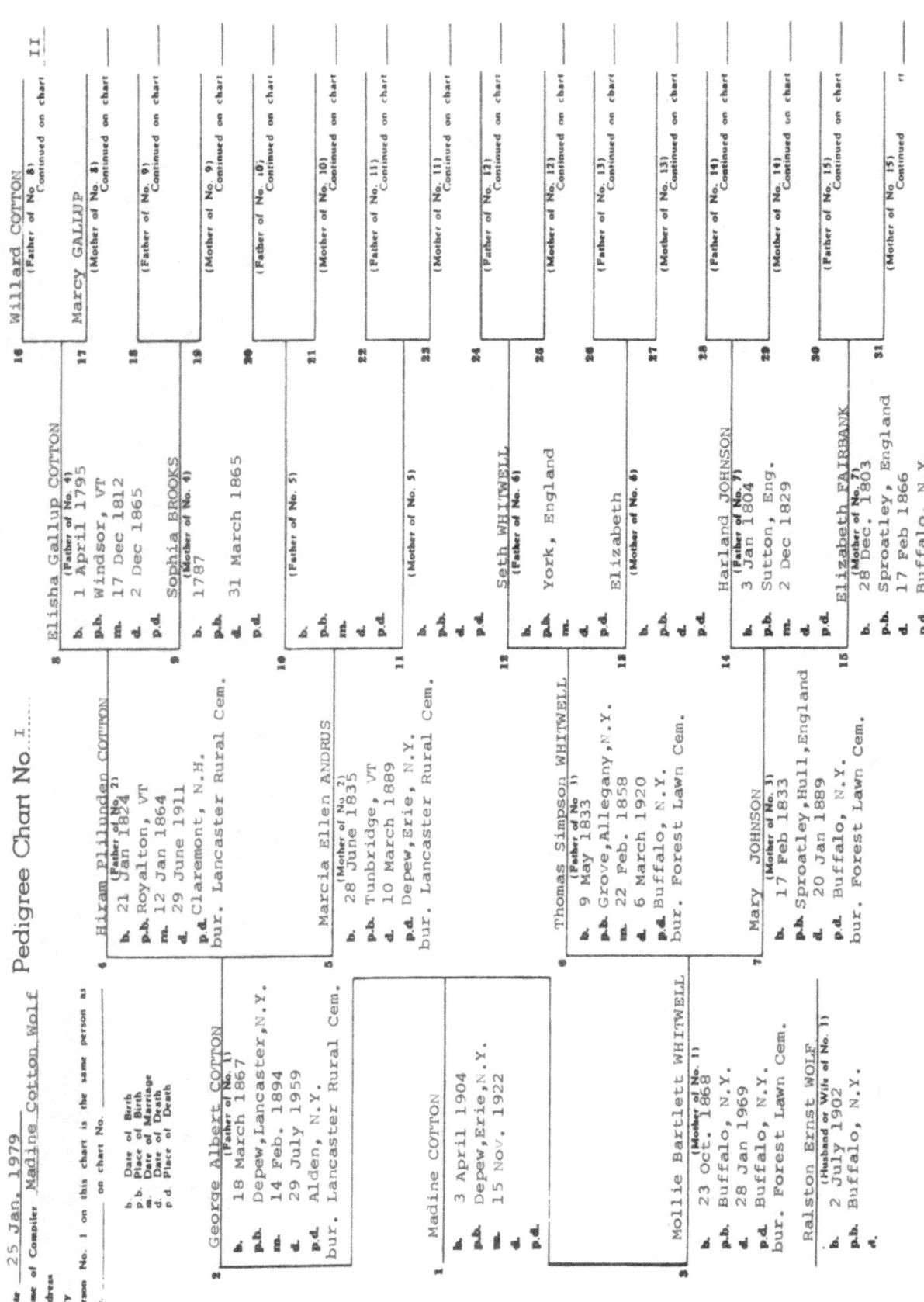

Date 25 Jan. 1979    Pedigree Chart No. 1

Name of Compiler Madine Cotton Wolf

Address

City

Person No. 1 on this chart is the same person as _____ on chart No. _____

    b.   Date of Birth
    p.b.   Place of Birth
    m.   Date of Marriage
    d.   Date of Death
    p.d.   Place of Death

**1   Madine COTTON**
b.   3 April 1904
p.b.   Depew, Erie, N.Y.
m.   15 Nov. 1922
d.
p.d.

**2   George Albert COTTON** (Father of No. 1)
b.   18 March 1867
p.b.   Depew, Lancaster, N.Y.
m.   14 Feb. 1894
d.   29 July 1959
p.d.   Alden, N.Y.
bur. Lancaster Rural Cem.

**3   Mollie Bartlett WHITWELL** (Mother of No. 1)
b.   23 Oct. 1868
p.b.   Buffalo, N.Y.
m.   28 Jan 1969
p.d.   Buffalo, N.Y.
bur. Forest Lawn Cem.

Ralston Ernst WOLF (Husband or Wife of No. 1)
b.   2 July 1902
p.b.   Buffalo, N.Y.
d.

**4   Hiram Philunder COTTON** (Father of No. 2)
b.   21 Jan 1824
p.b.   Royalton, VT
m.   12 Jan 1864
d.   29 June 1911
p.d.   Claremont, N.H.
bur. Lancaster Rural Cem.

**5   Marcia Ellen ANDRUS** (Mother of No. 2)
b.   28 June 1835
p.b.   Tunbridge, VT
d.   10 March 1889
p.d.   Depew, Erie, N.Y.
bur. Lancaster Rural Cem.

**6   Thomas Simpson WHITWELL** (Father of No. 3)
b.   9 May 1833
p.b.   Grove, Allegany, N.Y.
m.   22 Feb. 1858
d.   6 March 1920
p.d.   Buffalo, N.Y.
bur. Forest Lawn Cem.

**7   Mary JOHNSON** (Mother of No. 3)
b.   17 Feb 1833
p.b.   Sproatley, Hull, England
d.   20 Jan 1889
p.d.   Buffalo, N.Y.
bur. Forest Lawn Cem.

**8   Elisha Gallup COTTON** (Father of No. 4)
b.   1 April 1795
p.b.   Windsor, VT
m.   17 Dec 1812
d.   2 Dec 1865
p.d.

**9   Sophia BROOKS** (Mother of No. 4)
b.   1787
p.b.
d.   31 March 1865
p.d.

**10** (Father of No. 5)
b.
p.b.
m.
d.
p.d.

**11** (Mother of No. 5)
b.
p.b.
d.
p.d.

**12   Seth WHITWELL** (Father of No. 6)
b.
p.b.   York, England
m.
d.
p.d.

**13   Elizabeth** (Mother of No. 6)
b.
p.b.
d.
p.d.

**14   Harland JOHNSON** (Father of No. 7)
b.   3 Jan 1804
p.b.   Sutton, Eng.
m.   2 Dec 1829
d.
p.d.

**15   Elizabeth FAIRBANK** (Mother of No. 7)
b.   28 Dec. 1803
p.b.   Sproatley, England
d.   17 Feb 1866
p.d.   Buffalo, N.Y.

**16   Willard COTTON** (Father of No. 8)
Continued on chart II

**17   Marcy GALLUP** (Mother of No. 8)
Continued on chart _____

**18** (Father of No. 9)
Continued on chart _____

**19** (Mother of No. 9)
Continued on chart _____

**20** (Father of No. 10)
Continued on chart _____

**21** (Mother of No. 10)
Continued on chart _____

**22** (Father of No. 11)
Continued on chart _____

**23** (Mother of No. 11)
Continued on chart _____

**24** (Father of No. 12)
Continued on chart _____

**25** (Mother of No. 12)
Continued on chart _____

**26** (Father of No. 13)
Continued on chart _____

**27** (Mother of No. 13)
Continued on chart _____

**28** (Father of No. 14)
Continued on chart _____

**29** (Mother of No. 14)
Continued on chart _____

**30** (Father of No. 15)
Continued on chart _____

**31** (Mother of No. 15)
Continued

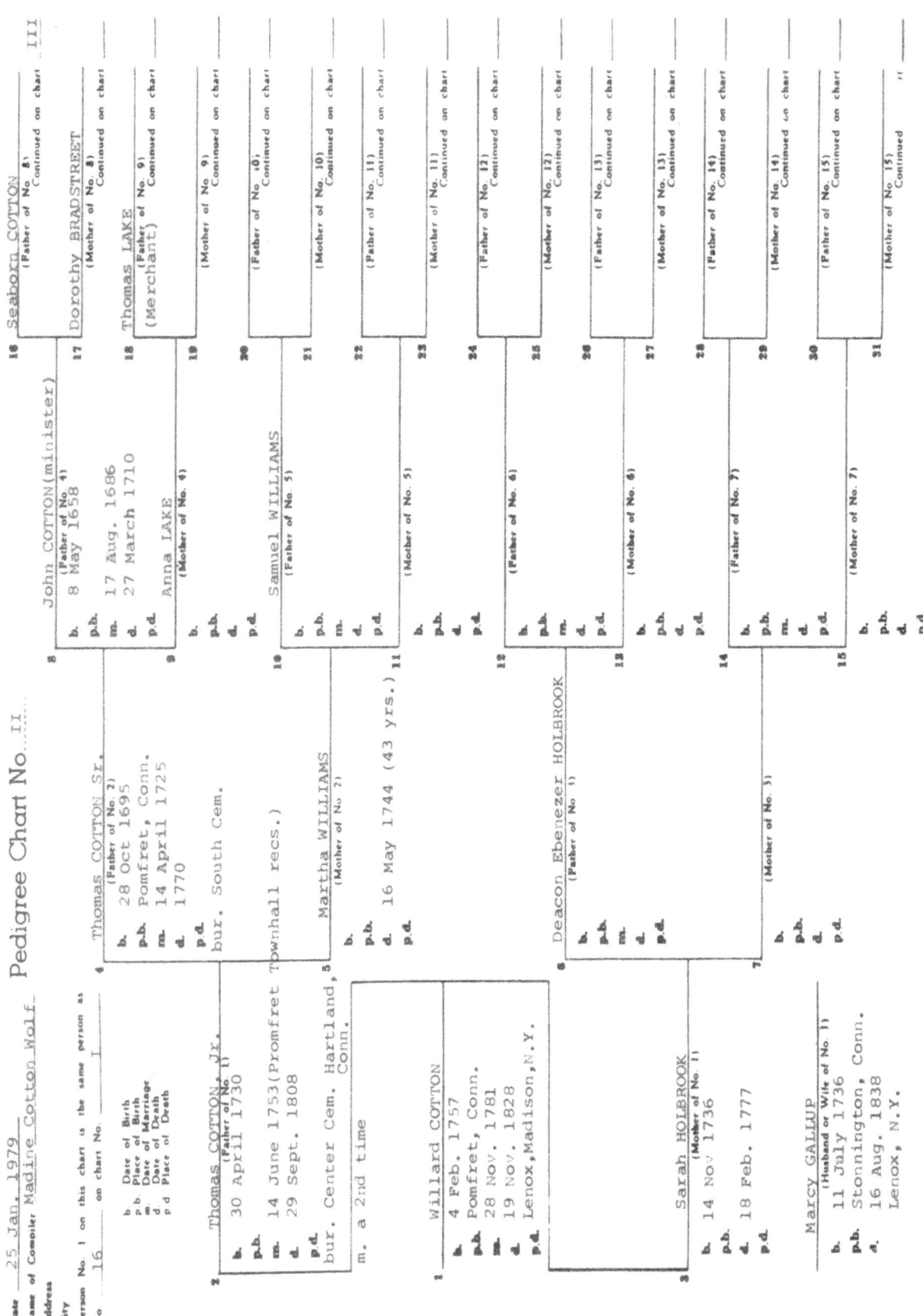

Pedigree Chart No. II

Date 25 Jan. 1979
Name of Compiler: Madine Cotton Wolf
Address
City
Person No. 1 on this chart is the same person as No. 16 on chart No. I

b. Date of Birth
p.b. Place of Birth
m. Date of Marriage
d. Date of Death
p.d Place of Death

1 — Willard COTTON
b. 4 Feb. 1757
p.b. Pomfret, Conn.
m. 28 Nov. 1781
d. 19 Nov. 1828
p.d. Lenox, Madison, N.Y.

Marcy GALLUP (Husband or Wife of No. 1)
b. 11 July 1736
p.b. Stonington, Conn.
d. 16 Aug. 1838
d. Lenox, N.Y.

2 — Thomas COTTON, Jr. (Father of No. 1)
b. 30 April 1730
p.b.
m. 14 June 1753 (Promfret Townhall recs.)
d. 29 Sept. 1808
p.d. bur. Center Cem. Hartland, Conn.
m. a 2nd time

3 — Sarah HOLBROOK (Mother of No. 1)
b. 14 Nov 1736
p.b.
d. 18 Feb. 1777
p.d.

4 — Thomas COTTON Sr. (Father of No. 2)
b. 28 Oct 1695
p.b. Pomfret, Conn.
m. 14 April 1725
d. 1770
p.d. bur. South Cem.

5 — Martha WILLIAMS (Mother of No. 2)
b.
p.b.
d. 16 May 1744 (43 yrs.)
p.d.

6 — Deacon Ebenezer HOLBROOK (Father of No. 3)
b.
p.b.
m.
d.
p.d.

7 — (Mother of No. 3)
b.
p.b.
d.
p.d.

8 — John COTTON (minister) (Father of No. 4)
b. 8 May 1658
p.b.
m. 17 Aug. 1686
d. 27 March 1710
p.d.

9 — Anna LAKE (Mother of No. 4)
b.
p.b.
d.
p.d.

10 — Samuel WILLIAMS (Father of No. 5)
b.
p.b.
m.
d.
p.d.

11 — (Mother of No. 5)
b.
p.b.
d.
p.d.

12 — (Father of No. 6)
13 — (Mother of No. 6)
14 — (Father of No. 7)
15 — (Mother of No. 7)

16 Seaborn COTTON (Father of No. 8) Continued on chart III
17 Dorothy BRADSTREET (Mother of No. 8) Continued on chart
18 Thomas LAKE (Merchant) (Father of No. 9) Continued on chart
19 (Mother of No. 9) Continued on chart
20 (Father of No. 10) Continued on chart
21 (Mother of No. 10) Continued on chart
22 (Father of No. 11) Continued on chart
23 (Mother of No. 11) Continued on chart
24 (Father of No. 12) Continued on chart
25 (Mother of No. 12) Continued on chart
26 (Father of No. 13) Continued on chart
27 (Mother of No. 13) Continued on chart
28 (Father of No. 14) Continued on chart
29 (Mother of No. 14) Continued on chart
30 (Father of No. 15) Continued on chart
31 (Mother of No. 15) Continued

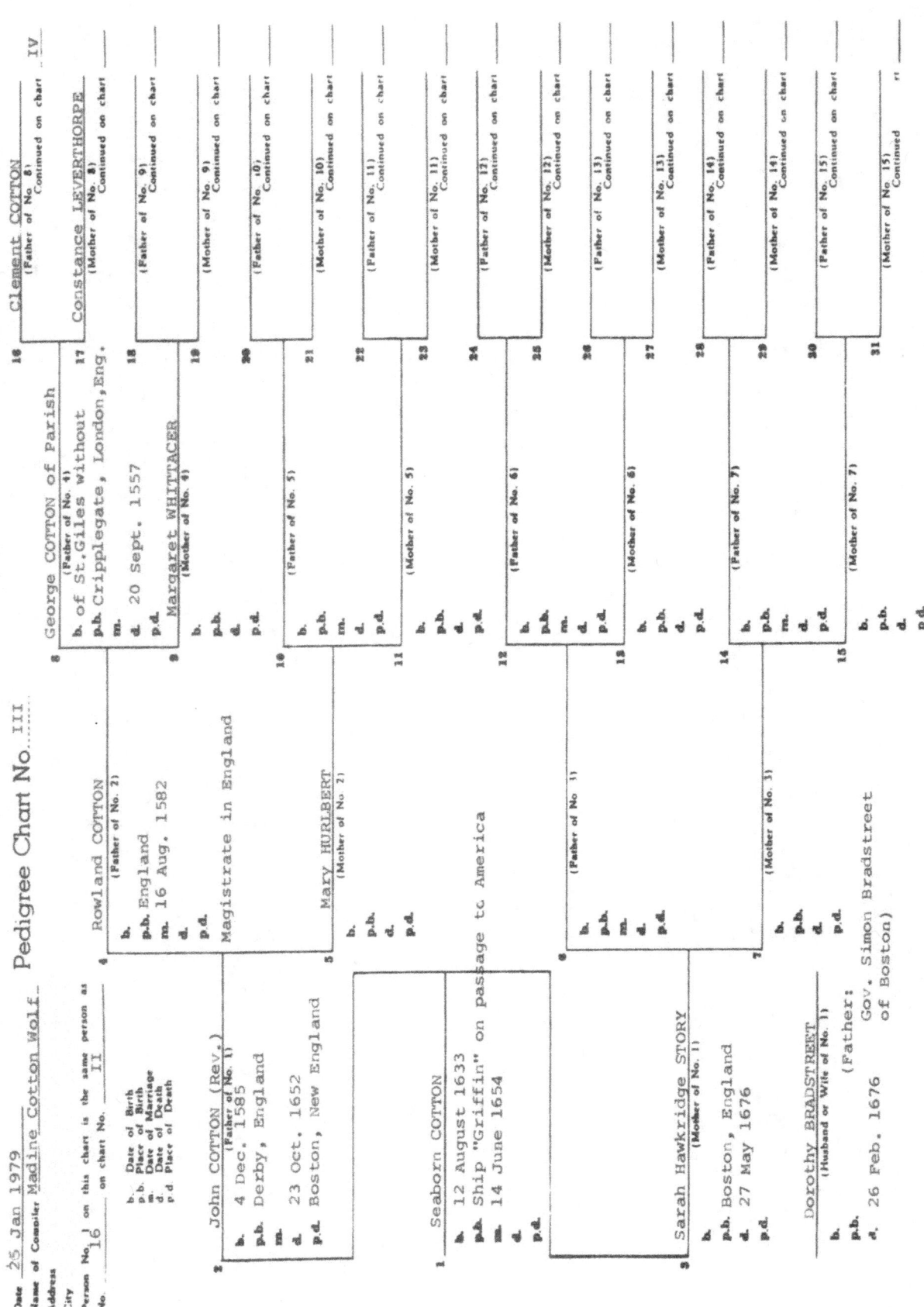

Pedigree Chart No. III

Date 25 Jan 1979
Name of Compiler Madine Cotton Wolf
Address
City
Person No. 1 on this chart is the same person as
No. 16 on chart No. II

b.  Date of Birth
p.b. Place of Birth
m.  Date of Marriage
p.d Place of Death

2  John COTTON (Rev.)
   (Father of No. 1)
b.  4 Dec. 1585
p.b. Derby, England
m.
d.  23 Oct. 1652
p.d. Boston, New England

4  Rowland COTTON
   (Father of No. 2)
b.
p.b. England
m.  16 Aug. 1582
d.
p.d.
Magistrate in England

5  Mary HURLBERT
   (Mother of No. 2)
b.
p.b.
d.
p.d.

8  George COTTON of Parish
   (Father of No. 4)
b. of St.Giles without
p.b. Cripplegate, London, Eng.
m.
d. 20 Sept. 1557
p.d.

9  Margaret WHITTACER
   (Mother of No. 4)
b.
p.b.
d.
p.d.

10  (Father of No. 5)
b.
p.b.
m.
d.
p.d.

11  (Mother of No. 5)
b.
p.b.
d.
p.d.

16  Clement COTTON
    (Father of No. 8)
    Continued on chart IV

17  Constance LEVERTHORPE
    (Mother of No. 8)
    Continued on chart

18  (Father of No. 9)
    Continued on chart

19  (Mother of No. 9)
    Continued on chart

20  (Father of No. 10)
    Continued on chart

21  (Mother of No. 10)
    Continued on chart

22  (Father of No. 11)
    Continued on chart

23  (Mother of No. 11)
    Continued on chart

24  (Father of No. 12)
    Continued on chart

25  (Mother of No. 12)
    Continued on chart

26  (Father of No. 13)
    Continued on chart

27  (Mother of No. 13)
    Continued on chart

28  (Father of No. 14)
    Continued on chart

29  (Mother of No. 14)
    Continued on chart

30  (Father of No. 15)
    Continued on chart

31  (Mother of No. 15)
    Continued on chart

12  (Father of No. 6)
b.
p.b.
m.
d.
p.d.

13  (Mother of No. 6)
b.
p.b.
d.
p.d.

14  (Father of No. 7)
b.
p.b.
m.
d.
p.d.

15  (Mother of No. 7)
b.
p.b.
d.
p.d.

6  (Father of No. 1)
b.
p.b.
m.
d.
p.d.

7  (Mother of No. 3)
b.
p.b.
d.
p.d.

1  Seaborn COTTON
b.  12 August 1633
p.b. Ship "Griffin" on passage to America
m.  14 June 1654
d.
p.d.

3  Sarah Hawkridge STORY
   (Mother of No. 1)
b.
p.b. Boston, England
d.  27 May 1676
p.d.

Dorothy BRADSTREET
(Husband or Wife of No. 1)
(Father:     Gov. Simon Bradstreet
b.
p.b.                    of Boston)
d.  26 Feb. 1676

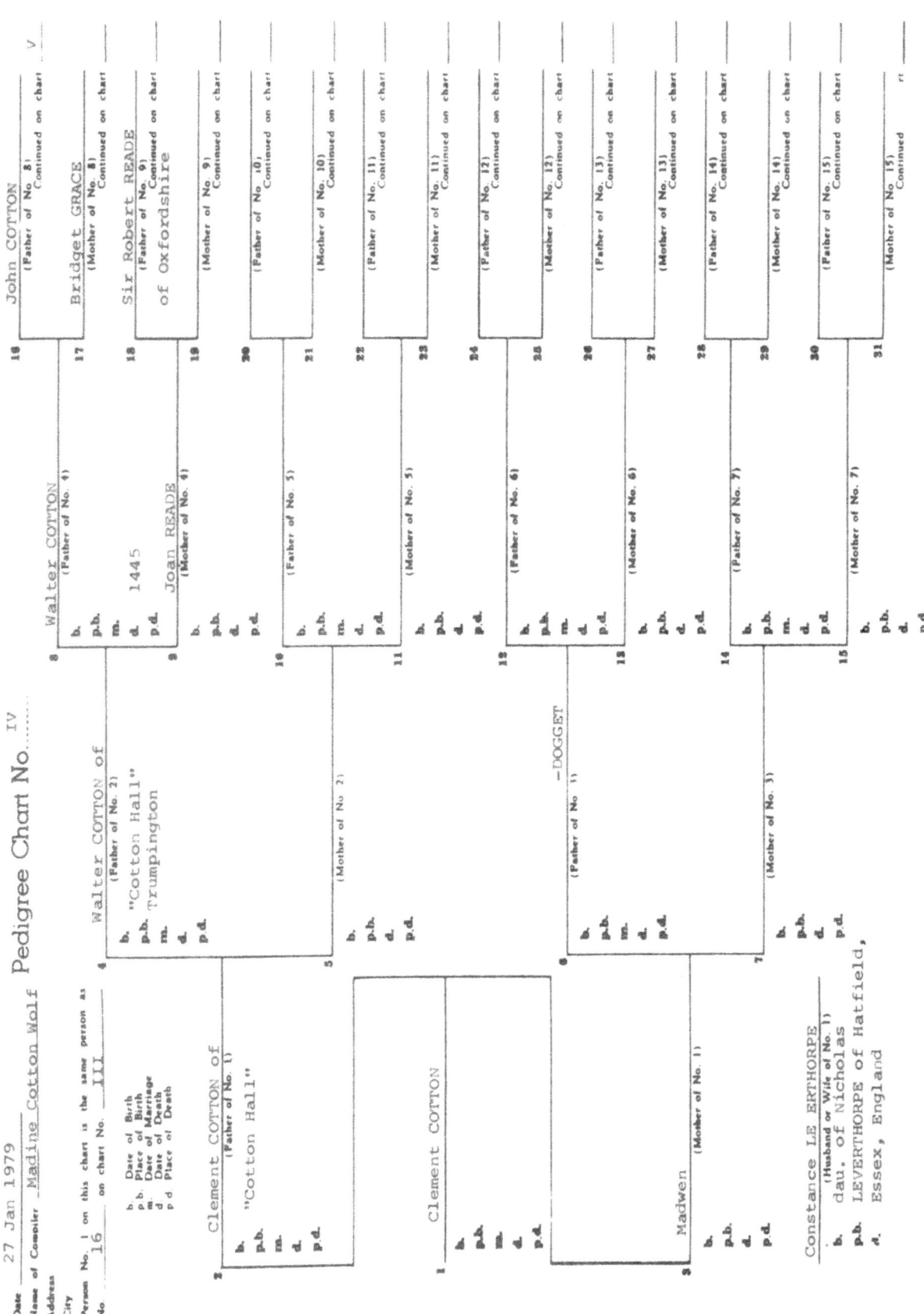

Pedigree Chart No. IV

Date 27 Jan 1979
Name of Compiler Madine Cotton Wolf
Address
City
Person No. 1 on this chart is the same person as
No. 16 on chart No. III

b. Date of Birth
p.b. Place of Birth
m. Date of Marriage
d. Date of Death
p.d Place of Death

16  John COTTON (Father of No. 8) Continued on chart
17  Bridget GRACE (Mother of No. 8) Continued on chart
18  Sir Robert READE (Father of No. 9) Continued on chart
     of Oxfordshire
19  (Mother of No. 9) Continued on chart
20  (Father of No. 10) Continued on chart
21  (Mother of No. 10) Continued on chart
22  (Father of No. 11) Continued on chart
23  (Mother of No. 11) Continued on chart
24  (Father of No. 12) Continued on chart
25  (Mother of No. 12) Continued on chart
26  (Father of No. 13) Continued on chart
27  (Mother of No. 13) Continued on chart
28  (Father of No. 14) Continued on chart
29  (Mother of No. 14) Continued on chart
30  (Father of No. 15) Continued on chart
31  (Mother of No. 15) Continued

8  Walter COTTON (Father of No. 4)
   b.
   p.b.
   m. 1445
   d.
   p.d.
9  Joan READE (Mother of No. 4)
   b.
   p.b.
   d.
   p.d.
10 (Father of No. 5)
   b.
   p.b.
   m.
   d.
   p.d.
11 (Mother of No. 5)
12 (Father of No. 6)
   b.
   p.b.
   m.
   d.
   p.d.
13 (Mother of No. 6)
   b.
   p.b.
   d.
   p.d.
14 (Father of No. 7)
   b.
   p.b.
   m.
   d.
   p.d.
15 (Mother of No. 7)
   b.
   p.b.
   d.
   p.d.

4  Walter COTTON of (Father of No. 2)
   b.
   p.b. "Cotton Hall"
   m. Trumpington
   d.
   p.d.
5  (Mother of No. 2)
   b.
   p.b.
   d.
   p.d.
6  —DOGGET (Father of No. 1)
   b.
   p.b.
   m.
   d.
   p.d.
7  (Mother of No. 3)
   b.
   p.b.
   d.
   p.d.

2  Clement COTTON of (Father of No. 1)
   b.
   p.b. "Cotton Hall"
   m.
   d.
   p.d.
3  Madwen (Mother of No. 1)
   b.
   p.b.
   d.
   p.d.

1  Clement COTTON
   b.
   p.b.
   m.
   d.
   p.d.

Constance LE ERTHORPE
   (Husband or Wife of No. 1)
   dau. of Nicholas
   p.b. LEVERTHORPE of Hatfield,
   d. Essex, England

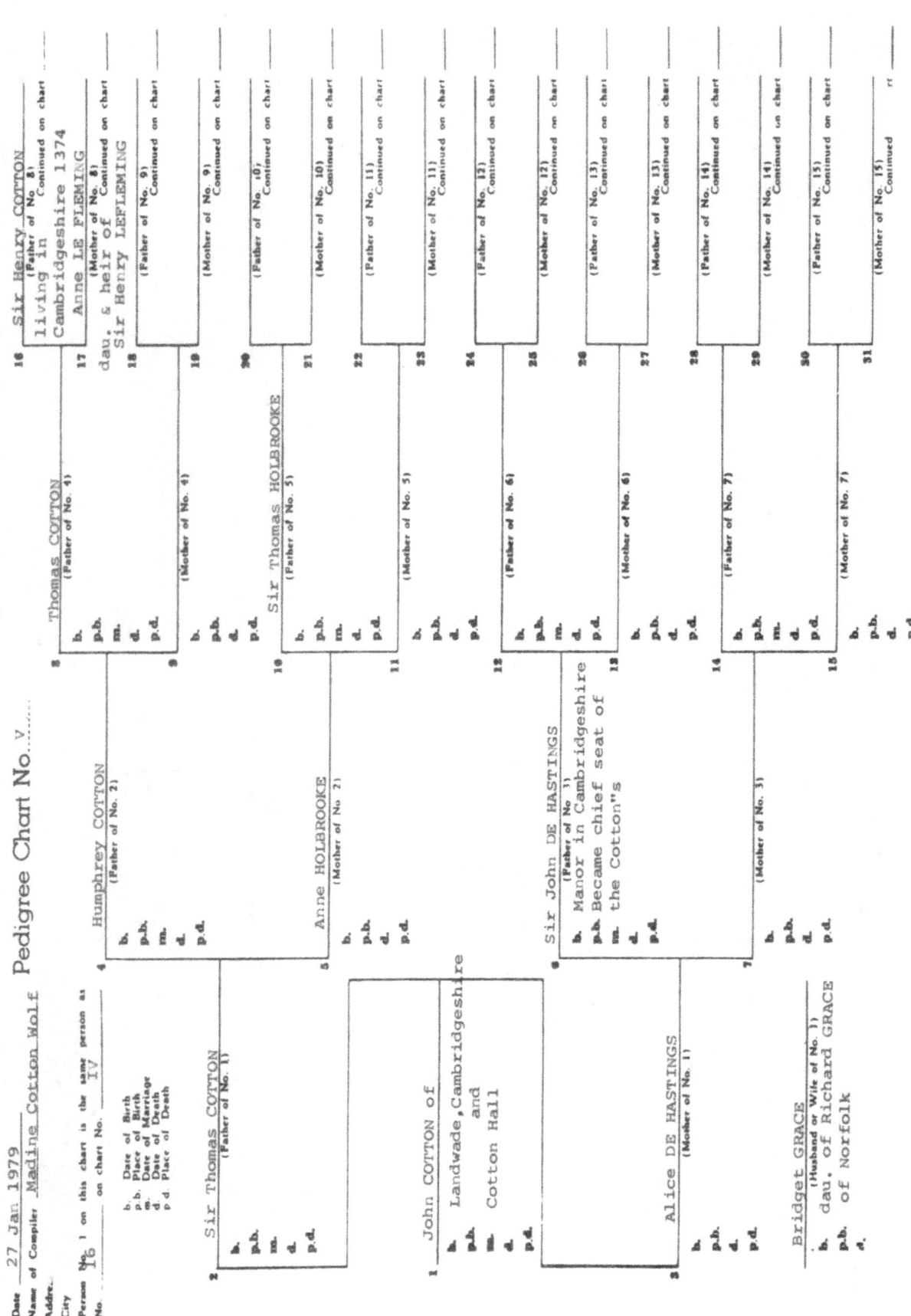

# Pedigree Chart No. V

Date 27 Jan 1979

Name of Compiler Madine Cotton Wolf

Address

City

Person No. 1 on this chart is the same person as No. 16 on chart No. IV

b. Date of Birth
p.b. Place of Birth
m. Date of Marriage
d. Date of Death
p.d. Place of Death

1 John COTTON of Landwade, Cambridgeshire and Cotton Hall

2 Sir Thomas COTTON (Father of No. 1)

3 Alice DE HASTINGS (Mother of No. 1)

. Bridget GRACE (Husband or Wife of No. 1) b. dau. of Richard GRACE p.b. of Norfolk

4 Humphrey COTTON (Father of No. 2)

5 Anne HOLBROOKE (Mother of No. 2)

6 Sir John DE HASTINGS (Father of No. 3) b. Manor in Cambridgeshire p.b. Became chief seat of m. the Cotton"s

7 (Mother of No. 3)

8 Thomas COTTON (Father of No. 4)

9 (Mother of No. 4)

10 Sir Thomas HOLBROOKE (Father of No. 5)

11 (Mother of No. 5)

12 (Father of No. 6)

13 (Mother of No. 6)

14 (Father of No. 7)

15 (Mother of No. 7)

16 Sir Henry COTTON (Father of No. 8) living in Cambridgeshire 1374 Continued on chart

17 Anne LE FLEMING (Mother of No. 8) dau. & heir of Continued on chart Sir Henry LEFLEMING

18 (Father of No. 9) Continued on chart

19 (Mother of No. 9) Continued on chart

20 (Father of No. 10) Continued on chart

21 (Mother of No. 10) Continued on chart

22 (Father of No. 11) Continued on chart

23 (Mother of No. 11) Continued on chart

24 (Father of No. 12) Continued on chart

25 (Mother of No. 12) Continued on chart

26 (Father of No. 13) Continued on chart

27 (Mother of No. 13) Continued on chart

28 (Father of No. 14) Continued on chart

29 (Mother of No. 14) Continued on chart

30 (Father of No. 15) Continued on chart

31 (Mother of No. 15) Continued

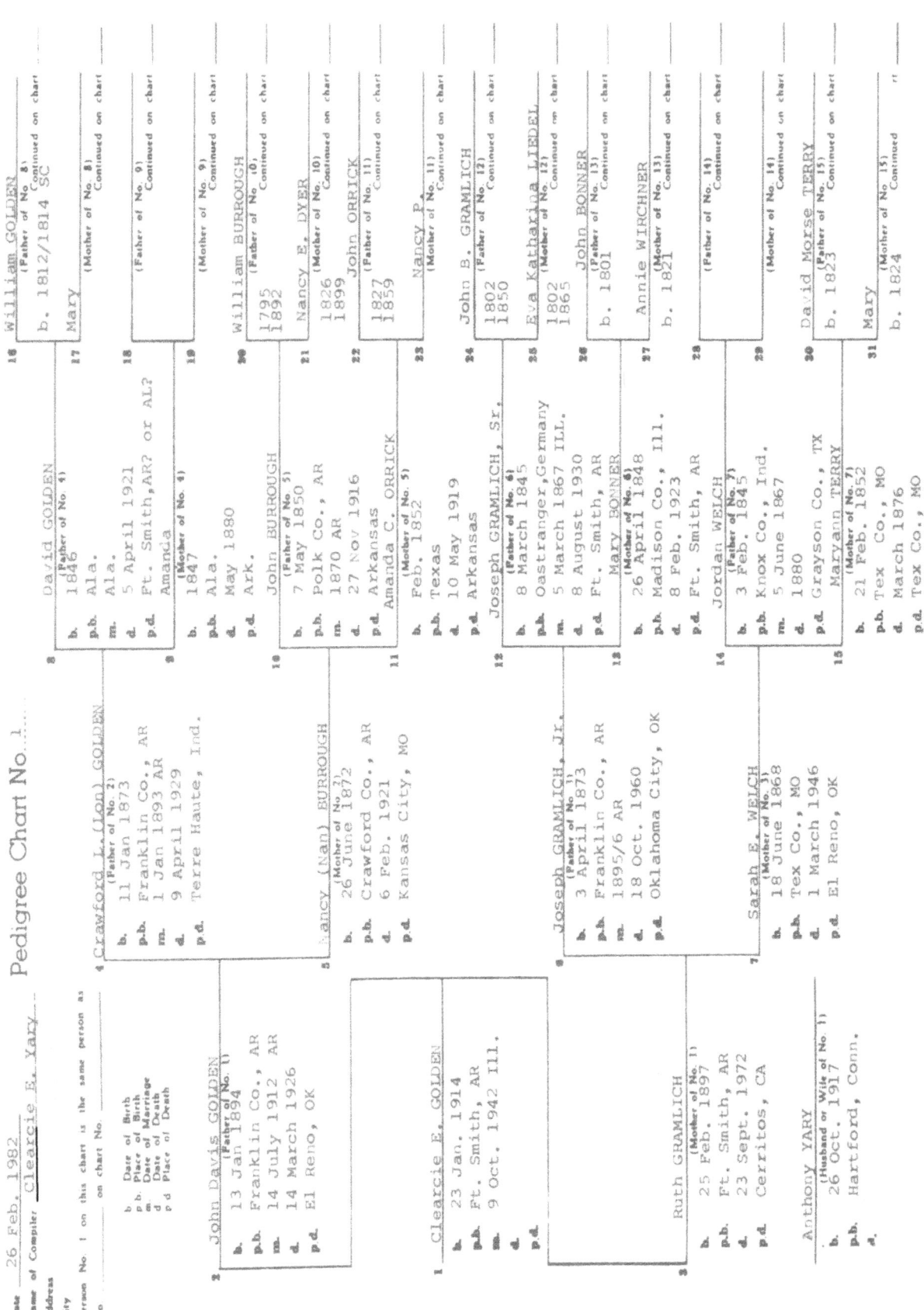

Pedigree Chart No. 1

Date    26 Feb. 1982
Name of Compiler  Clearcie E. Yary
Address
City
Person No. 1 on this chart is the same person as
No.                on chart No.

b    Date of Birth
p.b  Place of Birth
m    Date of Marriage
d    Date of Death
p.d  Place of Death

1  Clearcie E. GOLDEN
b.    23 Jan. 1914
p.b.  Ft. Smith, AR
m.    9 Oct. 1942 Ill.
d.
p.d.

(Husband or Wife of No. 1)
Anthony YARY
b.    26 Oct. 1917
p.b.  Hartford, Conn.
d.

2  John Davis GOLDEN
(Father of No. 1)
b.    13 Jan 1894
p.b.  Franklin Co., AR
m.    14 July 1912 AR
d.    14 March 1926
p.d.  El Reno, OK

3  Ruth GRAMLICH
(Mother of No. 1)
b.    25 Feb. 1897
p.b.  Ft. Smith, AR
d.    23 Sept. 1972
p.d.  Cerritos, CA

4  Crawford L. (Ion) GOLDEN
(Father of No. 2)
b.    11 Jan 1873
p.b.  Franklin Co., AR
m.    1 Jan 1893 AR
d.    9 April 1929
p.d.  Terre Haute, Ind.

5  Nancy (Nan) BURROUGH
(Mother of No. 2)
b.    26 June 1872
p.b.  Crawford Co., AR
d.    6 Feb. 1921
p.d.  Kansas City, MO

6  Joseph GRAMLICH, Jr.
(Father of No. 3)
b.    3 April 1873
p.b.  Franklin Co., AR
m.    1895/6 AR
d.    18 Oct. 1960
p.d.  Oklahoma City, OK

7  Sarah E. WELCH
(Mother of No. 3)
b.    18 June 1868
p.b.  Tex Co., MO
d.    1 March 1946
p.d.  El Reno, OK

8  David GOLDEN
(Father of No. 4)
b.    1846
p.b.  Ala.
m.    5 April 1921
p.d.  Ft. Smith,AR? or AL?

9  Amanda
(Mother of No. 4)
b.    1847
p.b.  Ala.
d.    May 1880
p.d.  Ark.

10  John BURROUGH
(Father of No. 5)
b.    7 May 1850
p.b.  Polk Co., AR
d.    27 Nov 1916
p.d.  Arkansas

11  Amanda C. ORRICK
(Mother of No. 5)
b.    Feb. 1852
p.b.  Texas
d.    10 May 1919
p.d.  Arkansas

12  Joseph GRAMLICH, Sr.
(Father of No. 6)
b.    8 March 1845
p.b.  Oastranger,Germany
m.    5 March 1867 ILL.
d.    8 August 1930
p.d.  Ft. Smith, AR

13  Mary BONNER
(Mother of No. 6)
b.    26 April 1848
p.b.  Madison Co., Ill.
d.    8 Feb. 1923
p.d.  Ft. Smith, AR

14  Jordan WELCH
(Father of No. 7)
b.    3 Feb. 1845
p.b.  Knox Co., Ind.
m.    5 June 1867
d.    1880
p.d.  Grayson Co., TX

15  Maryann TERRY
(Mother of No. 7)
b.    21 Feb. 1852
p.b.  Tex Co., MO
d.    March 1876
p.d.  Tex Co., MO

16  William GOLDEN
(Father of No. 8)
b. 1812/1814 SC        Continued on chart

17  Mary
(Mother of No. 8)
Continued on chart

18  (Father of No. 9)
Continued on chart

19  (Mother of No. 9)
Continued on chart

20  William BURROUGH
(Father of No. 10)
1795        Continued on chart
1892

21  Nancy E. DYER
(Mother of No. 10)
1826        Continued on chart
1899

22  John ORRICK
(Father of No. 11)
1827        Continued on chart
1859

23  Nancy P.
(Mother of No. 11)
Continued on chart

24  John B. GRAMLICH
(Father of No. 12)
1802        Continued on chart
1850

25  Eva Katharina LIEDEL
(Mother of No. 12)
1802        Continued on chart
1865

26  John BONNER
(Father of No. 13)
b. 1801        Continued on chart

27  Annie WIRCHNER
(Mother of No. 13)
b. 1821        Continued on chart

28  (Father of No. 14)
Continued on chart

29  (Mother of No. 14)
Continued on chart

30  David Morse TERRY
(Father of No. 15)
b. 1823        Continued on chart

31  Mary
(Mother of No. 15)
b. 1824        Continued on chart

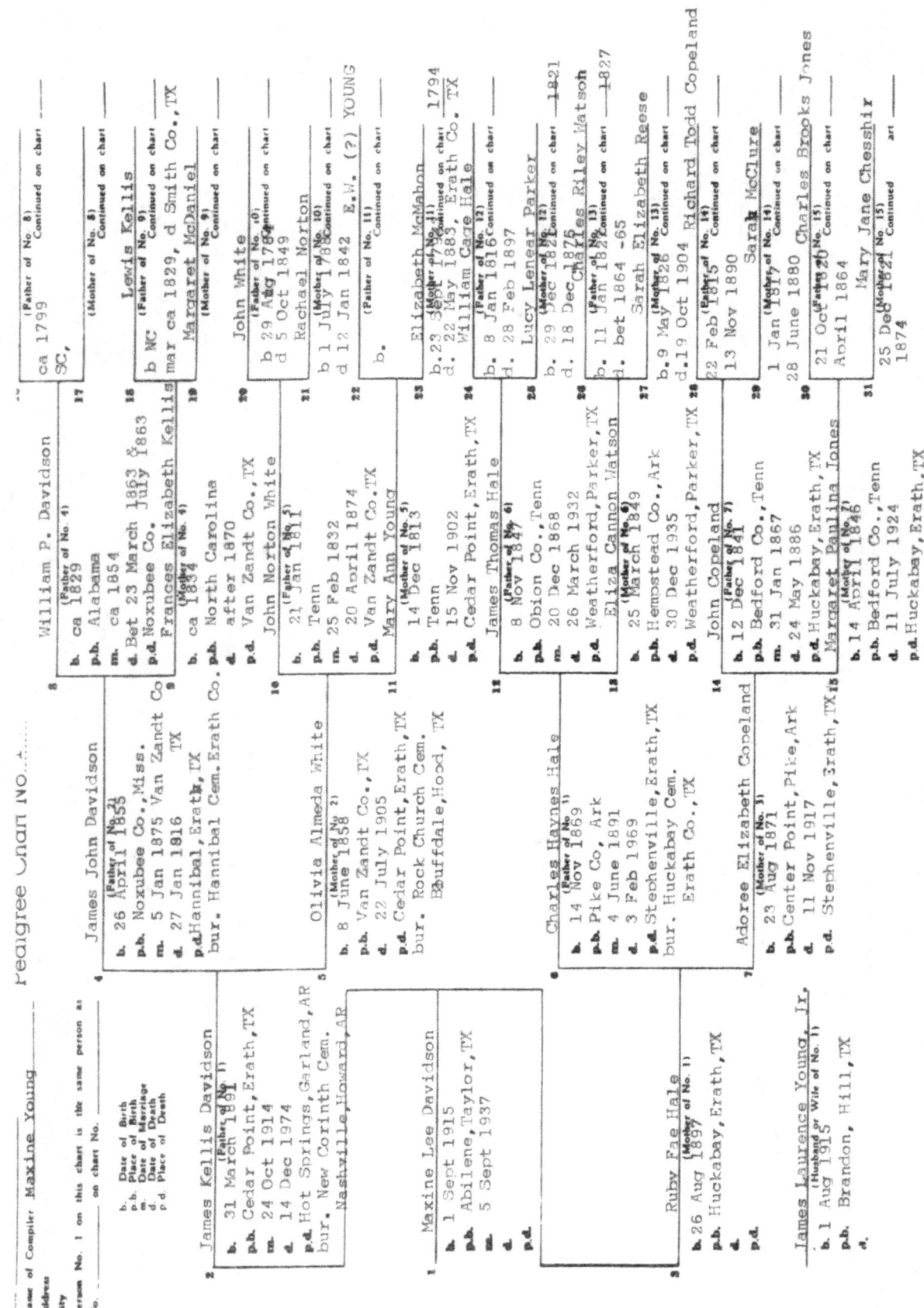

Pedigree Chart No. _____

Name of Compiler Maxine Young
Address
City
Person No. 1 on this chart is the same person as
No. _____ on chart No. _____

b.   Date of Birth
p.b.   Place of Birth
m.   Date of Marriage
d.   Date of Death
p.d.   Place of Death

**1**   Maxine Lee Davidson
b. 1 Sept 1915
p.b. Abilene, Taylor, TX
m. 5 Sept 1937
d.
p.d.

**2**   James Kellis Davidson (Father of No. 1)
b. 31 March 1891
p.b. Cedar Point, Erath, TX
m. 24 Oct 1914
d. 14 Dec 1974
p.d. Hot Springs, Garland, AR
bur. New Corinth Cem. Nashville Howard, AR

**3**   Ruby Fae Hale (Mother of No. 1)
b. 26 Aug 1897
p.b. Huckabay, Erath, TX
d.
p.d.

**4**   James John Davidson (Father of No. 2)
b. 26 April 1855
p.b. Noxubee Co., Miss.
m. 5 Jan 1875 Van Zandt Co
d. 27 Jan 1916   TX
p.d. Hannibal, Erath, TX
bur. Hannibal Cem. Erath Co.

**5**   Olivia Almeda White (Mother of No. 2)
b. 8 June 1858
p.b. Van Zandt Co., TX
d. 22 July 1905
p.d. Cedar Point, Erath, TX
bur. Rock Church Cem. Buffdale, Hood, TX

**6**   Charles Haynes Hale (Father of No. 3)
b. 14 Nov 1869
p.b. Pike Co, Ark
m. 4 June 1891
d. 3 Feb 1969
p.d. Stephenville, Erath, TX
bur. Huckabay Cem. Erath Co., TX

**7**   Adoree Elizabeth Copeland (Mother of No. 3)
b. 23 Aug 1871
p.b. Center Point, Pike, Ark
d. 11 Nov 1917
p.d. Stephenville, Erath, TX

James Laurence Young, Jr. (Husband or Wife of No. 1)
b. 1 Aug 1915
p.b. Brandon, Hill, TX
d.

**8**   William P. Davidson (Father of No. 4)
b. ca 1829
p.b. Alabama
m.
d. Bet 23 March 1863 & 1863
p.d. Noxubee Co.

**9**   Frances Elizabeth Kellis (Mother of No. 4)
b. ca 1834
p.b. North Carolina
d. after 1870
p.d. Van Zandt Co., TX

**10**   John Norton White (Father of No. 5)
b. 21 Jan 1811
p.b. Tenn
m. 25 Feb 1832
d. 20 April 1874
p.d. Van Zandt Co., TX

**11**   Mary Ann Young (Mother of No. 5)
b. 14 Dec 1813
p.b. Tenn
d. 15 Nov 1902
p.d. Cedar Point, Erath, TX

**12**   James Thomas Hale (Father of No. 6)
b. 8 Nov 1847
p.b. Obion Co., Tenn
m. 20 Dec 1868
d. 26 March 1932
p.d. Weatherford, Parker, TX

**13**   Eliza Cannon Watson (Mother of No. 6)
b. 25 March 1849
p.b. Hempstead Co., Ark
d. 30 Dec 1935
p.d. Weatherford, Parker, TX

**14**   John Copeland (Father of No. 7)
b. 12 Dec 1841
p.b. Bedford Co., Tenn
m. 31 Jan 1867
d. 24 May 1886
p.d. Huckabay, Erath, TX

**15**   Margaret Paulina Jones (Mother of No. 7)
b. 14 April 1846
p.b. Bedford Co., Tenn
d. 11 July 1924
p.d. Huckabay, Erath, TX

**16**   (Father of No. 8)
ca 1799
SC,
_____ (Continued on chart) _____

**17**   (Mother of No. 8)
_____ Continued on chart

**18**   Lewis Kellis (Father of No. 9)
b. NC
mar ca 1829, d Smith Co., TX
_____ Continued on chart

**19**   Margaret McDaniel (Mother of No. 9)
_____ Continued on chart

**20**   John White (Father of No. 10)
b. 29 Aug 1784
d. 5 Oct 1849
_____ Continued on chart

**21**   Rachael Norton (Mother of No. 10)
b. 1 July 1788
d. 12 Jan 1842
_____ Continued on chart

**22**   E.W. (?) YOUNG (Father of No. 11)
b.
_____ Continued on chart

**23**   Elizabeth McMahon   1794 (Mother of No. 11)
b. 23 Sept 1794
d. 22 May 1883, Erath Co., TX
_____ Continued on chart

**24**   William Cage Hale (Father of No. 12)
b. 8 Jan 1816
d. 28 Feb 1897
_____ Continued on chart

**25**   Lucy Lenear Parker   1821 (Mother of No. 12)
b. 29 Dec 1821
d. 18 Dec 1876
_____ Continued on chart

**26**   Charles Riley Watson   1827 (Father of No. 13)
b. 11 Jan 1827
d. bet 1864 -65
_____ Continued on chart

**27**   Sarah Elizabeth Reese (Mother of No. 13)
b. 9 May 1826
d. 19 Oct 1904
_____ Continued on chart

**28**   Richard Todd Copeland (Father of No. 14)
b. 22 Feb 1815
d. 13 Nov 1890
_____ Continued on chart

**29**   Sarah McClure (Mother of No. 14)
b. 1 Jan 1817
d. 28 June 1880
_____ Continued on chart

**30**   Charles Brooks Jones (Father of No. 15)
b. 21 Oct 1820
d. April 1864
_____ Continued on chart

**31**   Mary Jane Chesshir (Mother of No. 15)
b. 25 Dec 1821
d. 1874
_____ Continued on chart

Pedigree Chart No. _____

Name of Compiler: J. L. Young, Jr.
Address: _____
City: _____

Person No. ___ 1 ___ on this chart is the same person as
No. _____ on chart No. _____

b   Date of Birth
p.b   Place of Birth
m.   Date of Marriage
d.   Date of Death
p.d   Place of Death

**1** James Laurence Young, Jr.
b. 1 Aug 1915
p.b. Brandon, Hill Co., TX
m. _____
d. _____
p.d. _____

**2** James Laurence Young (Father of No. 1)
b. 10 Jan 1893
p.b. Brandon, Hill Co., TX
m. 31 Oct 1914
d. 4 April 1969
p.d. Weslaco, Hidalgo, TX
bur. Weslaco City Cem.

**3** Ruth Elzirah Millard (Mother of No. 1)
b. 1 Feb 1894
p.b. Woodford, Old Pickens, IT
d. _____
p.d. _____

**4** William Clayton Young (Father of No. 2)
b. 27 July 1853
p.b. Loundesville, Abbe., SC
m. 23 Dec 1889
d. 16 Jan 1952
p.d. Mineral Wells, Palo Pinto Co., TX
bur. Woodland Park Cem.

**5** Cora Day (Mother of No. 2)
b. 13 July 1871
p.b. Overton, Rusk Co., TX
d. 27 March 1920
p.d. Brandon, Hill Co., TX
bur. Brandon Cem.

**6** Isaac Millard (Father of No. 3)
b. 29 Aug 1855
p.b. Bluff City, Sullivan Co., TN
m. 4 Oct 1891
d. 15 July 1936
p.d. Hillsboro, Hill Co., TX
bur. Old Hillsboro Cem.

**7** Emma Laura Mead (Mother of No. 3)
b. 13 Sept 1873
p.b. Prairie Co., AR
d. 10 Oct 1949
p.d. Hillsboro, Hill, TX
bur. Old Hillsboro Cem.

**8** James Martin Young (Father of No. 4)
b. 29 Nov 1819
p.b. Loundesville, Abbe., SC
m. 8 Nov 1842, Pickens Co.
d. 24 July 1905
p.d. Loundesville, Abbe., SC

**9** Mary Elizabeth Clayton (Mother of No. 4)
b. 1825
p.b. Pickens Co., SC
d. 23 Oct 1856
p.d. Loundesville, Abbe., SC

**10** Jacob Laurence Day (Father of No. 5)
b. 21 July 1845
p.b. Pickens Co., SC
m. _____
d. 30 Oct 1870
p.d. Overton, Rusk Co., TX

**11** Georgia Florence (Mother of No. 5)
b. 26 Feb 1850
p.b. Montgomery, Ala.
d. 26 March 1886
p.d. Overton, Rusk, TX

**12** George Millard (Father of No. 6)
b. 25 April 1823
p.b. Sullivan Co., TN
m. 21 Nov 1844
d. 18 May 1864
p.d. KIA CSA below Richmond, VA,

**13** Elzirah Morrell (Mother of No. 6)
b. 5 June 1836
p.b. Sullivan Co., TN
d. 10 Sept 1884
p.d. Hillsboro, Hill, TX

**14** Henry Clay Mead/Meade (Father of No. 7)
b. 2 Aug 1844
p.b. Hendricks Co., Ind.
m. ca 1867
d. 3 May 1912
p.d. Lane, Atoka Co., OK

**15** Mary Frances Ann Rooks (Mother of No. 7)
b. 6 Aug 1848 or 1847
p.b. Tennessee
d. 21 July 1932
p.d. Atoka Co., OK

**16** John Clayton (Father of No. 8)
d. 7 June 1864    Sarah Pratt, b. 18 Feb 1796
   d. 22 Jan 1868

**17** (Continued on chart)
John Clayton
d. Before 1850

**18** Hannah --- b. ca 1800 (Father of No. 9)

**19** (Mother of No. 9)
Benjamin Day, Jr.
d. Bef. Nov 1848

**20** (Father of No. 10)
Jane Elizabeth Geurin or Guerin
b. 1825
d. before 1855

**21** (Mother of No. 10)
Simeon Florence
b. 7 Dec 1823
d. 26 Oct 1909

**22** (Father of No. 11)
Frances Muckelroy
b. ca 1825
d. ca 1881

**23** (Mother of No. 11)
Abia Millard
b. 7 May 1789
d. 17 Jan 1846

**24** (Father of No. 12)
Mary Weaver, b. 20 Oct 1791
d. 23 March   1884

**25** (Mother of No. 12)
Isaac Morrell, b. 18 May 1799
d. 7 Oct 1870

**26** (Father of No. 13)
Susannah Crumley, b. 6 Jan 1802
d. 29 May 1878

**27** (Mother of No. 13)
John Adam Mead/Meade
b. Bet.1804-1806
d. Bet. 1860-1870

**28** (Father of No. 14)
Sarah Amanda Clay
b. ca 1801 died ca 1896

**29** (Mother of No. 14)
---Fullerton? Brooks? or Rooks

**30** (Father of No. 15)
Mary F. Canada

**31** (Mother of No. 15)

Maxine Lee Davidson (Husband or Wife of No. 1)
b. 1 Sept 1915
p.b. Abilene, Taylor Co., TX
d. _____

# SURNAME INDEX

| Surname | Page | | | | |
|---|---|---|---|---|---|
| Lou | 33 | | | | |
| Loyd | 67 | | | | |
| Lynch | 57 | | | | |
| Lynn | 33 | 40 | | | |
| Lyons | 11 | | | | |
| Mahoney | 43 | | | | |
| Man(u)ery | 59 | | | | |
| Mann | 16 | 19 | | | |
| Manning | 68 | 69 | 73 | 67 | |
| Maquire | 23 | | | | |
| Marberry | 16 | | | | |
| Martin | 25 | 63 | 64 | | |
| Mason | 53 | | | | |
| Masterson | 17 | | | | |
| Mathews | 69 | | | | |
| Matlock | 43 | | | | |
| Mauldin | 74 | 76 | | | |
| Maupin | 12 | | | | |
| May | 22 | | | | |
| Mayhan | 43 | | | | |
| Mazzini | 44 | 45 | | | |
| McAlester | 41 | | | | |
| McCharen | 23 | 27 | | | |
| McClure | 92 | | | | |
| McCollum | 60 | 63 | | | |
| McCurry | 50 | | | | |
| McDaniel | 66 | 92 | | | |
| McDonald | 50 | 66 | | | |
| McEache | 23 | | | | |
| McEachern | 27 | | | | |
| McFarland | 13 | | | | |
| McGill | 48 | | | | |
| McGrew | 57 | | | | |
| McKiever | 18 | | | | |
| McKinley | 27 | | | | |
| McKinney | 57 | | | | |
| McLevaine | 78 | 79 | | | |
| McMahon | 92 | | | | |
| McMurry | 66 | | | | |
| McWhorter | 65 | | | | |
| McWilliams | 14 | | | | |
| Mead | 93 | | | | |
| Meade | 93 | | | | |
| Meador | 46 | | | | |
| Meadows | 46 | | | | |
| Meek | 44 | | | | |
| Merrick | 66 | | | | |
| Merriott | 53 | | | | |
| Metsker | 11 | | | | |
| Middleton | 50 | | | | |
| Miles | 69 | | | | |
| Millard | 47 | 93 | | | |
| Miller | 11 | 48 | 63 | 64 | |
| Milley | 17 | | | | |
| Minton | 49 | | | | |
| Mitchell | 48 | 51 | 61 | | |
| Montgomery | 21 | | | | |
| Moore | 11 | 24 | 47 | 58 | |
| Morrell | 93 | | | | |
| Morris | 13 | 33 | 39 | | |
| Moseley | 11 | 82 | | | |
| Motley | 14 | | | | |
| Muckelroy | 93 | | | | |
| Mulanax | 11 | | | | |
| Munger | 60 | | | | |
| Murphy | 84 | | | | |
| Mynne | 71 | | | | |
| Neisler | 81 | | | | |
| Nelson | 11 | | | | |
| Nesbitt | 72 | | | | |
| Nester | 49 | | | | |
| Nettles | 12 | | | | |
| Norton | 92 | | | | |
| Orrick | 91 | | | | |
| Owen | 50 | 51 | | | |
| Owens | 43 | | | | |
| Owsley | 15 | | | | |
| Ozier | 23 | 28 | | | |
| Parham | 74 | 75 | | | |
| Parker | 28 | 52 | 92 | | |
| Parks | 74 | 77 | | | |
| Parrish | 47 | | | | |
| Parsons | 60 | 61 | | | |
| Patrick | 21 | | | | |
| Pearce | 68 | | | | |
| Peebles | 80 | | | | |
| Pettiet | 65 | | | | |
| Philips | 63 | | | | |
| Phillips | 53 | | | | |
| Pierce | 43 | | | | |
| Piles | 21 | | | | |
| Pitts | 53 | | | | |
| Ponder | 16 | | | | |
| Poole | 22 | | | | |
| Posey | 49 | | | | |
| Pratt | 51 | 93 | | | |
| Price | 19 | | | | |
| Pruitt | 46 | | | | |
| Purser | 41 | | | | |
| Pyland | 53 | | | | |
| Raley | 73 | | | | |
| Rawls | 22 | | | | |
| Reade | 89 | | | | |
| Reed | 42 | 71 | | | |
| Reese | 92 | | | | |
| Reid | 54 | 55 | | | |
| Revels | 66 | | | | |
| Rhodes | 50 | | | | |
| Rich | 71 | | | | |
| Rider | 52 | | | | |
| Riggs | 12 | 72 | | | |
| Riley | 44 | 73 | | | |
| Ritter | 53 | 82 | | | |
| Roberts | 21 | 33 | 36 | 37 | |
| Robinson | 23 | 27 | | | |
| Robison | 26 | | | | |
| Roby | 80 | | | | |
| Rodgers | 33 | 34 | 35 | 79 | |
| Rogers | 13 | 41 | | | |
| Roggs | 67 | | | | |
| Rooks | 93 | | | | |
| Rushing | 20 | | | | |
| Saint | 18 | | | | |
| Sammons | 48 | | | | |
| Sandlin | 82 | | | | |
| Satterfield | 66 | | | | |
| Schilling | 50 | 51 | | | |
| Schmitz | 51 | | | | |
| Scobee | 17 | | | | |
| Scott | 44 | | | | |
| Sharp | 12 | | | | |
| Shaw | 57 | | | | |
| Sherry | 67 | 68 | | | |
| Shoemake | 18 | | | | |
| Shy | 42 | | | | |
| Simpson | 57 | | | | |
| Sims | 80 | | | | |
| Skelton | 48 | | | | |
| Slaughter | 23 | 28 | | | |
| Slocum | 14 | | | | |
| Smith | 23 | 30 | 31 | 32 | 53 | 74 |
| Smith | 76 | 78 | 79 | 84 | |
| Sneed | 46 | | | | |
| Snook | 22 | | | | |

# MEMBERS LISTING

| Mem # | Last Name | First Name Street Address | City | St | Zip + 4 |
|---|---|---|---|---|---|
| B07 | BARNES | Jane | Deceased | | |
| B14 | BOLTON | Chas | | | |
| B03 | BROWN | F. E. | Deceased | | |
| B16 | BRYANT | Mr. Vaughn | Deceased | | |
| B10 | BURNS | B.A. | | | |
| | | 14019 E Cypress Forest Dr. | Houston | TX | 77070-3009 |
| C01 | CLEMENTS | Enon & Margaret | Deceased | | |
| D01 | DILLARD | Marcile | Deceased | | |
| E01 | EATON | Evelyn | Deceased | | |
| | FRANCES | Ena Mae | | | |
| G07 | GREER | Richard D. | | | |
| | | P.O. Box 7193 | Monroe | LA | 71203-7193 |
| H04 | HOLDER | Donna | | | |
| H07 | HUDGENS | Marilyn | | | |
| H11 | HUGHES | Carol D. | Deceased | | |
| J04 | JONES | Jimmie Lois (Caton) | | | |
| | | 258 Catherine Hts. Rd. | Hot Springs | AR | 71901-8306 |
| M04 | MAHONEY | Mary Eliz. | Deceased | | |
| M08 | MAZZINI | Shirley | Deceased | | |
| M07 | MEADOR | Anita | Deceased | | |
| | MILLARD | Sidney J. | | | |
| M06 | MILLER | Paul & Ena | Deceased | | |
| M05 | HILL | Sharon (Minton) & Darrell | | | |
| | | 173 Duke Trail | Hot Springs | AR | 71913-8114 |
| O1 | OWEN | Mary (Mrs. Ernest T.) | Deceased | | |
| | PARKER | Winnie Parker | | | |
| S09 | SMITH | Jerry Ray | | | |
| S07 | STEPHENS | Lewis C. | Deceased | | |
| S03 | STEVENS | Arthur | Deceased | | |
| S10 | SUIT | Glenda | | | |
| | | 3060 S Blackhills Dr. | Boise | ID | 83709-4002 |
| S06 | STEVENSON | Nadine | | | |
| | | 345 Tulip St. | Fairfield | CA | 94533-1534 |
| T07 | THOLBORN | Wanda J. | | | |
| | | 1980 Michigan | Stockton | CA | 95204-4143 |
| W02 | WILLIAMS | Gertrude | Deceased | | |

| Mem # | Last Name | First Name Street Address | City | St | Zip + 4 |
|---|---|---|---|---|---|
| W05 | WILLIAMS | Letha | Deceased | | |
| W03 | WOLF | Nadine C. | Deceased | | |
| Y3 | YARY | Mrs. Clearcie | Deceased | | |
| Y1 | YOUNG | Maxine | Deceased | | |
| Y2 | YOUNG | James L. | Deceased | | |

### THE MELTING POT
### Genealogical Society

**649-B Ouachita Ave**
**Please Send Mail To: P. O. Box 936**
**501-624-0229**
mpgs@att.net

Membership in the Melting Pot Genealogical Society is open to anyone interested in genealogy.

All memberships are on a calendar year basis and all memberships are due as of January 1st. Your membership entitles you to a copy of our annual publication, *"The Kettle"*, which may be picked up at the library, after publication each year. If you wish your book mailed, please include an additional fee of $4.00 with your dues. Your membership also entitles you to check out 4 books for a two-week period (each visit to the library) and a monthly newsletter. Our meetings are the fourth Tuesday of September – May at 1:30 p.m. at our library. Our library is open Monday and Friday (or by appointment) from 10:00 a.m. to 2:00 p.m.

| --Regular Member $25.00 | --Lifetime Member $250.00 | --Benefactor $500.00 | Corporate Membership $1,000.00 |
|---|---|---|---|

All memberships entitle the member to the same benefits. Membership in one of the higher categories helps to provide more support to the Society. In addition, any level above the regular membership rate qualifies as a tax-deductible donation.

**Please type or print very clearly:**

Name_____

Address_____

City_____ State_____ Zip_____ + _____

Telephone (_____)_____-_____ E-mail _____

Mail with your check to:
**Melting Pot Genealogical Society**
(Location) 649-B Ouachita Ave.
(Please Send Mail to**) P. O. Box 936**
**Hot Springs, Arkansas 71902-0936**

# (Please do not forget to complete the reverse side)

The MPGS wants to know what information you wish to appear in the Melting Pot's periodical and in our website; therefore, we are asking for your input. _We will be listing your name in the periodical as a member but nothing else without your permission. The website will not contain your name unless permission is given._

## The *KETTLE*

| | Yes | NO |
|---|---|---|
| May we publish your **address** in *The Kettle?* | | |
| May we publish your **telephone number** in *The Kettle?* | | |
| May we publish your **E-mail address** in *The Kettle?* If Yes Please list your E-mail address. | | |
| May we publish the **surnames** that you are researching? If Yes, Please list what you would like listed. | | |
| Do you have a personal website that you want listed? If Yes, What is the URL? | | |

## MPGS WEBSITE

| | Yes | No |
|---|---|---|
| May we publish your **name** in the website? | | |
| May we publish your **address** in the website? | | |
| May we publish your **telephone number** in the website? | | |
| May we publish your **E-mail address** in the website? If Yes, Please list your E-mail address. | | |
| May We publish the **surnames** that you are researching? If Yes, Please list what you would like listed. | | |
| Do you have a personal website that you want listed? If Yes, what is the URL? | | |

Signature (may be typed if sent via e-mail)

_____ Date _____

Address, telephone # and E-mail address if permission to use:

Address: _____

Telephone: (_____) _____

E-mail: _____@_____